SOFTWARE QUALITY ASSURANCE—A STUDENT INTRODUCTION

THE McGRAW-HILL INTERNATIONAL SERIES IN SOFTWARE ENGINEERING

Consulting Editor

Professor D. Ince
The Open University

Titles in this Series

Further titles in this Series are listed at the back of the book

SOFTWARE QUALITY ASSURANCE—A STUDENT INTRODUCTION

Darrel Ince
Professor of Computer Science
Open University

McGRAW-HILL BOOK COMPANY

London · New York · St Louis · San Francisco · Auckland
Bogotá · Caracas · Lisbon · Madrid · Mexico
Milan · Montreal · New Delhi · Panama · Paris · San Juan
São Paulo · Singapore · Sydney · Tokyo · Toronto

Published by

McGRAW-HILL Book Company Europe

SHOPPENHANGERS ROAD · MAIDENHEAD · BERKSHIRE · SL6 2QL · ENGLAND

TELEPHONE 01628 23432

FAX 01628 770224

British Library Cataloguing in Publication Data

Ince, Darrel

   Software Quality Assurance: Student

   Introduction. – (McGraw-Hill

   International Software Quality Assurance

   Series)

   I. Title   II. Series

   005.10685

   ISBN 0-07-709096-9

Library of Congress Cataloging-in-Publication Data

Ince, D. (Darrel)

   Software quality assurance: a student introduction/Darrel Ince.

     p. cm.

   Includes index.

   ISBN 0-07-709096-9

   1. Computer software—Quality control.   I. Title.

QA76.76.Q35I536   1995

005.1'068'5—dc20   95-7040

                                             CIP

12345 CUP 98765

Typeset by the author

Printed and bound in Great Britain at the University Press, Cambridge

Printed on permanent paper in compliance with ISO Standard 9706

CONTENTS

PREFACE

During the eighties computer science courses were severely technical. A casual browser through college and university prospectuses would, quite rightly, gain the impression that the lecturers based their courses on the presupposition that the only solution to the problems that beset our software projects are technical ones—that all you need are the right tools, development methods and programming languages to achieve major productivity gains. The evidence over the last ten years has been that while some small gains have been achieved, there are a number of other solutions which promise much higher gains—especially to those companies whose software development is in a rudimentary state. One of these solutions is the disciplined application of software quality assurance. I know of many companies who, admittedly starting from a low baseline, have achieved gains of 30 per cent in productivity and error reduction through mainstream quality methods.

While the educational world now regards quality assurance as important there is still a shortage of accessible textbooks. There have been few written; these are referenced in the body of this book. However I believe they do not have the breadth of coverage of this book.

This book is aimed at a number of audiences. It is intended for students on quality assurance courses which are run in either the second or third year of a degree. It used to be that computing degrees relegated quality assurance to a third year option; there are now encouraging signs that the topic is being introduced to the mainstream curriculum. It is also intended for self study. In order to give the student who is studying this book alone some idea of progress—over and above that of page numbering—I have included a large number of self assessment questions. These questions have a number of functions:

- They reinforce the section which precedes them, often testing an understanding of a main point in that section.
- They extend the reader a little and place him or her in a position where the ideas of the following section will be a little more congenial and understandable.
- Occasionally they provide a reminder of major concepts introduced a number of chapters ago and which are to be used in the chapter in which the self assessment question is included.

Once again I have to thank my wife Stephanie who has tolerated my continual occupancy of our study with her usual good humour. I would also like to thank Rupert Knight, my commissioning editor at McGraw-Hill. His driving optimism has kept me working on the book at times when even clearing out the garage seemed a more congenial task than finishing the book. I would also like to thank Tony Pearce of Network Consultants; his company has allowed me to practise my ideas on a large number of industrial staff over the past four years.

Darrel Ince
Milton Keynes

WHAT IS SOFTWARE QUALITY?

AIMS

- To describe the nature of software quality assurance.
- To introduce the idea of a quality factor.
- To describe some common quality factors.
- To show how consideration of quality factors drives the quality planning process.
- To show how a quality system affects different members of staff associated with a software project.
- To describe what exactly a quality system is and how it is used in software development.

1.1 INTRODUCTION

The building that I visited was very quiet, considering that software was developed in it—normally programmers are quite a boisterous bunch and the offices had the ambience of a funeral parlour. The reason I was in the building was that I had been called in as a consultant to carry out a post-mortem on three software projects that had failed dismally. The quietness arose from the fact that morale in the company was low after the three disasters, and also from the fact that quite a large number of staff had been made redundant—including many of the senior managers responsible for software development.

A revealing question to ask a programmer who has participated in a disaster, in order to get some idea about the reasons for it, is: 'What tasks do you enjoy doing, and what tasks do you not enjoy doing?' One programmer told me that he enjoyed programming, and even testing, but what he hated was the process of retesting. He used the programming language C to produce coded functions (a function is a module in C) which, he claimed, were well tested and were then consigned to a project library ready for subsequent development. This part of his job he thoroughly enjoyed doing. However, he often found that the functions which he produced were returned to him a few weeks later with a change request. These change requests arose for two reasons. The first was that the company's marketing department, who was, in effect, the internal customer for the software, continually generated new requirements. Members of the department often talked to external customers who would buy the software only if it did something extra and, being a good marketing department, they promised the changes in order to generate potential revenue.

The second category of change came from modifications to hardware. The software developer produced systems which were intended to run on interface hardware; this was often being enhanced in parallel with the software development. Each time a new feature was added to the hardware, or a feature modified, it resulted in a large number of software change requests.

The programmer explained to me that when he received one of his original functions back from the project library he would have major problems trying to remember his original test data, and would end up spending a considerable amount of time doing this, together with thinking up new test data which checked out the requested modifications to the function.

I asked him whether he had thought about storing his original test data in a file and, perhaps, storing the test outcomes in the same way. These files could easily be retrieved whenever a modification was requested, and the only work required from the programmer would have been the derivation of additional tests which checked out the modifications. When I suggested the use of these files the programmer looked at me as if I had solved every problem in his life. All I had done was to suggest something that a good quality system should have insisted he do anyway.

The reason for the three software disasters that I had to investigate was an inadequate quality system. The company had what it called a 'quality manual'. This was a sort of rudimentary quality system, but it suffered from two problems: one managerial and one technical. The managerial problem was that it was not mandatory for project managers to use the system. Software projects in the company had achieved the status of medieval Italian city states, with individual project managers having a huge degree of independence—even over the pitifully small quality assurance department.

The technical problem was that the quality system did not insist on developers carrying out tasks in such a way that changes such as the requirements modifications demanded by the marketing department could be coped with, for example, by insisting on the storage of test data. The three projects that bottomed up were all affected by changes which gave rise to a massive amount of unnecessary work—work which a good quality system could have minimized. Later in this chapter I will return to this problem of change, as it forms a major input into the process of developing a quality system.

In order to convince the management of the company that they needed to invest in a good quality system I carried out an exercise with one of the luckier project managers who remained on the payroll. We calculated the average amount of time required for programmers to retest C functions on the three projects, and then calculated the time taken if a quality system had insisted on the storage of the test data. Admittedly this was quite a rough calculation, but in the end we had enough confidence in the assumptions that we had made to predict that just by addressing one small aspect of the development process the company could have saved a programmer's salary for the five years during which the projects were live.

This is a very minor example of how a component—albeit a small component—of a quality system, in this case a procedure which instructs a programmer to store test data on a file, is able to not only save a company money, but also make a software developer's life easier.

I hope that this anecdote might act as an antidote to the view of quality assurance which many people still have. It is a view exemplified by the story related to me by a senior programmer who, at the start of his career, joined a company which developed real-time software. On his first day he was befriended by a helpful senior colleague who pointed out to him where the best bar was in the area, where the best sandwiches were to be bought, which project manager to work for, which project manager not to work for, and which secretary to ask for stationery. During the process of communicating this advice on a tour of the building the senior colleague pointed at a door and said: 'Whatever you do, don't go through that door, the people in there have been given the job of stifling our creativity.' The door, of course, belonged to the quality assurance department. I hope that this book will go some way towards overcoming the prejudice which I still encounter—albeit in less extreme forms than that just described.

1.2 THE MEANING OF QUALITY

If you look at many of the books that have already been published on quality assurance you will see that they generally agree on the meaning of quality. Usually, their agreement is enshrined in the phrase 'fitness for purpose'; that is, a quality product—be it a car, refrigerator, hair dryer or any other item—is one which does what the customer expects it to do. Fitness for purpose is an important concept, and forms a central tenet of quality assurance. However, later in this chapter you will see that it is not the only property of a quality product.

Before examining the full story it is worthwhile looking at a particular implication of the phrase 'fitness for purpose'. This implies that somewhere there will be a description of the purpose for which an item is intended. For very simple objects this description might mainly be contained in the name of the article; for example, the term 'hair dryer' conveys the vast majority of the functionality of a device used to dry hair. The description of the purpose of some articles might be contained in a user manual which, as well as providing details about how to use them, might also include some technical specification. For large items—for example, software or hardware systems—the purpose is enshrined in a document usually known as the *requirements specification*, sometimes known as the *system specification*. In Chapter 4 I shall describe in some detail what can be found in a requirements specification for a software system. In reading this chapter all you need to know about a requirements specification is that it contains a description of what a software system is to do, together with descriptions of constraints such as response time which are to be associated with the system. The requirements specification is the most important document generated in a software project, and it is around this document that a quality system revolves.

The modern view of quality assurance takes a more sophisticated view than that of fitness for purpose. A high quality product is one which has associated with it a number of *quality factors*. The quality factors, often known as *quality attributes*, could be described in the requirements specification; they could be cultural, in that they are normally associated with the object through familiarity of use and through the shared experience of users; or they could be factors which the developer regards as important, but which are not considered by the customer and, hence, are not included in the requirements specification.

It is instructive to examine some examples of each of these three categories of quality factors. The first category comprises those which would be contained in the requirements specification. An example of this is *portability*. A customer for a software system may require a system to be executable across a diverse range of hardware architectures. Consequently, these architectures would be described in the requirements specification.

An example of the second category, comprising cultural factors, is *usability*. Because a customer may have experience of systems in which it is relatively easy to communicate with a computer, he or she may not specify how an interface is to be implemented in detail in a requirements specification. In the specification there may be a brief directive to use a WIMP interface or a line-by-line command interface, but because of the same shared assumptions with the developer, the details of the interface would normally be omitted from the requirements specification.

The third category consists of those quality factors which may be of interest to the developer, but not of direct interest to the customer. An example of this might be *reusability*: the ability to transfer modules constructed for one software system into another software system. For example, a software developer may be currently producing a software system for one customer which is somewhat similar to a system that he or she hopes to construct for another customer. If the second system is being bid for by a number of software developers, then the producer of the first system could gain a major commercial advantage during the bidding process by ensuring that the first software system is highly reusable. This advantage would, of course, be obtained by making a very low bid since little new programming would be required. This category of quality factor is, at best, only of indirect interest to the customer, and would not be contained in a requirements specification. In the case of reusability a customer, while not perhaps asking for reusability in the requirements specification, may be interested in receiving a licence fee for the software that is reused.

It is important to point out that the three categories of quality factor do not represent a hard and fast taxonomy. What category a factor is placed in really depends on the customer, the customer's circumstances, the application area, and the developer's circumstances. For example, I described usability as a cultural quality factor in that everybody expects their systems to be usable; this is usually the case in a large number of software systems. However, there are some categories of software systems used for safety-critical applications where usability is of such importance that it is included in the requirements specification, for example by specifying a metric which quantifies the unacceptable frequency of erroneous commands being initiated by the operators of the system.

Even though the three categories are not hard and fast, what is important is for a quality system to recognize that they exist, and to ensure that right at the start of the project the manager examines all the quality factors that may be necessary before deciding on the quality controls that are required for a project. A project manager should not just assume that 'fitness for purpose', as exemplified in a requirements specification, is enough.

Self Assessment Question 1.1 What are the three categories of quality factor?

Solution They are those which might appear in the requirements specification, those which are cultural in nature and those which are of interest to the developer but only of indirect interest to the customer.

It is now worth examining some of the important quality factors. The list that is presented here can be found in McCall *et al.* (1978), although I have amended it somewhat. It is worth pointing out that there is some overlap within the quality factors described by McCall: that aspects of one quality factor can be found in another quality factor. Nevertheless, his categorization forms a good basis for a quality system.

The first factor is *correctness*, that is, that a software system actually conforms to its requirements specification; naturally, this factor should be totally present in any system.

The next is *maintainability* or *modifiability*. This describes the ease with which a software system can be changed. In the original paper written by McCall, the term *maintainability* had a very limited meaning—it referred to the ease with which errors could be located and fixed. McCall's original paper was written at a time when the changes which a software system experienced were due to errors being discovered—either during development or during maintenance, when the software was in operation.

However, over the last decade or so it has become quite evident that many other categories of change occur. There are, of course, changes due to errors being committed—these will always be with us, although I would hope that, as technology improves, the extent of this category will lessen. There are also changes due to requirements volatility. Paradoxically, one of the indicators for a software developer that a good system has been developed is to receive numerous requests from a customer for changes in requirements; these are often framed in terms of new functions. Also, the developer will receive requests for modifications due to changes in a customer's external circumstances. For example, an accounting package may have been delivered which, although it satisfied the original customer's requirements, now has to be modified because tax laws have changed. Thus nowadays, because customers demand more and more from successful systems, and external circumstances change, a high level of modification can be attributed to changes in requirements. There is another category of change which McCall did not envisage: changes which somehow improve a system without changing its functionality; for example, tuning a system in order to give it a faster response time, or rewriting a device handler to cope with a new output device.

The first category of modifications—those due to error fixing—are known as *corrective changes*, the second category—due to the developer responding to changes in requirements—are known as *adaptive changes* and the third category—changes which improve a system—are known as *perfective changes*.

What is important is not the categories of change, but the fact that as a result, many software systems have a very high level of maintenance, with the majority of the changes being adaptive. Moreover, many of these changes will not only occur during maintenance but, for projects which have a long time duration, will occur during the project itself. For this reason alone I would say that the maintainability factor should always be present to a very great extent in a software system. After correctness, I would regard it as the next most important quality factor.

Self Assessment Question 1.2 Into what category of change would you place a design and code modification which speeds up a system?

Solution This is a perfective change because it improves the system.

Maintainability is normally only of indirect interest to the customer. Very few customers, indeed, include directives about maintainability in the directions they give to a software developer, apart, of course, from those customers who intend to carry out the maintenance of a system themselves. However, it is worth pointing out that there will be an indirect interest in that software developers who build maintainability into their systems have a much greater chance of delivering a correct system within time and within budget. For example, if changes to a system are going to take a long time to apply, then there is always the possibility that when a high level of errors are discovered the duration of the project will overrun the estimated delivery time for the software.

Another quality factor, which has already been mentioned previously, is *portability*. This is the effort required to transfer a system from one hardware platform to another. Normally, portability will be detailed in a requirements specification. However, for commercial reasons it is sometimes of direct interest to the developer but only of indirect interest to the customer, as in the example cited earlier, where portability was built into a system in order to give the customer a competitive edge during the process of tendering for another system.

Testability is another factor which is of direct interest to the developer but is very rarely directly specified by the customer. It describes the ease with which a system, or part of a system, can be tested. For example, a system which has a very poor requirements specification that contains a large amount of ambiguities and platitudes is very difficult to test, because the staff responsible for system testing will have major problems in specifying the tests which check out the requirements specification.

Another important factor is *usability*. This is the effort required to learn, operate and interrupt a functioning system. Usability is often a major problem with systems: many software developers tend to think about the functions of a system at the front-end of a project, and then only bolt on an inadequate interface in its dying stages. If anyone asks me to justify my obsession with quality factors and my contention that 'fitness for purpose' is not a wholly adequate basis for quality assurance, then I give them the example of the system which, when implemented, satisfies all the functions in its requirements specification but, because of a very poor interface, is highly unusable.

Reliability describes the ability of a software system to carry on executing with little interruption to its functioning. This factor is normally expected to be ultra-high in certain classes of safety-critical systems, and will often be specified in terms of metrics involving factors such as mean time between failure. For other types of system, this factor will be cultural in that it will not usually be specified in a requirements specification, but will be assumed by the customer to be present to a high level in a system.

Efficiency is another important quality factor. It is used to describe the degree to which computing resources—file-space, memory and processor time—are used in an application. This is a difficult factor to categorize: many requirements specifications will contain detailed descriptions of the amount of hardware available and the desired response time. However, I would say that there are features which make it cultural, in that a customer will expect, but not explicitly specify, that a software developer will make efficient use of the computing resources available to him or her.

Integrity is used to describe the extent to which the system and its data are immune to access by unauthorized users. Again, this is a quality factor which cannot be precisely categorized: some systems, for example those used in financial applications, will have requirements specifications which describe the level of access allowed to such systems. However, there is a cultural assumption that a delivered system should not be capable of being tampered with by unauthorized users or intruders.

Reusability is also becoming increasingly important, and describes the ease with which chunks of software in one system can be moved to another system. This is normally a quality factor which is only of indirect interest to a customer.

The final quality factor which I will describe is *interoperability*. This is the ability of a system to operate in conjunction with another software system, for example a spreadsheet. Normally this factor is specified in a requirements specification and is of direct interest to a customer.

This, then, is a brief discussion of what a quality factor is. Many of you might have been tempted to regard it as somewhat academic; indeed, it has been something of an academic game to derive longer and longer lists of quality factors.

However, there is a very practical reason for discussing quality factors this early in the book. It is connected with the fact that a quality system should be flexible. Normally, a quality system is embodied in a document known as a *quality manual*. At the beginning of a software project a project manager should decide which elements of the quality system should be used to ensure the quality of the software that is to be delivered. In order to do this, the quality manager should examine a list of quality factors; identify those parts of the quality system which should be used to enforce the level of quality factor required; identify those parts of the quality system which should not be used; or even develop some new quality controls which may not be in the quality manual. A consideration of the quality factors to be built into a system, and the level to which they are to be built in, is often embodied in a checklist. Consideration of the checklist by a project manager at the beginning of a project drives this process.

Obviously there will always be components of a quality system which will be used in every software project; for example, a standard for the requirements specification will always be needed. However, depending on the customer, application or software technology to be used, the project manager will decide what components of a quality system will be either used, strengthened or omitted. In order to understand this link between quality factors and the quality system it is worth examining some examples.

> **Self Assessment Question 1.3** How is a quality manual used on a software project?
>
> **Solution** The quality manual will contain facilities such as standards and procedures which are extracted for a particular project. Which of these are extracted depends on the quality factors for a project.

The first concerns a system which is to be developed where the management of the company decides that reusability will be high in the system. This decision would normally be made by the manager of a software project during the process of examining a quality factor checklist which contains a list of questions relevant to the particular factor. When the quality factor heading for reusability is encountered by the project manager there will be a number of questions which will drive the manager's thinking about that factor. For reusability there will be questions such as:

- Are we thinking of developing a similar software system in the future?
- Does our company have a policy of developing a reusable library of components?
- Are we currently bidding for a software system which has similarities to the one which is to be developed?

Let us suppose that the answer to the third question is yes, and the project manager decides to use a programming language such as C^{++} which has a high degree of reusability. A consequence of this might be that the quality system does not contain a programming standard for C^{++} and one has be developed, or an existing programming standard for C has to be modified since C^{++} is based on it.

Another example involves the development of a safety-critical system. Such systems have to have an extremely high correctness quality factor. On examining the quality manual prior to starting such a project, the manager may decide that because this factor is so high every technique for ensuring correctness which is contained in the quality manual has to be used. This armoury of validation techniques may be much larger than those which the manager would normally deploy on a project for which the correctness quality factor was lower, for example in developing software for a clerical application.

A third example might be where a transaction-based system is to be produced, where the customer employs keyboard operators in an area of the country where such staff are in short supply. The project manager may decide—either after reading documents provided by the customer or in conversation with the customer—that a high degree of usability is required. This would mean that some usability studies would need to be carried out and usability testing would need to be scheduled during the later stages of the software project. The quality manual would be consulted and any sections pertaining to usability would have to be taken on board the project or, if non-existent, would have to be developed. The topic of the human–computer interface and quality assurance is discussed in Chapter 10.

Thus quality factors, or more correctly a consideration of quality factors, forms the basis for the quality controls that are going to be applied in a software project. Before examining some of the principles behind a quality system—many of which constitute the main themes of this book—it is worth looking at who the users of the quality system are. There is a popular misconception that the only users tend to be management: a misconception which I would wish to quash as early as possible. Before doing this, it is worth briefly introducing some terminology which is used in the next section.

A quality system contains procedures, standards and guidelines. A *procedure* is a description of the actions which are to be carried out when a particular project task is to be executed for example, the production of a system design. I shall define a *standard* as a directive which describes how a particular document is to be structured, and what data is contained in the document. A *guideline* is a series of instructions which provide advice on carrying out a task. For example, a guideline might specify that normally five members of staff are to attend a particular project meeting. The difference between a guideline and the other two types of document is that a guideline represents advice, while the others represent activities which *have* to happen on a project. Normally, the advice enshrined in a guideline is taken; however, the instructions in procedures and standards must be followed.

It is worth making the point that the vocabulary which I have introduced is not used by some companies; for example, some software developers use the term 'standard' to cover both procedures and standards. However, for standardization reasons I shall use the terminology above.

Self Assessment Question 1.4 What is the difference between a standard and a procedure?

Solution A *standard* describes the format of some document such as the requirements specification. A *procedure* details the steps that are to be taken in carrying out some software task such as testing a module.

1.3 SOME USERS OF A QUALITY SYSTEM

1.3.1 The project manager

In this book the term 'project manager' is used to describe a member of staff who has day-to-day control of a software project. Such a person carries out a number of functions: planning, monitoring, controlling, innovating, and representing. *Planning* involves a number of tasks; these include estimating the risk of a project, estimating its overall cost, deciding which quality controls are to be used, identifying the tasks that make up a project, scheduling these tasks, deciding on the particular project organization to be used, and establishing the interfaces between the project and both the customer and the senior management of the software development company. It is worth stressing that planning is not just a one-off activity: in the vast majority of cases a manager will, of course, carry out quite a large amount of planning at the beginning of a project, but will also undertake replanning, for example when a change in requirements to a project is notified by the customer.

Monitoring involves checking the progress of the project against an overall project plan and evaluating the performance of staff on the project. Monitoring is intimately connected to *controlling*: the process of taking actions to ensure that when a project starts to diverge from the project plan, it is brought back on target. This will involve some degree of planning, or rather replanning.

Innovating involves the introduction of some new innovation, for example a new development method, project organization, or testing tool, and evaluating the effect.

Representing is the final function carried out by a project manager. He or she represents his or her project in dealings with the customer, the senior management of the software company and other agencies such as the quality assurance department, the marketing department and the personnel department.

It is worth exploring some of the ways in which a quality system is able to support these managerial functions:

- A quality system should provide facilities whereby a project manager can consider the vast majority of possible risks which could affect a project. Risk analysis is an important, but much neglected, activity; for example, consideration of risk is used as one of the factors to be taken into consideration when making a decision about whether a project should be started or even bid for. As a minimum, the quality system should provide a checklist which would outline those factors which might result in a project being late or over-budget. These include factors such as the degree of familiarity that the customer has with the application which is to be computerized; the degree of knowledge the customer has about software practice; and the reliance of the project on outside agencies who may not be trusted to deliver on time, such as hardware providers and external software contractors. More sophisticated quality systems provide spreadsheet programs which prompt the user about these factors, and give a numerical risk factor which might then be used by the project manager in adjusting upwards a rough estimate for the cost of the project in order to build in some contingency.

- A quality system should specify standards which will enable staff to report on their activities in a uniform way. Such reports should be able to be easily processed by a project manager in order to give some idea of how close to schedule a project is.

- Software estimating is still quite a hazardous process, even for medium-sized projects. A quality system should lay down standards and procedures which ensure that cost and expenditure records from earlier projects are kept in an easily accessible form, so that a project manager can check that the estimate for a project is not too different from a similar project; or, more likely, that parts of a system to be produced have similar costs to those parts of systems already developed.

- A quality system should provide a way of collecting and analysing defect statistics: data about errors, their severity, and when they occur on a software project. This data can be used in a number of ways: in analysing staff performance; as one of the inputs into the process of evaluating whether an innovation has been a success; or in predicting the pattern of errors in a product when it is released.

- A quality system should contain a standard for a project plan which gives details about the capabilities of the staff who are to carry out project tasks such as system testing. This enables the project manager, when he or she is representing a project with some resourcing department within the software company, to specify what staff are needed, or what training is required for staff who are available for a project but who do not have requisite skills.

This is just a subset of some of the facilities that should be provided by a quality system. However, it does give an idea of the huge influence of these facilities.

1.3.2 The programmer

I shall assume that a programmer is a member of staff who is given a specification for a chunk of software—it could be a subroutine or a program—and who then has to produce program code which he or she tests for correctness. Most programmers are not only involved in programming, but also carry out a large amount of reprogramming, for example when a requirements change occurs. Some of the help that a quality system should provide a programmer is shown below:

- The quality system should set programming standards which determine the way that a program is to be constructed and displayed, for example by insisting that certain layout conventions are adhered to. A good programming standard—and I must say there are some pretty terrible ones—should enable a programmer to read source code, and understand the contribution of each part of the source code to the overall function of the chunk of the software that he or she is examining. In this way, testing and debugging becomes easier, and the effort to understand the software after perhaps many weeks of absence is minimized.
- It should provide directions to the programmer to store away test data and test outcomes in files. In this way, reprogramming becomes much easier. The programmer can retrieve the test data, modify it in response to, say, a requirements change, and then apply it again. Obviously, this is preferable to trying to reconstitute the whole data set again.
- It should provide a standard which insists that the names of the program chunks which have been produced by a programmer have a correspondence to the files used to store the source code, object code, test data, and test outcomes for the software. For example, if a program has a name *Update*, then a quality standard should insist that if it was programmed in COBOL the file holding the source code should have the name, *Update.cbl*, the object code the name *Update.obj*, the test data file *Update.tda*, and the test outcome file *Update.out*. If this trivial standard is used, then programmers who are asked to reprogram the work of other staff do not need to waste time trying to find the location of the software in a project library—a search which often involves long, time-consuming phone calls.

Self Assessment Question 1.5 What quality factor does a procedure which directs a programmer to store test data away in a file address?

Solution This mainly addresses the maintainability quality factor.

1.3.3 The system designer

I shall assume the existence of a member of staff known as the system designer. He or she will be responsible for processing a description of the software system that is to be produced—normally, the requirements specification—and providing an architecture which implements the functions demanded by the customer, but which at the same time respects constraints such as response time which have been specified by the customer. The system designer usually produces a process architecture which describes the inter-relationship of the modules which make up a system, and a data architecture which describes any databases that are to be used by the system. A number of the facilities that a good quality system should offer the system designer are shown below:

- It should provide a standard which describes how the process architecture and data architecture are to be written down. A good standard should enable the designer to check that the system which has been designed actually implements the functions described in the requirements specification.
- It should also specify standards which lead to a system that should be easily maintainable. For example, a good standard for design is the insistence that each module in a system carries out one function—and one function only. Systems designed in this way tend to be far easier to maintain than systems containing modules which each carry out large sets of functions.
- It should provide standards which lead to a good requirements specification. For a system designer, the word 'good' implies that the requirements specification should contain no ambiguities, contradictions or platitudes, and that constraints such as response time are directly cross-referenced to the functions to which they apply.

1.3.4 The analyst

I shall assume that an analyst is a member of staff who liaises with a customer and produces a requirements specification which is then extensively used by staff, such as the system designer, who carry out different functions. The analyst's needs tend to be centred around the requirements specification. Some examples of how a good quality system is able to satisfy those needs are shown below:

- It should provide a standard for the requirements specification which, among other concerns, specifies an organization of the requirements specification in which related functions are textually close to each other. For example, in a stock control system the descriptions of the functions associated with querying a database of information about products which are out of stock should be physically close to each other.

  One of the implications of this is that it makes it easier for the analyst to check for contradictions. It also makes it easier for the customer to check the requirements specification: related groups of functions are usually the province of one person—in the case of this example the purchasing manager— who, in accessing the requirements specification for text which relates to his or her work, does not want the relevant text to be cluttered up with a description of functions for which another member of the customer's staff is responsible.

- It should provide a number of checklists which enable the analyst to ensure that features or issues associated with a software system that is to be developed are not forgotten. Such checklists are usually general, and might include questions such as: 'Have you specified what should happen when the system exhausts a hardware resource such as main memory?' Sometimes software developers who work in a narrow application area will have, as part of their quality system, an application-specific checklist. For example, a developer who produces software for stock-control applications might have a checklist which includes questions such as: 'Do the customers who are on a back-orders queue have some priority which will determine the order of the items on the queue?'

- It should provide a description of the processes involved when an analyst liaises with a customer; for example, specifying the way in which functions in the requirements specification are checked against the customer's requirements.

1.3.5 Senior management

By the term 'senior management' I mean those members of staff who work at the next level of the management structure above project managers. They are often called *business managers*, and usually supervise a number of projects. Such staff will require the quality system to provide a number of facilities, for example:

- It should provide senior managers with reports of achievement against targets for each of their projects; for example, what tasks should have been completed by a certain date and what tasks have, in fact, been completed; what expenditure should have been incurred by a certain date and what expenditure has actually been incurred.

- It should provide direction on the setting up of documentation audit trails. Such a trail might consist of memoranda which have been generated by checklists; for example, when the analysts in a project have queried a particular set of requirements with the customer. Such audit trails are useful for members of senior management; for example, when resolving some dispute about requirements which has escalated out of a project to his or her level of responsibility.

- It should provide facilities whereby reports on defects discovered during development are issued regularly. Such reports are not only of value to the individual project manager, but are also useful for senior management. For example, where a senior manager is actively involved in a management team which is attempting to carry out some process improvement, diagrams showing where defects were introduced during development, and where they were discovered, would be a major input into the task of determining what processes need to be improved.

1.3.6 The maintainers

In many companies the vast majority of resources is spent maintaining existing software: responding to error reports and changes in system functions by modifying the existing code of a system and changing documentation. In order for the staff charged with maintenance to do their job efficiently the quality system should provide a number of facilities, for example:

- It should insist on programming standards which ensure that maintainers can easily determine the function of modules in a system.
- It should provide traceability features which ensure that the process of determining which part of the system is executed when a particular function is exercised can be easily carried out.
- It should provide facilities which enable staff to track and monitor the various versions of a system which are created during the maintenance process.
- It should ensure that staff who created a system store away their test data so that the maintainers do not have to create fresh test data.

1.3.7 The staffing department

I shall use this term to describe a central function which is responsible for human resourcing on projects; sometimes this department also has a training role. There are a number of ways in which a quality system could serve the interests of this department; for example:

- The standards for a project plan should insist that the skills level of the staff on the project is properly specified. This obviously helps the staffing department to allocate the right people to the project, and to detail requisite training if staff with the specified skills are not available.
- The quality system should provide instructions on the activities carried out when the project has been completed. One activity relevant to a staffing department, which also has a personnel function, is for the project manager to produce a written report on the effectiveness of the staff on the project. There should be a standard format for this report, defined in the quality system, so that comparisons can be made between staff, for example when they are being interviewed or reviewed for senior positions.

1.3.8 The customer

The customer is also a user of the quality system. The customer's concerns are rather different from those of the developer; for example, he or she is concerned that adequate means are going to be used to develop the software and to check that it meets requirements; that adequate reporting facilities are provided which enable the progress of the project to be monitored; and that adequate liaison occurs during the period in which the developer is demonstrating that the system actually meets user requirements. Some examples of the type of facilities that a quality system should provide for the customer are:

- It should provide directives which specify how progress meetings are to be organized: who should be invited from the developer's staff, when meetings should be scheduled, what physical arrangements, such as the booking of a room, should be made, and how issues arising from a progress meeting are to be resolved.

- It should provide guidelines about how facilities provided are to be extracted and used as quality controls for a project. This list of controls would be specified in the quality plan. This is often a contractual document, or is at least signed off by the customer. The document should be a complete description of the way in which the developer intends to check that the system meets customer requirements, and the role of the customer in this process.
- It should specify the format of reports that are to be sent to the customer concerning progress and how to determine the frequency with which these reports are sent.

> **Self Assessment Question 1.6** What part of the quality system provides the best means for enabling a customer to check that software will be developed adequately?
>
> **Solution** The best part is the project plan, or rather the project plan standard. This contains details such as the technical solution adopted, the experience of the development staff to be used and how project monitoring is to be carried out.

1.3.9 The testers

Two critical activities on a software project are system testing and acceptance testing. Either developmental staff or staff from the quality assurance department derive a series of tests from the requirements specification, which are intended to check that the system which has been developed meets customer requirements. Such staff require a number of facilities from a quality system. Some examples follow:

- It should ensure that the requirements specification is constructed in such a way that system tests can be easily derived and related back to the functions that they test.
- It should ensure that procedures are in place which enable test data and test outcomes to be stored somewhere in a project library. The test files in the project library can be easily retrieved when retesting takes place.
- It should ensure that procedures are in place which ensure that those responsible for test planning can check that adequate resources are available during the test phase; for example, that during the development of a software system intended for a mainframe computer, the computer is actually available for testing and is not too heavily loaded by existing applications.

1.3.10 The marketing department

The marketing department sells software. In a company which develops one-off systems the effectiveness of this department will determine the profit levels. A quality system should offer facilities to staff involved in marketing. For example, every project should, as part of the debriefing process, produce a list of subsystems and modules which the project manager feels could be reusable. Given this list the marketing department, in conjunction with project staff, may be able to produce a bid for a future project which is substantially lower than a competitor's bid, because of the potential high reuse of previously written modules.

These, then, are some examples of which staff use the quality system. In summary, everybody uses it and, hence, everyone in a software company should be responsible for quality assurance.

1.4 SOME PRINCIPLES

There are a number of important principles which have to be borne in mind when implementing a quality system. These issues permeate the book, and it is worth collecting them here for reference.

1.4.1 Independence

The first principle is of independent validation. In order to describe this, it is worth telling you a short story. But first, some background to give an added dimension to my story. I was brought up in South Wales where religion plays an important part in the life of very many communities. It certainly played a major part in the life of my own village: my brother and I were packed off to chapel three times on Sunday and at least once during the week. We were preached at by a white-haired priest who harangued us about almost every evil in the world. The priest never hesitated to remind us that if we worked hard in this world, then we would get both the rewards of this world and the rewards of the next world. I was impressed by this message: that if I worked hard for a comparatively short time—say 40 years—then not only would I get rewards for 40 years, but also for the possible infinity that followed.

Because I took the preacher seriously I worked hard at school and university. I also worked hard at the first job that I took: as a programmer developing real-time software for mainframe computers in the mid-sixties. I used to come in early with my ham sandwiches—for I worked through lunch, sandwich in one hand and core dump in another—and worked very late.

One of the tasks that I had to carry out was to develop a 12k assembler program which implemented a high degree of parallelism. Undoubtedly, it was the most difficult program that I had to deal with. I came in every morning and spent hours working through core dumps, sometimes spending days trying to track down errors. One error caused me major problems. I took the best part of a week tracking it down and the way that it was discovered was, I thought, remarkable.

I shared an office with another programmer who did not share my attitude to work. He would come in late, leave early and have long lunches—liquid lunches. Being friendly, he would often lurch into the office, look over my shoulder and tell me what was wrong with my software, and collapse into his office chair. I ignored his attempts at being helpful since I assumed a drunk would have little, if any, debugging skills. However, in this particular instance I listened to him and he was right. For the next few days I listened to him again, and he pinpointed my errors with a remarkable accuracy.

This made me very depressed: here was a drunk, debugging better than myself who had believed the preacher of my childhood who told me that hard work leads to rewards. I went to see a senior programmer and explained my problem. He pointed out something which I have tried to implement ever since. He told me that a programmer is so bound up with a program that it takes a totally independent view of that program in order to debug it effectively. He also told me that individual programmers find it very difficult to detect errors because this detection is concrete evidence of what they might perceive as their own incompetence.

Because of the difficulty that staff have in validating their own work a good quality system should provide facilities whereby the validation of any product is decoupled from those who produced it. There are a number of examples of this principle, and it is worth briefly exploring some of them here. Later sections of this book will look at these techniques in much more detail.

A good example of this decoupling occurs with the programming of a module. Normally, on a software project, a programmer codes a module, generates test data and then checks that the execution of the module matches his or her expectation of the test output. A good way of ensuring a high degree of independence is to have a procedure which insists that, after producing a module, a programmer sits down with another programmer and describes in detail to the second programmer what the module does. My experience is that even if the second programmer says nothing, the very act of explaining the function of the module usually leads to the first programmer detecting errors. Once this code reading process has finished, the second programmer then tests the module. This puts the onus on the second programmer to listen during the read through. A clever project manager will usually ensure that the second programmer is one who the first programmer respects, fears, or is in awe of. This tightens the validation and usually results in the first programmer delivering high-quality program code which is easy to test.

Another example of independence in a quality system concerns the organization of the quality assurance function. I have experienced a number of quality assurance regimes, and the best tend to be those which are organized as a separate department, with the head of the department having a separate reporting line—often up to board level. Projects would normally then have a member of the quality assurance staff attached to them. This form of organization usually means that the project manager is unable to browbeat quality assurance staff into relaxing standards when a project has time or budget difficulties.

Two more extreme examples of independence are *black teams* and *bug bounty hunters*. Both are American phenomena. The former are aggressive testing teams which virtually attack a software system before it is handed over to the customer for acceptance testing. Such teams are often made up of staff who hate project managers and those who enjoy the act of destruction. Bug bounty hunters are companies who specialize in independent testing. Normally, you pay a bug bounty hunter a fixed fee, together with a sum of money for each bug detected in system testing.

1.4.2 Maintainability

Another principle involves maintainability. Figures gathered over the last decade have indicated that software developers can spend as much as 75 per cent of their project budgets on software maintenance: the process of modifying a system once it has been made operational. There are a number of reasons for this high figure. The main reason is that a software system is a reflection of the world, and since the world changes the system must change. For example, an existing accounting package has to change when taxation laws are changed. A good quality system should have standards and procedures which ensure that the process of changing a document or program code is as easy as possible; for example, by insisting on naming conventions for test files so that they can be easily found in the project library.

Another implication of the fact that maintenance is a high resource consumer is that a software quality system should incorporate something known as a *configuration management system*, the components of which are described in Chapter 8. This is a set of standards and procedures which govern the process of modifying a system both during development and maintenance: how changes are proposed, agreed, applied and validated, together with procedures for notifying relevant staff of changes.

1.4.3 Traceability

I am often asked to pass judgement on a software developer, usually on behalf of a customer who may be thinking of using the developer to construct a system. One strategy which I use to judge the quality of the software developer's quality system is to ask for the source listing of a finished project and flip over some pages until I find a module. I then ask the staff concerned what functions in the requirements specification that module helps implement. If they can tell me in ten minutes, then I know that their quality system—or at least that part of it which is concerned with the requirements specification—is good; if they take hours to tell me, then it usually indicates that the software developer will have problems, especially during maintenance.

This is an example of something known as *reverse traceability*: the ability to trace from the source code of a module back to a function in a requirements specification. There is also *forward traceability*, which describes the ability to trace from a function to a module.

Why is traceability important? The reason is connected with maintainability. In order to see why a good quality system should establish linkages between program code and a requirements specification, consider the process of acceptance testing. This is the final stage of the software project when the customer, in conjunction with the software developer, checks that a system is ready for handover. If an acceptance test for a function fails, then there is usually a lot of embarrassment, and the developer has to fix the error.

If the test that failed was test n, then a poor software developer will correct the error, repeat acceptance test n, and move on to test $n + 1$. This is certainly the wrong thing for the software developer to do, for in fixing the error that leads to the failure, he or she may have inserted another error into the system which could only be detected by tests carried out prior to test n. If the documentation for a project does not support traceability then, when an acceptance test fails, the customer has every right to ask the developer to start the acceptance test process again.

However, if the quality system does support traceability, then all the software developer has to do is to identify the modules which have been changed, trace back to the functions which have been affected, and then re-execute the acceptance tests which check out those functions.

> **Self Assessment Question 1.7** Explain the difference between reverse and forward traceability.
>
> **Solution** *Forward traceability* describes the ability to trace easily from a function in the requirements specification to the modules that implement that function. *Reverse traceability* describes the ability to trace from a chunk of code—usually a module—to the functions that it helps implement.

1.4.4 Incrementalism

One of the unpleasant facts about software development is that it exhibits what is known as *combinatorial explosion*. This means that as a system gets larger and a certain task is applied to the system, such as testing, the degree of difficulty of that task does not increase linearly as a function of the size of the system but often rises exponentially.

A good quality system should provide facilities whereby software development is split up into small manageable tasks. A good example of this is integration testing. *Integration* is the process whereby a project builds up a software system a chunk at a time, with integration testing being the tests which take place after each chunk has been added. Most companies claim that they carry out integration. However, the integration that they practise is very coarse-grained: usually subsystems are integrated. An integration strategy which adds single modules, or small numbers of modules, invariably leads to a system testing phase which is less error-prone than would be the case if integration was not carried out.

In order to see why integration is such a useful technique it is worth looking at system testing. When an error occurs in system testing the software developer is faced with a massive task: that of detecting where an error occurs in a system which may contain hundreds, if not thousands, of modules. Because of this, debugging during system testing is a highly resource-intensive process. Now, if a software developer practised integration and integration testing, the process of debugging would be much easier. If an error occurred after an integration test, then the error is normally found in one of the small number of modules which have been added to the system at the last integration. By devoting some extra resources to integration, the developer will normally remove many of the errors which would have been detected during system and acceptance testing, and which would have consumed an inordinate amount of resources.

1.4.5 Early validation

A good indication of the quality of a quality system is how much direction it devotes to the process of early validation: the checking of a system during the early stages of software development—during requirements analysis, requirements specification and system design. The reason for this is that if a developer commits an error early on in the software project, and it is not detected until the later stages, then the resources devoted to rectifying the error can often be far greater than the resources which would have been needed if the error was detected and rectified at an early stage. Many software projects have failed because of requirements errors which were only detected towards the end of the testing phase. There are a whole battery of techniques that can be used for early validation: these include technical reviews, meetings where staff examine a document for correctness; prototyping, where an early version of a system can be shown to the customer during requirements specification; and simulation.

The quality system should offer facilities for all these; for example, for reviews it should provide direction on how many staff should attend a review, how a review is set up, its ideal duration, what documentation is required, and what documentation needs to be completed after the review.

Self Assessment Question 1.8 Why do you think late detection of an error leads to major costs?

Solution An error discovered late in a project can lead to a major resource expenditure in respecifying, redesigning and reprogramming a system. If the error was discovered at the time it was made all that might be needed would be a small change in, say, the requirements specification.

1.4.6 The importance of the requirements specification

One of the key documents in a software project is the requirements specification. It is used by the system designer when deciding on a software architecture, by the staff responsible for writing user documentation, by testing staff to generate tests, and also by project managers when predicting the resources on a software project. This importance should be reflected in the amount of effort which the quality system devotes to the requirements specification: its form, the way it is developed and the way it is validated. All too often I see quality systems which have excellent standards for program code, but perfunctory ones for the requirements specification.

1.4.7 The dynamic nature of the quality system

There are two aspects of this. First, when a quality system is used by a manager on a project it is often just taken down off the shelf with little consideration of whether some of the facilities offered by the quality system are not needed or whether some need to be strengthened. Every software project is different, even those within a narrow application band. The next section of this chapter will stress that at the start of each project—usually during project planning—a software developer will need to look at what a quality system offers and decide whether some facilities need to be dropped or others need to be augmented before including them in a quality plan for a project. For example, the quality system of a management information company may be directed towards assurance activities for mainstream applications such as retailing and banking where, perhaps, the customer knows the application area well and is computer-literate. However, a new project may involve a customer who knows nothing about computers. The project manager, in that case, may have to augment the facilities available in the quality system to keep closer track of the progress his staff are making in eliciting customer requirements.

Secondly, the quality system requires periodic review. There are a number of reasons for this. In the early days of deployment of a quality system there will be a surprisingly large number of deficiencies reported: producing a good quality system is very much like developing a software system, and you should not be surprised that some of the standards that were initially documented do not work as well as they should. In the longer term, the business progress of the software developer, together with the availability of better technology such as software tools, new programming languages and software development methodologies, should mean that aspects of the quality system will be incomplete or out-of-date. Because of this, a quality system should be periodically reviewed during its lifetime, with the review periods being shorter during its initial life. This is a requirement which many external quality standards place great emphasis on.

1.5 QUALITY AND THE QUALITY SYSTEM

The last theme—that of the flexibility of the quality system—leads naturally on to a description of how quality systems work. The aim of this section is to describe the relationship that a quality system has with software development, and provide the reader with some terminology which will ensure that the remainder of the book can be properly accessed. At the heart of the application of quality assurance there is something called a *quality system* (sometimes known as a *quality management system*). This consists of the managerial structure, responsibilities, activities, capabilities and resources which ensure that software products produced by projects will have the desired quality factors that both the customer and the developer decide will be built into them. This means that a quality system encompasses activities such as:

- The auditing of projects to ensure that quality controls are being adhered to.
- The review of the quality system in order to improve it.
- Staff development of personnel employed within the quality assurance area.
- The negotiation of resources which enable staff who carry out quality assurance activities to function properly.
- Providing input into development-oriented improvement activities; for example, the adoption of a new notation for requirements specification.
- The development of standards, procedures and guidelines.
- The production of reports to high-level management which describe the effectiveness of the current quality system.
- The production of reports to high-level quality management which enable them to put into action activities that aid the improvement of the quality system.

These, then, are a selection of activities normally associated with a quality management system.

The concrete details of a quality system will be held in a *quality manual*—sometimes erroneously called a quality system. Such a manual will normally contain standards for the quality and developmental activities that may be applied to a project. A short extract from a quality manual is shown below. It shows the directions given to programming staff about the testing of a module in a system:

7 Module testing

One of the most important tasks to be carried out by the programmer is the testing of individual modules. Normally the module which is to be tested will be one which has been created by the programmer who is to carry out the test. Each module will have a name and will be found in a file whose name consists of the name of the module with the extension *pas, cob* or *for* depending on whether the module was programmed in Pascal, COBOL or FORTRAN. The programmer should carry out two types of test: a functional test and a structural test. The aim of the functional test is to check that the function of the module has been implemented correctly. The function of a module can be found in the comment which forms the header of the module. The aim of a structural test is to generate test data which exercises some proportion of a structural metric of the module—usually 100% of statements.

The relationship between international standards, the quality system and individual projects is shown in Fig. 1.1. International standards such as ISO 9001 provide guidance to companies on how they should organize their quality system. A component of the quality system is the quality manual which describes the variety of standards and quality controls available to projects. When a project is in its formative stages—normally during planning—a project manager will identify the quality factors that are important, and extract from the quality manual those standards and procedures which are necessary to ensure that the software product to be developed will contain those factors. These are placed in a document known as a *quality plan*, which forms part of the overall project plan for a software project.

A quality plan will contain a list of quality tasks such as the application of a particular system test, when the task is to be carried out and who is to carry it out. The quality plan will also contain other information such as any quality standards that are to be adopted, any quality tools which are to be used and the way in which the quality assurance is to be organised.

Thus, international standards often—but not always—drive the production of a quality system which then provides facilities for a project manager to produce a quality plan—there being separate quality plans for each project undertaken by a software developer.

As an example of the latter parts of this process, consider a software project whose manager decides that portability is to be a major quality factor for a particular product. The manager will consult the quality manual for those parts which address portability and incorporate them as quality controls in his or her project. There are a number of ways in which the quality manual can provide facilities for ensuring portability; for example, by providing standards for:

- The language chosen for the project which ensures that non-standard features are not used by staff.
- Portability testing across a wide range of computers and operating systems.
- Checking the output from any one-off or proprietary tools which process program code and detect non-portable features.
- Development techniques such as information hiding which enable a high degree of portability to be achieved.

A quality plan will embody a number of *quality controls* which check that particular quality factors are present in a system. A quality control is normally associated with

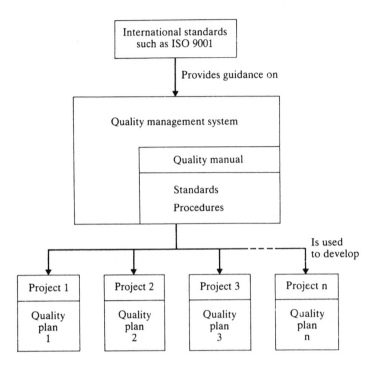

Figure 1.1 External standards, a quality management system and quality plans.

documentary evidence that the quality factor is present. Some examples of quality controls are:

- A system test which checks that a particular function has been properly executed. The documentary evidence would be a test record.
- The code review which, as part of its agenda, has been asked to check for portability concerns. The signed minutes of such a review would be the documentary evidence.
- The execution of a tool which checks program code for adherence to programming standards. The printout from the tool indicating the absence of standards violations would be the documentary evidence.
- The execution of a tool which gives a numerical readability index for the requirements specification. The printout from the tool indicating a high readability index would be the documentary evidence.

The first control is associated with the correctness quality factor, the second with the portability quality factor, and the third and fourth with the maintainability factor.

Self Assessment Question 1.9 A dynamic analysis tool instruments modules written in a third-generation language and provides a report on the execution of the module when it is supplied with test data, for example the percentage coverage achieved by the data. Could this tool act as a quality control? If so, what quality factor does it address and what documentary evidence would be associated with it ?

Solution There a number of quality factors that could be associated with this tool. The main one is correctness. If the tool provides a report on structural coverage achieved by test data, then provided the tests were correct the tool would address the correctness quality factor. The documentation associated with the tool's use as a quality control would be its printout reporting on the coverage.

1.6 STANDARDS AND PROCEDURES

In order to conclude this chapter, and to complete the process of providing a vocabulary, this section briefly describes the major tools provided in a quality manual: standards, procedures and guidelines. This topic will be treated in much more detail in Chapter 13; however, since these terms will be used frequently before that it is worth defining them.

First, a warning. Paradoxically, for such a precise subject as quality assurance, nomenclature is still quite loose and the definitions given here are accepted by a large number of software developers and books, but by no means the majority. I shall define a *standard* as an instruction about how a document should be laid out on paper or on a computer screen. For example, a requirements specification standard would specify all the sections expected in such a document and how each section is to be structured.

By a *procedure* I mean text which describes how a particular software task is to be carried out. For example, a procedure for programming would describe what standards to apply, where to store the source code and object code of a program or module, how to carry out certain categories of test, and what documentation to fill in when the process of programming and testing have been completed. The important point about both procedures and standards is that once they have been adopted for a particular project they have to be adhered to.

A *guideline* is text which provides advice on an activity. It is not prescriptive like a standard or a procedure. For example, a company may have a guideline which governs the conduct of project progress meetings which, for example, specifies who should normally attend such meetings. Although guidelines offer advice you would normally expect them to be followed by projects most of the time. Often, procedures and guidelines are found combined, where a procedure will mainly contain mandatory instructions but also provide advice, for example about how many staff should attend a particular meeting. The important point about such a combined document is that it should be made clear what exactly is mandatory and what is advice.

It is worth pointing out that some companies collectively refer to standards and procedures as standards, and sometimes as guidelines.

1.7 SUMMARY

The main points embodied in this chapter are:

- A quality factor is an aspect of a software product which is important to the customer or the developer. Sometimes it is important to both.
- A quality system is intended to ensure that quality factors identified at the beginning of a project are present in a completed software system.
- A standard is a description of the way in which a project document is structured and how information in the document is presented.
- A procedure is a set of instructions which describe how a particular software task should be carried out.
- A quality control is an activity which ensures that a particular quality factor is present in a software system and its associated documentation. It gives rise to documents which provide assurance that a particular quality factor is present.
- A quality manual is a document which contains standards, procedures and guidelines which can be adopted by a project manager for a particular software project.
- A quality plan embodies the standards, procedures and quality controls which are to be used on a project.

1.8 FURTHER READING

There are few good books on software quality assurance topics. Dunn and Ullman (1982) and Lewis (1992) are excellent American books; the latter is particularly good on the need for independence in the quality assurance process. Ould (1990) is an excellent British tutorial which can be read in an evening and Gillies (1992) is a superb British introduction to quality assurance. Crosby (1979) is a book which is not specifically about software, but does address the cultural and managerial aspects of implementing a quality system in a very effective way. Finally, Boehm (1981) is an excellent book which describes the economics of software production.

PROBLEMS

1.1 Which of the quality factors mentioned in the chapter does the following activity address: the application of a static analysis tool to program code which detects certain types of errors such as the fact that a variable is declared but never used.

1.2 Which of the quality factors mentioned in the chapter does the following activity address: the application of a tool to the requirements specification which produces an index that quantifies how readable that document is.

1.3 Which of the quality factors mentioned in the chapter does the following activity address: the use of a guideline which ensures that all project documents are stored in a central project library.

1.4 What particular quality factors does the process of acceptance testing address?

1.5 Service staff are normally part of the maintenance function. They are the people who the customer usually telephones whenever an error is discovered in a system during its operation. What sort of facilities should a quality system offer such staff?

1.6 If you were to convince your senior management that software quality assurance needs to be taken seriously in your company what would be the main points that you would make in a report?

1.7 Why do you think each project will require its own quality plan? Would it not be simpler to apply the quality manual to each project?

SOFTWARE TASKS AND QUALITY ASSURANCE

AIMS

- To describe the developmental tasks which make up the software production process.
- To describe the validation and verification tasks which are used to check the correctness of a software system.
- To outline some of the problems with developmental, validation and verification tasks which software quality assurance is intended to address.

2.1 INTRODUCTION

Before looking at the various elements that make up software quality assurance it is worth describing a number of technical tasks which are carried out by software developers. The main aim of this chapter is to provide the reader with a vocabulary which will enable subsequent chapters to be easily accessed. In order to describe these tasks two models of software development will be presented. The first is normally used by developers of system software, real-time software and telecommunications software, where the data complexity of the product is small. The second is found within companies which produce information systems where the stored data can be very complex. If you think that you are familiar with conventional software development then it is worth skipping to Sect. 2.5 which describes some of the problems that affect software activities and which quality assurance is intended to address.

2.2 A SOFTWARE DEVELOPMENT MODEL

The majority of today's software projects are partitioned into a number of phases—*requirements analysis, requirements specification, system design, detailed design,* and *programming.* Each of these phases corresponds to a distinct activity that gives rise to some end-products, which are then fed into the next phase. The starting point in any software project is a customer *statement of requirements*. This is a document, produced by the customer, which expresses his or her aspirations about a future computer system.

The quality of the statement of requirements varies considerably: customers with little experience of software systems, specifications and information technology will produce short, very abstract documents which perhaps only give broad hints about their requirements. The more sophisticated customer, e.g. a major computer manufacturer who is subcontracting a system, might develop a statement of requirements which is a multi-volume work, containing descriptions of every facet of the system to be developed.

The statement of requirements is communicated to the software developer, who then carries out *requirements analysis*: the task of attempting to discover what the proposed system is to do. To carry out this task, analysts from the developer's staff study any existing systems—manual, automated, or semi-automated—which the proposed system is to replace, interview the customer's staff, and carry out some form of technical analysis of the statement of requirements.

When the process of requirements analysis is complete, the analysts write down a description of the properties of the system that is to be developed. This process is known as *requirements specification*, and gives rise to a document known as the *requirements specification*, often referred to as the *system specification*. This contains a detailed description of all the tasks that a system is to carry out, any constraints such as response time or memory utilization, and any design directives or implementation directives such as insistence on a particular file organization for a database. The requirements specification also contains a number of appendices that address issues which, although important, are not directly relevant to the description of the system, e.g. they may detail the maintenance support for the system and the training of the customer's staff to be be carried out. The major feature of a requirements specification relevant to the subject matter of this book is that it contains a large amount of detail about what a system should do, i.e. its functions.

The requirements specification is a key document in the software project for a number of reasons. First, it is a major input into the next task in the project: system design. Second, it is used, either in its final form or, more realistically, in outline form, by a project manager to estimate the resources that are required for a project. Third, it is used by either quality assurance or development staff to develop the system tests and acceptance tests which will check the correctness of the system. Fourth, it is consulted by staff responsible for developing system documentation when constructing the user manual.

Because the requirements specification is such an important document, the software developer will expend a large amount of resources on its construction, and will ensure that everything is defined in minute detail. Errors in the requirements specification that remain undiscovered until late in a software project, say during system testing, have been a major cause of project overruns, and have even led to the cancellation of major projects.

The next stage in the development process is *system design*. This consists of processing the requirements specification and producing an architecture which implements the functions contained in the requirements specification and also respects the constraints specified in that document. The architecture of the system is expressed in terms of self-contained chunks of program code which I shall call *modules*. If the programming language used was Pascal, modules would correspond to procedures or functions; if the

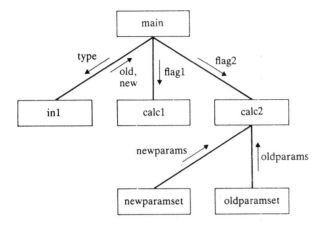

Figure 2.1 A system design notation.

language was FORTRAN or COBOL, then a module would correspond to a subroutine.

The system architecture can be specified using a number of notations—probably the most common class of notation uses graphics. An example is shown in Fig. 2.1. This represents the design of a system which contains six modules. The lines joining the modules are calls, and the items attached to lines represent the parameters that are passed between the modules. Thus, in Fig. 2.1, the module *main* calls the modules *in1*, *calc1* and *calc2,* and the interface between *main* and *in1* is the collection of parameters *old, new* and *type*. The arrows indicate the direction in which data is passed between the modules. Thus, *type* is passed to *in1*, and *in1* passes *old* and *new* to *main*.

Self Assessment Question 2.1 Can you think of the type of facility that a quality system should provide for staff who check the correctness of a system design?

Solution Generally the quality system should provide standards, procedures and guidelines which enable staff to check that a design meets both the functional and non-functional properties detailed in the requirements specification. For example, there should be a procedure which governs review meetings which check system design correctness.

The next stage of development is *detailed design*. During system design the staff allocated to this task will have specified what each module in the system should do. The task of the detailed designers is to take this description and fill in the processing details inside the modules. These processing details are usually expressed in terms of some specialized detailed design notation, e.g. a flow chart or a program design language. An example of part of a module expressed in terms of a program design language is shown below. It counts up the number of items in the array *a* that are greater than the value *maxvalue*. The notation is very similar to that of a programming language, in that all the standard control constructs are used, the only difference being that it uses natural language for the specification of the detailed processing that occurs:

```
PROCEDURE Checkup(a, sum)
BEGIN
Set sum to zero
FOR i FROM 1 TO n DO
    IF a[i] is greater than maxvalue THEN
        Add 1 to sum
    ENDIF
ENDFOR
END
```

The task of detailed design is an optional one. Many software developers prefer to miss it out, and program directly from the system design. Detailed designs tend to be used by software developers who are interested in portability—especially when they are implementing a number of versions of a system using a variety of programming languages. A detailed design represents a good, language-independent description of what a system does, and can be easily hand-translated into any programming language—be it an assembler language or a very high-level language such as Ada.

After detailed design, *programming* begins. This involves the programmer taking a module specification, which is either extracted from a detailed design—assuming such a document is constructed—or from a system design if it is not. If a developer constructs a detailed design, the process of programming is easy: all it involves is a hand-translation of the detailed design into the program code of the chosen implementation language. However, if the developer has not constructed a detailed design, then programming is a more intellectual task, which involves selecting an algorithm that carries out the processing required by the system design.

This marks the end of the development activities in the software project. Fortunately, this is not the whole story. Overlaid with all the developmental activities that have been previously described, there is the continual application of a series of activities which check that the developer is carrying out software tasks correctly, and that the system which is being specified and programmed meets user requirements. These tasks are collectively known as *verification* and *validation* and are described in some detail in Sect. 2.4.

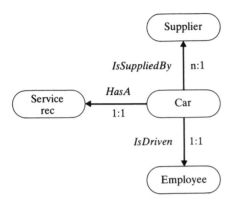

Figure 2.2 An example of an entity-relation diagram.

2.3 ANOTHER DEVELOPMENT MODEL

The model presented in the previous section is a fairly common one. It, or a variant, is usually adopted by the developers of software systems which are dominated by software processes and have little data associated with them; for example, those systems found in application areas such as railway signalling, military command and control, and avionics. These systems are not devoid of data but have relatively simple data architectures compared with application areas such as retailing, banking, and strategic information provision. It is also a model employed by developers of data-rich systems who use third-generation languages such as C and COBOL. Developers of data-rich systems who use fourth-generation languages usually adopt a slightly different life-cycle model in which the data architecture is considered well before the development of a program architecture. Such developers use a variety of notations to characterize the data in a system. One of the first notations often produced is known as an *entity-relationship diagram*, often abbreviated to an E-R diagram. This describes the relationships between the entities in a system. An example of an E-R diagram is shown in Fig. 2.2, and describes the data for a simple system which administers company cars.

This simple diagram describes the fact that the system is made up of cars, employees, and the service records of cars. Each arrowed line represents the fact that an entity is related to another entity. The name of the relationship is written close to a line; thus, the vertical line labelled *IsDriven* between cars and employees describes the fact that a car is driven by an employee. A relation can be one-to-one or one-to-many; in the former case only one entity is associated with an occurrence of another entity, while in the latter case one occurrence of an entity is associated with a number of occurrences of another entity. Thus, in Fig. 2.2 the fact that only one employee is associated with one car is indicated by the characters 1:1, and the fact that a car supplier will supply a number of cars is indicated by the characters n:1.

Another notation which is produced by the developers of data-rich systems is the

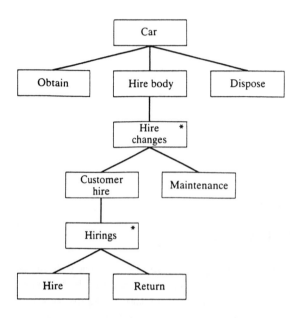

Figure 2.3 An example of an entity life-history.

entity life-history. An example of such a diagram is shown in Fig. 2.3.

This shows the ordering of actions on the entity *car*, which is an entity in a system for a car hire company. The top level of the diagram gives the name of the entity. The next level states that a car will first be obtained, it will then undergo hirings, and finally will be disposed of. The box marked *hire body* describes what the hiring part of the system entails: it first involves customer hirings, followed by maintenance on a car. The box marked *customer hire* describes the fact that a repeated number of hirings is to take place, the asterisk in the box *hirings* indicates that all the boxes underneath it are to be repeated a number of times. Finally, the boxes underneath the box marked *hirings* show that a customer hire is always followed by a return.

This diagram, therefore, describes a situation whereby a car is obtained, and then a series of actions consisting of hires and returns followed by a maintenance action is executed, the whole process being terminated by the action of disposing of a car.

Such diagrams are a good aid to validation and verification: they enable the analyst to discover whether any events in the system have been missed. Indeed, in Fig. 2.3, an event has been missed: that of a customer crashing a car, and the car being written off.

Diagrams like the ones shown in Fig. 2.2 and Fig. 2.3 represent a logical view of the data that is inherent in an application; they are produced during the requirements analysis and specification process. The functions of the system may be written down at this stage, although many software developers will delay this part until the last possible

Table 2.1 A relational table

Worksno	Name	Salary	Grade
1244	Cleland	45000	A
2894	Lee Yok	23400	D
8871	Roberts	12500	E
3349	Rolands	12800	E
1900	Ince	23450	D
4545	Williams	12500	E
1444	Dickins	23450	D
2928	Hoare	34000	B
9876	Khan	12500	E
4588	Rimbaud	35000	B
2358	Proust	25000	D

moment as the functional specification will be more volatile than the specification of the data; this means that if the functional specification is delayed, then the developer's staff do not prematurely commit themselves to a functional specification which may change drastically during the early stages of a project.

For those developers who do wish to commit themselves to a functional specification at this stage it would either be expressed in terms of text or in some graphical notation such as a data flow diagram. Once the requirements specification has been completed, the next stage is to design the data and, in a fourth-generation language environment, provide a specification of the programs which are to access the data. The architecture of the data is usually expressed in terms of tables known as *relations*. An example is shown in Table 2.1.

This table represents employees in a rather simple personnel management system; each line of the table represents an occurrence of an employee. Each employee occurrence is distinguished by a field known as a *key field* which uniquely identifies the employee. In the case of Table 2.1 the key field is *Worksno*. A number of these tables will be developed, and each will contain linking information; for example, another table in the personnel management system might contain employee performance figures. This table would contain a field which held the unique works number of each employee.

Once these tables have been completed, the specification of individual programs can be refined and their action expressed in terms of operations on the tables. An example of such a specification is shown below:

Program PersonnelQuery1
This program retrieves all the employees in the staff table who have a salary greater than a specific amount and who have reached a specific employee grade.

Another task which is carried out at this stage is to design the human–computer interface: how individual programs will be linked together and how the user will interact with these programs. This topic is addressed in Chapter 10.

The final development task is that of *programming*. Often a fourth-generation language is used, which interfaces directly to a relational database management system that supports tables such as that shown in Table 2.1. Such a language enables program code and interfaces to be produced much more easily than languages such as COBOL.

During the development process, validation and verification occurs. This will largely be similar to that described in Sect. 2.4. However, there will be some differences; for example, in the life-cycle I described first a practice increasingly insisted on by quality manuals is to achieve a coverage of 100 per cent statements during unit testing. With a fourth-generation language there is no direct analogue of statement coverage. Also, with fourth-generation language development there is much more of an opportunity to carry out prototyping: the early development of a software system which is used to improve tasks such as requirements elicitation and the selection of appropriate designs.

2.4 VERIFICATION AND VALIDATION

Verification is concerned with checking that a particular task has been carried out correctly, e.g. that a programmer has correctly implemented a detailed design. *Validation* is concerned with checking that a system meets customer requirements; system testing—executing a system in order to check that it meets customer requirements—is an example of validation. There are many verification and validation activities which occur during a software project. In this section they will be described in the order in which they occur in the conventional software project.

Self Assessment Question 2.2 Is unit testing, sometimes known as module testing, a verification or validation activity?

Solution Unit testing involves the checking of a module to ensure that the task of programming has been carried out correctly. Hence it is an example of verification.

During requirements analysis and requirements specification two validation activities can be carried out and one can be started. The first two activities are the execution of the software requirements review, and prototyping; the third is preparing for the system testing and acceptance testing phases.

A *review* is a meeting of a number of staff who spend some time—no more than two hours—reading a document or a segment of program code and checking it for correctness. Reviews are highly effective: staff who attend such reviews tend to bring a fresh mind to a problem, and are able to check a document or program code more thoroughly. Many programmers, analysts and designers find it very difficult to detach themselves from what they produce, and hence find it very difficult to detect errors. The technical review overcomes this problem in that staff who are completely detached from a document, or software product, do not have any misconceptions about that product.

Normally a review involves between three and five members of staff. In a requirements review, which is normally attended by five staff, these would normally be the analyst who produces the requirements specification—or more realistically, the part of the requirements specification—that is being reviewed; a member of the developer's quality assurance department; a member of staff from another project; another analyst; and a customer representative.

The requirements specification is examined in detail, together with the statement of requirements. The participants' main concern is that the requirements specification actually represents an adequate description of the system that the customer wants. The meeting also addresses problems such as ambiguities and contradictions in the requirements specification. A review is an error detection process, and not an error rectification process, and hence there is little discussion about what needs to be done in order to improve the specification—all that is produced is an action list of errors that have been discovered, and which need subsequent attention.

Self Assessment Question 2.3 Reviews are a highly effective validation or verification process. Why do you think this is?

Solution The main reason is that it brings a high degree of independence to checking. Many of the staff involved in a review will have no vested interest in the correctness or otherwise of the item being reviewed and hence they will have an objective viewpoint.

Prototyping involves the early production of a version of a system that can be used as a learning medium by both the developer and the customer. There are a number of ways of developing such a prototype. If the application is for a commercial data processing system, then a fourth-generation programming language would, almost invariably, be used. Such languages enable large amounts of functionality to be expressed in a small amount of programming code. Other techniques for prototyping involve the use of very high-level languages such as LISP and PROLOG, the UNIX operating system, relaxing the quality assurance standards on a project, or only implementing part of a system.

Prototyping is a highly effective process for carrying out requirements analysis. Requirements specifications are becoming so complex and large that both the customer and the developer have major difficulties understanding them. A prototype represents the most concrete manifestation of a software system that is possible, and is able to give the customer an exact and complete idea of what will be delivered.

Another validation process that occurs towards the end of the requirements specification is the process of deriving the system tests and acceptance tests. These are the final checks on a system which confirm that it meets user requirements. The system and acceptance tests are carried out at the end of the development of a system after all the correctly programmed modules of the system have been brought together. The *system tests* are a set of preliminary tests carried out within the developer's environment as a last check that acceptance will not be too much trouble. The *acceptance tests* are carried out in the environment in which the system is to be installed—each test being witnessed by the customer or a representative. These tests are crucial since, if the system fails an acceptance test, the customer has every right to refuse to take delivery of a system and, hence, to pay for it. Also, the failure of an acceptance test often involves the developer in a large amount of respecification and redesign.

Because the acceptance tests are so critical, the developers carry out a series of preliminary tests in their workplace. These so-called system tests have, as a subset, the acceptance tests, but also contain a large number of other tests which give the developers considerable confidence that there will be no embarrassment during the acceptance test phase. The major difference between the system tests and the acceptance tests is that items of equipment, such as a nuclear reactor or an aeroplane, will not be available in the developers' workplace and, hence, will need to be simulated—either by software or by special-purpose hardware.

During the latter stages of requirements specification the developers will start to develop the system and acceptance test suite. By the end of the system design phase they will have a description of the tests expressed in outline form. An example of such an outline is shown below. It represents some of the tests for a stock control application:

> **TEST 1.4** This test checks that when an order is processed by the system and the order is for an item that is out of stock then a suitable message is displayed at the originating VDU.
>
> **TEST 1.5** This test checks that when the query command is processed by the system the correct price of the item that is queried is displayed on the originating VDU.
>
> **TEST 1.6** This test checks that when the back orders command is processed by the system the list of orders which cannot be currently satisfied is displayed.

There are a number of reasons why the system test process is started so early. First, it helps the developer's analysts in carrying out requirements analysis. One of the toughest questions to ask of a statement in a requirements specification is: 'How do I test that?' Many analysts have reported to me that they carry out their job more effectively if there is a tester continually looking over their shoulder at the requirements specification, asking difficult questions about how functions and constraints are to be checked during system testing. It is an excellent way of detecting functions and constraints that are expressed ambiguously.

Second, the early development of the system and acceptance tests enables the early prediction of the resources required for these activities. The high-level management of a software company would look askance at a project manager who asked for staff for acceptance and system testing a few days before those activities started. They require as much notice as possible. A set of outline system tests provides the basis for at least a rough estimate of project resources early on in a project.

Finally, many software projects either require special-purpose testing tools, or the development of large test data suites. Only by deriving the system and acceptance tests early will the developers be able to anticipate these needs well in advance of requiring them.

After requirements analysis and requirements specification is complete, system design begins. The main validation and verification activity associated with this is the design review. The conduct of such a review is similar to that of the requirements review, the major differences being that the customer is not usually invited to such reviews, and the nature of the questions asked will be different.

A design review concentrates on two types of issues. First, it addresses issues concerning the degree to which the system design meets the description of the system contained in the requirements specification. Second, it concentrates on structural issues: is the specification of a module's function expressed clearly and correctly; are there any features of the design that will give rise to problems during software maintenance; and will the design produce a system that will satisfy memory constraints?

An important activity commenced during system design is *integration testing*. During the later stages of the design process the developers decide on an integration testing strategy. Integration testing occurs during the integration process. The developers build up a system a few modules at a time; after each addition of modules, a series of tests are carried out in order to check that the interfaces between the integrated modules and the system that is being built up are correctly implemented.

There are a number of decisions that software developers have to make about integration and integration testing. First, they have to decide on an overall strategy. There are essentially three options for integration: top-down integration, bottom-up integration, and inside-out integration. Each has its advantages and disadvantages. For example, top-down integration enables an early, albeit partial, version of a system to be available, but is not very good at detecting errors in modules that lie at the bottom of a system.

Self Assessment Question 2.4 Can you think of any other advantage of top-down integration?

Solution It enables early functional testing to be carried out in advance of system testing and hence reduces rectification costs.

Another decision that has to be made concerns the granularity of integration: the number of modules that are to be added at a time. The developers may decide on an overall figure; for example, that three modules are to be integrated at a time. Or they may decide on integrating a variable number of modules at a time, for example, they may integrate one module where that module is very complex, or 20 where the modules are relatively simple.

The developers also have to decide whether to execute any early system tests during integration. The developer may find that after carrying out a number of integrations, enough of the system has been constructed for some system tests to be executed. It is often a good idea to carry out these tests: a maxim for all software developers is that if it is possible to check something early in the software project, then do so, and save yourself the considerable redesign and respecification costs which would arise if the checking was carried out later.

By the end of the system design phase the developers will have constructed an *integration and test plan.* This plan will specify the order of integration, what modules are to be integrated, the degree of testing that is to be carried out, and a list of any system tests that are to be exercised.

As early as the latter stages of the system design process, coded and tested modules will start emerging from the project—usually from subsystems that have been designed early. The process of testing which these modules undergo is known as *unit testing.* This involves the programmers who programmed a module developing test data which checks out the function of the module. For example, if the module sorted an arbitrary collection of integers, the programmers would check the module with one integer, 50 integers, and a large number of integers; they would also select a sequence of integers that was already sorted, one which was already sorted except for one integer, and a sequence that was sorted in reverse order. After this functional testing is complete, the programmers check that their test data has achieved a high coverage of a structural element of their module—typically, they might check that their test data has exercised all the statements in a module and a very high proportion of branches.

The tested modules are then placed in a project library and withdrawn from this library during integration testing, as and when they are needed. Eventually, after all the integrations have taken place, and all the integration tests are complete, the final system will emerge from development. The only validation and verification activities that remain will be system testing and acceptance testing. By this stage of the software project the outline system tests, which, you will remember, were generated during the late stages of requirements specification and the early stages of system design, will have been expanded until they have become step-by-step descriptions of the tests to be carried out. In this state they are known as *test procedures*. An example of a test procedure is shown below. Ideally, such procedures can be given to staff who have little knowledge of the system which they are to test:

> **TEST-PROC 3.4** Attach test file ATEST14.TST to the system stored in file SYSV3.OBJ. Execute the system and type in a variety of product numbers between 1 and 1000 when prompted by the character =. If the product number is not found in the product database then a message, *error-unknown product*, will be displayed. A list of the product numbers that are in the test database can be found in the file PRODT.TXT: use this to check on the correctness of the response.

The test procedures for the system tests are then executed against the final system. If there are any errors the system is debugged, the errors rectified, and the test repeated, together with any tests that exercise the program code which was modified when the error was rectified. Eventually, the system will have passed its system tests, and all that remains is the execution of the acceptance tests. By the beginning of the system test phase the customer, in conjunction with the developers, will have selected the subset of the system tests that will be the acceptance tests. These tests will be applied to the software in its operational environment. If the developers have done their job correctly, then the execution of the acceptance tests will be a formality!

2.5 SOFTWARE PROBLEMS AND QUALITY ASSURANCE

The aim of this section is to describe a number of the problems that affect some of the developmental, validation and verification activities described previously and which software quality assurance is intended to address.

2.5.1 Requirements analysis and specification

The requirements analysis and specification process is one of the most important on the software project. Unfortunately, it suffers from major problems. A selection is shown below:

- The requirements specification which is so ambiguously written that the software developer misunderstands the customer's requirements and delivers a system which only meets a fraction of the requirements.

- The requirements specification which is so badly structured that large amounts of unnecessary resource is expended by both the customer and developer in reading the specification.
- The requirements specification which does not contain the full set of functions demanded by the customer, the result being the delivery of a particular system which is functionally deficient.
- The liaison with the customer being so badly organised that changes to the requirements specification are not adequately documented. This often results in major arguments between the developer and the customer during acceptance testing.

Self Assessment Question 2.5 What facility might a quality system provide to ensure that the problems associated with the fourth bullet point above are eliminated?

Solution The main facility would be a procedure which described how communication between the customer and the developer is carried out. For example, it might specify the documentation to be filled in when a telephone call is made which affects the requirements specification.

2.5.2 System design

System design is still quite an important activity, although less so than requirements specification. Unfortunately, it still suffers from major problems. A selection is shown below:

- A design being produced which is not adequately validated. This would result in the programmers producing a system which did not meet some of its requirements.
- A design being so poorly specified that the programmers are unable to understand the function of individual modules in the system and so produce incorrect code.
- A design so badly expressed that the maintainers are unable to understand the components of the design and either create errors or consume major amounts of resource in making correct amendments.

2.5.3 Programming

Programming is an activity for which errors are less serious. However, programming errors can result in major amounts of resource being consumed during system testing by staff trying to track down coding errors which manifest themselves as failed system tests. Some of the problems with programming are shown below:

- The programmer not providing enough commenting to enable maintenance staff to understand the function of a module.
- A poorly structured module being produced which is difficult to understand.
- A programmer choosing poor names for variables which do not express the role that the variables play in the module.

- The programmer storing a module away in a file which is difficult to find by staff who have to maintain the system in which the module is contained.

> **Self Assessment Question 2.6** What facility might a quality system provide to ensure that the first three bullet points above are eliminated?
>
> **Solution** A programming standard would provide direction on commenting, structural issues and variable-naming conventions.

2.5.4 System testing

System testing is an activity which is of prime importance. It aims to check out a system before acceptance testing is started. Problems during system testing can lead to delays in acceptance testing, with the almost invariable delay in delivery of a system to the customer. Some of the problems encountered with this activity are shown below:

- Poorly specified system tests used by the system testers, who then produce an inappropriate or even incorrect test. This often results in the real functions of the system not being tested until acceptance testing starts.
- The wrong system tests being specified which check out properties that a system should not have.
- Poor planning giving rise to the testers being available for testing but the test databases having not been produced.
- A lack of cross-checking between the system test descriptions and the requirements specification. This might lead to the system test process not checking important components of a system.

All these, and many more, problems can be eliminated or at least severely limited by a good quality system. For example, a good standard for the expression of system tests would eliminate many of the problems encountered when system testing staff read test descriptions. The aim of the rest of this book is to describe how the detailed components of a quality system address these problems.

2.6 SUMMARY

The main aim of this chapter has been to describe developmental activities and provide the reader with two views of how software developers organize their software processes. In doing this, the chapter has also provided a vocabulary of developmental, validation and verification terms. It is worth pointing out that the two models described in this chapter are ideals; for example, the model described in the first section is for large systems, often split into a number of parallel developments, with a number of separate teams carrying out the development of subsystems. Also, it is worth pointing out that there are a number of other life-cycle models which are available; for example, those which cater for rapid change or those which have been specifically developed for new or unusual software technology.

The concluding section looked at a small selection of the problems that bedevil software projects. The aim of any quality system is to eliminate or at least severely mitigate these problems by means of tools such as reviews, procedures, standards and guidelines.

2.7 FURTHER READING

It is important that anyone learning about the software quality assurance function have some knowledge of the development process. If they do not, they soon lose the respect of development teams. The two books that I recommend are Pressman (1994) which is far and away the best general book published on software engineering, and McDermid (1990). The publication of the latter was *the* book event of 1990; it is a superb reference book which covers the vast majority of software topics that the student or the professional need to know about—and even some that they do not.

PROBLEMS

2.1 Examine the list of problems in Section 2.5 that arise during system design and describe the specific components of a quality system that you would use to eliminate them.

2.2 Examine the list of problems in Section 2.5 that arise during system testing and describe the specific components of a quality system that you would use to eliminate them.

2.3 *Throw-away prototyping* is a term used to describe the process of quickly building a working model of a system and then continually showing it to the customer and modifying it until he or she is happy with the result. Once the customer is happy, the prototype is thrown away and conventional development starts using a description of the prototype. What problems would you expect with this process?

2.4 A technical review is a meeting of staff who examine a document— usually a requirements specification or a design—and check it for correctness. What problems do you think would arise in a technical review where a system design was examined?

2.5 A software developer uses the system design notation shown on page 29. What do you think should be in a standard used to describe how such a notation should be displayed?

2.6 What do you think should be in a programming standard for a language such as Pascal?

3

PROJECT PLANNING

AIMS

- To describe the general process of project planning.
- To outline the role of risk and risk planning on the software project.
- To describe how a quality plan is developed.
- To outline how the form of a particular configuration management system is decided upon.
- To describe the two main tasks that make up the project planning process: costing and task identification, and outline the quality implications of these tasks.

3.1 INTRODUCTION

Project planning is one of the first steps in a software project and one which, in my experience, is poorly carried out. There are a number of planning tasks which the quality system must address via standards, procedures and checklists. They are:

- The identification of the quality factors which are relevant to the software system that is being developed. These quality factors will either be extracted from the customer statement of requirements or from discussions with the customer.
- The development of a quality plan which details how the developer is going to ensure that the identified quality factors are going to be met and validated within the software which is to be developed.
- The estimation of the resources for the project, not only human resources, but also equipment, software such as tools, and laboratory facilities.
- The identification of the tasks which make up the project and the specification of the temporal relationships between the tasks; for example, whether one task has to be completed before another or whether two tasks can be carried out in parallel.
- The estimation of the resources required for each task that has been identified as contributing to the development of the software.

- The estimation of the overall cost of a project.
- The specification of the risks inherent in a project.
- The specification of how a project might cope when events associated with the most probable risk areas occur.
- The development of a suitable project organization which will effectively deliver the required software system.
- The development of subcontracting plans which specify how the activities of the subcontractor are to interface with project tasks.
- The selection of subcontractors.

There are a number of problems that occur during project planning that a quality system needs to address. However, before describing these problems it is worth making a point about the development of a quality system—or rather, the quality manual.

Many developers ask me how they should go about developing standards and procedures. Many ask, for example, whether the process should be driven by external standards such as ISO 9001: whether the first step to take is to read such external standards and, based on a reading of those documents, develop the standards and procedures necessary to implement the standard. The answer I give is that the best starting-off point for the development of a quality manual is not external standards, but a consideration of the errors and problems which have afflicted projects in the past. As you will see in Chapter 14 the main external standard, ISO 9001, is written at a rather abstract level, and does not provide specific guidance on particular topics such as testing. A better strategy to adopt is to look at all the problems that have been encountered in previous projects, attempt to predict future problems, and then base your standards and procedures on eradicating these problems. In my experience, companies who do this develop excellent quality systems which, almost invariably, meet external quality standards such as ISO 9001.

Many of the problems which arise during planning or which occur later on in a software project because of poor planning, are detailed below:

- An event associated with a risk occurs; for example, the late delivery of hardware, with not enough information being available on alternative actions which enable the project manager to react efficiently to the event, and put the project back on course.
- Inadequate liaison with the customer over quality factors, leading to major reworking later in the project when missing or incompletely specified quality factors need to be implemented.
- Project costing being badly carried out, leading to an underestimate in the project budget. This often manifests itself in a truncated testing phase due to the project manager trying to save costs at the back-end of a project.
- Inadequate information available about project progress. One of the most frequent telephone calls received by a project manager comes from his or her manager asking about progress according to plan or according to budget. Many projects are so badly planned that such information is often not immediately available, or, at best, is available only after a number of hours spent searching for inadequate documentation.
- Skill mismatches between staff allocated to a project and the tasks carried out. This often leads to tasks which are poorly performed.

- A poor project organization which is not the most efficient for the software being developed; for example, adopting a life-cycle which is intended for conventional software development for a new development method such as prototyping.
- The selection of a subcontractor who is not capable of producing the hardware or software that is contracted for.
- A project plan being produced which does not interface properly with project plans produced by subcontractors, or does not mesh with the project plan produced by the customer for liaising with the software project.
- Activities in the project plan being described at too high a level; for example, an activity might be described as 'Develop subsystem A'. This high level of abstraction does not provide adequate facilities for the project manager to monitor progress on a week-by-week basis.
- Documentation on project assumptions being omitted; for example, statements such as 'the developer will assume for the basis of planning that the customer will read, and either sign-off or query, major project documents such as the requirements specification no later than two weeks after receipt' being omitted. If these assumptions are not documented somewhere in the project plan, then their absence could lead to major time slippages, with the blame for slippage being ascribed solely to the developer.
- The costings for a project omitting factors such as travel, computer time or consultancy fees.
- The assumption that a resource will be available at a particular time, and that full use can be made of that resource. For example, a common problem with mainframe computer projects arises from the fact that the project manager has assumed the availability of the computer at a certain time, without checking that no other teams are using the computer for resource-intensive activities such as system testing.

These, then, are many of the problems afflicting the project planning process. The remainder of the chapter discusses project planning activities and how they should be carried out. The final section summarizes the standards and procedures necessary to support this best practice.

> **Self Assessment Question 3.1** What facility could a quality system offer that overcame the problem of activities being expressed at too high a level? (Bullet point 9 above)
>
> **Solution** First, the standard that covered the specification of tasks could describe some hierarchical notation. Second, if the quality system provides standards and procedures for reviewing the project plan, then a checklist for staff involved in the review might include a reminder to check for too abstract a task specification.

3.2 RISK ANALYSIS

Every project should carry out a risk analysis. There are a number of reasons for regarding this activity as very important. First, by estimating the risk inherent in a project a software developer will have a good idea of what financial contingency to build into the budget of a project in order to cope with those risks which could manifest themselves during the project. Second, by carrying out a risk analysis a project manager is able to devise alternative actions which could be taken in order to minimize the effect of the risk. For example, a project manager may have discovered during the process of subcontractor evaluation that there is a finite but quite high risk of the chosen subcontractor not developing some software on time. In this case, the project manager may decide to issue a contract to the software developer which includes penalty clauses. If invoked, these penalty clauses would generate revenue at a later stage of the project; this revenue can then be used to employ more staff in order to speed up activities such as programming and system testing. The top ten risks in a project are, according to Boehm (1989):

- *Staff deficiencies.* The project may be staffed with personnel who may not be technically equipped for the task assigned to them, or may have not performed optimally on previous projects.
- *Unrealistic schedules and budgets.* For example, the project may have been given an unrealistic budget prior to the process of calculating what the budget will be—an occurrence which often happens, particularly with in-company software development departments.
- *The wrong software functions may be developed.* This may occur as a result of inadequate liaison with the customer. There can be many reasons for this: the customer may not be readily available; there may be a lot of substitution of customer representatives, with the analysts meeting one customer representative one week and another the next; or the customer may be totally ignorant about information technology or even the application area.
- *The wrong kind of interface may be developed.* One reason for this may be the fact that the customer may not allow the analysts to talk to the real users of the system and confines discussions about human–computer interface issues—such as the capabilities of users—to staff who, although they are employed within the department in which the software is to be installed, would not necessarily have been in contact with the application for a number of years.
- *Over-engineering.* Here there may be a temptation to cram too much functionality into a system, or to produce an exotic interface.
- *Requirements volatility.* This is where requirements for the system may change during the course of a project. There are a number of reasons for this, many of which are unavoidable: inadequate analysis may have been carried out, the results of which are only discovered after the requirements specification has been frozen; the underlying hardware or operating system software on which the software is to be built may change; the business circumstances of the customer may change, for example a new management team may be put into place who require new data from the system being developed; and, finally, the outside world may change, for example new tax laws may require a change in an accounting package.

- *Deficiencies in externally developed items.* This is where a subcontractor—either for hardware or software—may not have the degree of quality assurance that is present on the main project to which they are subcontracted.
- *Shortfalls in externally performed tasks.* This not only includes software and hardware tasks carried out by a subcontractor, but also shortfalls in tasks carried out by the customer and any providers of external facilities such as documentation services.
- *Performance problems.* Real-time response is becoming an increasing problem on projects—not just real-time projects—but those which involve the development of software that accesses large external databases.
- *Strains on current computer technology.* This means that the software developer may use a technology which has not yet become state-of-the-art, but which he or she assumes will provide the same profit and lack of problems as existing mature technology.

The assessment of risk can be a highly complicated numerical exercise. However, for the vast majority of software developers a simple risk analysis can be carried out using a checklist. Such a checklist would ask questions about the ten areas above. Typical questions are shown below:

- Is this the first time that the project manager has managed a project?
- Is this the first time that the project manager has managed a project in this application area?
- Are any of the items developed by external subcontractors critical items, for example in performance terms?
- Is there a wide variety of users interacting with the system?
- Is the hardware technology upon which the application is to be run new?
- Have we achieved a similar response-time on comparable projects in the past?
- Is this the first time that the customer has been exposed to computer technology?

> **Self Assessment Question 3.2** If the answer to the first bullet point above is yes, then what actions might be taken by the management of the software developer?
>
> **Solution** This depends on the project. If it was very critical, then the project manager might be assigned to another project and be replaced by a more experienced manager. If the project was less critical, then the senior manager who the project manager reports to might monitor his or her activities a little more closely than normal.

Most of the questions are self-explanatory except, perhaps, the fourth one. The point of this question is to gauge the complexity of the human–computer interface: the wider the variety of users who interact with a computer system, the more complex the interface becomes. An extract from a risk questionnaire is shown below:

Project Management

For the project manager answer the following questions and enter your answers on the sheet provided.

1. Has the project manager been identified yet?

2. Is this the first time that the project manager has managed any project?

3. If the project manager has had no experience in managing a project before, has he or she had experience in a supervisory capacity such as being a senior programmer?

4. Is this the first time that the project manager has managed a project in this application area?

5. Has the project manager undergone the PM3 modules of the company management programme?

The Customer

For the project manager answer the following questions and enter your answers on the sheet provided.

1. Is this the first time that we have contracted a software system for this customer?

2. If this is not the first time that we have contracted a software system for this customer, is this the first time that we have contracted for this department?

3. Have customer liaison staff been identified yet?

4. Has the customer agreed that, except in exceptional circumstances, the same liaison staff will meet our staff?

5. Would you consider that the customer is familiar with information technology and the use of computers?

6. Is this the first time that the customer has gone outside his or her company for software development?

7. Is the customer liaison team familiar with the application area?

A very sophisticated quality system would ask the project manager to submit his or her answers to the questionnaire to a software tool or a spreadsheet which would give an overall risk factor value.

A good quality system should insist that once such a questionnaire or checklist has been filled in, the next step is for the project manager to list the most likely risks and describe what actions are to be taken to minimize the effect of those risks. For example, the project manager may have decided that because a particular project delivers a system which has a large database, and the implementation is via a somewhat inefficient fourth-generation language, then the project is risky and a number of risk avoidance tactics need to be put in place. One way to reduce this risk could be to organize the project with a simulation or prototyping front-end that would provide valuable information about potential problems. Another option would be for the project manager to decide to partially staff the project with some programmers who have third-generation language expertise so that, assuming the database system allowed access to such languages, critical parts of the system can be recoded in a more efficient way. Another option would be to plan for the in-house development of an instrumentor which is able to detect those parts of a system that are being executed frequently and are candidates for optimization. The quality manual should provide some documentation—usually a risk minimization guideline—which provides the project manager with guidance about the various options that are available to reduce the impact of risk on a project.

Some more sophisticated risk questionnaires provide data which can be processed by a spreadsheet and which enable the project manager to fix on a figure which is then used to add contingency to an estimated overall cost of a project.

A final part of the planning of the software project associated with risk analysis is the determination of how the effects of risk are to be monitored, and the actions which are subsequently taken reported on. Normally, a quality system will have standards and procedures for risk monitoring. The standards will describe documentation which gives details of which risks have recently occurred, how important they are, how they are being resolved, and the effect of the risks on the project.

3.3 OUTLINE DESIGN

An important project planning task is outline system design. Many other project planning tasks depend on this being carried out correctly. The main reasons for carrying out an outline design are so that the tasks in a software project can be identified, preliminary sizing studies of the software can be carried out, and the testing philosophy that is to be adopted can be specified.

A later section of this chapter describes the process of task identification and task specification, where the individual tasks that make up a software project are collected together and incorporated in the project plan. Without at least an outline architecture of a system it would be virtually impossible to identify these tasks. The development of an outline design should be described by standards and procedures.

Normally, the procedure will describe the analysis that is required to carry out the design. The standard will describe some design notation for expressing the outline design. This notation is usually similar, or the same as, that which will eventually be used for full design. The outline design standard will usually describe how to express a design in terms of subsystems or in terms of the first two or three levels of module hierarchy, and will include a description of the boundary between the user and the system. Some procedures insist that the project manager also includes a technical implementation strategy in this part of the project plan, although many specify that it is a separate chapter.

3.4 THE IDENTIFICATION OF QUALITY FACTORS

One of the main points made in Chapter 1 was that one of the first jobs that a project manager has to carry out is that of determining which quality factors are important for the system that is to be developed. If a feasibility study precedes the project planning part of the software project, then an outline consideration of quality factors would take place here. However, it is during project planning that this activity comes to the fore.

The project manager will, by examining the customer statement of requirements and by meeting the customer, gain an idea of which quality factors are important and which are not. Correctness will usually be a prime quality factor and, almost invariably, maintainability will be important.

Self Assessment Question 3.3 Can you think of any projects where the correctness quality factor might not be the prime one?

Solution Such projects occur in the finance and banking sectors where a product may be developed quickly and which requires IT support quickly. Here a customer may tolerate a system with minor functional errors provided that it is delivered quickly.

Once this analysis of quality factors has been completed the project manager then decides, in conjunction with staff who carry out the quality function, which quality controls are to be applied to a project. For example, one quality factor which may be important to the customer is that of interoperability: the ability to interface effectively with other software systems such as operating systems, word processors and spreadsheets. A customer may have specified that certain files for a financial application should have a format which would enable the user of a spreadsheet package to access them. This means that the project manager may have to specify standards which govern the output of the system, and employ a series of tests which check that the files can be processed by the spreadsheet, for example by exercising many, if not all, of the spreadsheet functions. The quality factors, together with their associated controls, are placed in a document called the *quality plan*. An extract from a quality manual section detailing quality factors, and the options that should be used in implementing them, is shown below:

3. Quality factors

Our company recognizes a number of different quality factors. Part of the planning process involves the project manager deciding what quality factors are important for a particular system and using a number of technical facilities to build in these quality factors, together with a number of quality controls which check that the factors have been implemented. The remainder of this document describes these quality factors and a number of technical options which can be pursued in order to implement them.

3.1 Maintainability

Maintainability is defined as the characteristic of a system which enables changes to be applied easily—this includes both changes during maintenance and development. Many of the quality standards and procedures which form part of the company quality manual are aimed at achieving maintainability, for example the programming standards specified in section 12.6 of the manual; however, there are a number of additional options which are available to the project manager. These options are:

1. The use of software tools for the storage of test data. The main software tool which we employ for this is *TransSave* which saves menu-based transactions to a file. The quality control which would be employed to ensure that this tool has been used is to amend the normal program testing standard to ask programmers to include the *TransSave* file listing within the program testing documentation.

2. The use of design metrics. Two metrics are used by the company: an information flow metric which measures the amount of data passing through a module or program, and the IF4 metric due to Ince and Shepperd which measures the interface in a program or module. Details of these metrics, and the tools which we use, can be found in the Metrics Guidelines Document. The project manager will stipulate a metric threshold; no module will be allowed to exceed this threshold. The quality control which is used to check that the metrics have not been exceeded is to insist that the designer produces a printout of the metric values of the modules in a system as part of the system documentation.

3. The stipulation that modules carry out only one function. Such modules tend to be easy to maintain. The quality control which is associated with this is that design reviews should be asked to check that all modules in the designed system carry out the one function.

4. The use of software tools for retesting. The tool that the company uses for this is *TestManager*. This enables tests to be specified in a form such that when a module is changed, a whole test suite corresponding to the module is re-executed. The quality control associated with this is to insist that the system testing documentation is amended with a listing of the retest commands used by the *TestManager* tool.

In the extract above there is a reference to design metrics. A *metric* is a numerical value which reflects a quality factor. These are discussed further in Chapter 11.

3.5 DEVELOPING THE QUALITY PLAN

The quality plan is a description of how the developer is to ensure that the quality factors identified at the beginning of a project are going to be validated, i.e. what activities are to be carried out to check that a particular quality factor is present in a software system. It can be seen as a subset of the project plan which deals with verification and validation activities.

The quality plan should:

- list the quality factors for a system;
- describe the quality controls which are to be applied; for example, reliability testing, prototyping and usability reviews;
- describe the skills of the staff who are to carry out the control activities;
- describe any special tools which will be necessary;
- specify the standards, procedures and guidelines from the quality manual which will be adopted by the project;
- describe any new standards and procedures, or modified standards and procedures, from the quality manual which are to be used on the project;
- reference any external standards or customer-imposed standards and procedures which are relevant to the project;
- specify, in detail, the individual tasks which implement a quality control: their nature, duration, when they can be started and the amount of resources needed. Each task should be cross-referenced to the quality factor which it is intended to validate.

The last item forms part of conventional project planning. Because of this many companies do not put detailed descriptions of the quality controls in the quality plan, but place them in a project plan. However, such companies do have some form of cross-referencing system so that quality control tasks can be easily extracted from the project plan. One way of doing this is to give each project task a unique name in the project plan, but give tasks associated with quality controls some prefix which indicates that they are quality tasks. The quality plan would then simply contain the unique identifiers of tasks, together with their associated quality factors.

Whether your project planning standards insist that quality control tasks are detailed in the quality plan, or cross-referenced in the quality plan to the project plan, is really just a matter of taste. I normally favour the former as it usually means that there is less turning of pages. It is worth pointing out that during the early stages of a project the description of quality control tasks will be at a high level of abstraction. Not enough will be known about the project at this stage for any level of detail to be achieved. However, as the project proceeds, this part of the quality plan should be expanded.

An important section of the quality plan will contain the *verification requirements*. These are external manifestations that the system is behaving as the requirements specification demands. These verification requirements will be used to produce the final system and acceptance tests, and work is normally started on these as soon after the completion of the requirements specification as possible. Two examples of such verification requirements are shown below:

> When the system receives any emergency signal from a reactor monitor a shut-down signal should be sent to the hardware which controls the main inlets and outlets.

> When the out-of-stock command is initiated with a correct product identifier, then the system will respond with the time periods during which the product was out of stock.

Both these statements describe events which are of importance to the customer and represent external manifestations of the behaviour of the system. The first event is detected by examining some electronic circuitry; the second by looking at a VDU. Since these verification requirements can only be extracted after requirements analysis is complete, this section of the quality plan will be left blank during the planning process.

Self Assessment Question 3.4 Can you remember why verification requirements are extracted at an early stage in a software project?

Solution There are three reasons: first, in order to gain an early idea of the resources required for system testing and acceptance testing; second, to provide an early indication of whether special-purpose software testing tools or hardware testing equipment is needed; and, third, to provide a powerful validation of the requirements specification.

An extract from part of a quality manual dealing with the identification of verification requirements is shown below:

17 Verification requirements

A verification requirement is a requirement which is extracted from the requirements specification. It represents some external behaviour of a system which can be detected by the customer, and will eventually be expanded so that it becomes a system test and often an acceptance test. Some examples of verification requirements are shown below:

1. When an update command is typed with a correct product identifier, the system will display the number of updates for that product over the last financial year.

2. When the out-of-stock command is initiated, the system will produce a hard copy report that will detail the items which are currently out of stock, together with the number of back orders for the products.

3. When the flow command is initiated, the flow meter will be repositioned so that it receives the maximum flow from the outlets of the nuclear reactor.

Some examples of requirements which are not verification requirements are:

The system should keep an up-to-date queue of messages waiting to be processed.

The system should produce accurate data on the state of the nuclear reactor.

The former is a requirement which has to be satisfied for a system but which can only be observed by actions which correspond to verification requirements; for example, by a command which displays the current state of the message queue. The second requirement is at too high a level of detail and requires further decomposition in order to produce adequate verification requirements.

Self Assessment Question 3.5 Is the statement: 'The system will respond to a hardware error by producing error messages on the main monitoring console which identify the hardware involved and suggest a possible cause' a verification requirement?

Solution Yes it is, albeit at a high level of abstraction. It describes a function of the system.

3.6 DETERMINING THE PROJECT ORGANIZATION

Another important task which the project manager has to carry out is to determine how a project is to be organized. Most projects tend to be organized as a hierarchy similar to that shown in Fig. 3.1, with staff reporting to senior staff above them who, in turn, report to their seniors, and so on. Figure 3.1 shows that the hierarchy is confined to development with quality assurance and testing outside the hierarchy. This is often the way that large software developers carry out their production, but it is by no means the only way. The project manager should look at the particular system to be developed and determine the project organization. Normally, a company will have a preferred organization—usually some form of hierarchy—but guidance should be provided in the quality manual about other forms of organization.

As an example of this, consider a system where the functions can be neatly partitioned into functional subareas; for example, a system for monitoring and controlling a chemical plant can normally be partitioned into functional areas concerned with monitoring, control, and management information. If this neat form of division occurs, then

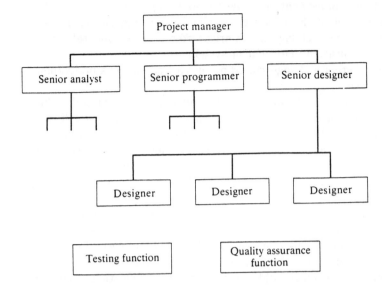

Figure 3.1 One popular form of project organization.

it is worth the project manager splitting the project up into mini-projects, each of which is managed by, say, a senior analyst, and each of which is responsible for the production of a subsystem, with the project manager mediating on design decisions which are made by teams but which may affect other teams.

There are two advantages with this form of organization. First, it cuts down on the communicational overhead in a project. As projects get bigger and bigger, the amount of work that staff have to do in terms of attending meetings, reading memos, inducting new staff, increases, sometimes to the point where it dominates useful work such as coding a module or designing a subsystem. By organizing the project as parallel teams with, perhaps, each team using the same office, the communicational overhead can be substantially reduced. Second, it gives technical staff some management experience which they may not get in a strictly hierarchical project.

This is just one form of organization; there are many others. The important point is that the quality system, via the quality manual, should provide guidance about the most relevant form of organization.

3.7 DETERMINING THE CONFIGURATION MANAGEMENT SYSTEM

Chapter 1 made the point that change is a fact of life for a software developer—not only during maintenance but also for the duration of a project. In order to cope with change, software developers have a set of standards and procedures in their quality manuals which detail how change is to be handled. This topic is dealt with in more detail in Chapter 8. But since the determination of configuration management practices is a task carried out during project planning it is worth including some material on it at this point in the book. The term *configuration management* describes the following:

- The interface between the remainder of the project and the configuration management system; for example, how a change which arises from a developmental error is communicated to the configuration management system.
- The process of deciding whether a change should occur, carried out by a body known as the *Change Control Board.*
- The establishment of baselines. A *baseline* is a document or program code which comes under configuration control. Up to the point that a document or a collection of program code is baselined, change can occur freely. However, after baselining, a formal process of evaluating whether the change is to be allowed to be carried out, documenting the change, and checking that only the change has occurred, has to take place. The items which are baselined are known as *configuration items.*
- The updating of the system documentation to reflect the changes that have occurred, and the broadcasting of that documentation to parts of the development team that need to know about the change.
- The proper accounting of change. This would include details of the reason for change, when the change occurred, and what other items had to be changed.
- Checking that a change which occurred did not include any modifications that were not sanctioned.

These are the main features of configuration management. More details can be found in Chapter 8. A project manager has to examine the configuration management system and ask how it is to be tailored to a project; for example, who should carry out the functions of the Change Control Board. Often this is a project manager's responsibility, but for large projects it may be necessary for the board to contain more than just the project manager.

Another example of tailoring occurs during prototyping. This form of software development is highly dynamic and relies on rapid feedback from the customer to the developer and the rapid implementation of changes. Configuration management systems which are tailored to conventional phase-oriented projects tend to slow down the prototyping process considerably, so the project manager has to make the very difficult decision whether to drop the configuration management system for the prototyping phase or to considerably ease the application of the system.

3.8 THE EVALUATION OF SUBCONTRACTORS

Large software projects often use subcontractors for the development of software or hardware. The quality system should provide procedures whereby the project manager can issue calls for bids, and evaluate those bids on the basis of the competence of the subcontractor to produce hardware or software which is at least of the same standard as that which is to be developed by a project. A subcontractor selection procedure should provide guidance on evaluation, and will often incorporate a checklist of questions, such as whether the subcontractor has an adequate configuration management system. It will also offer advice about questioning previous customers of the subcontractor. A section of part of a quality manual dealing with the evaluation of subcontractors is shown below:

23 Subcontractor evaluation

Occasionally we use subcontractors for software development; normally these subcontractors are used when we do not have enough experience with a particular programming language or computer. Care has to be taken over the selection of such subcontractors. It is important that the subcontractor(s) chosen for a project develop software which is at least to the quality of the software that your project is to deliver. The following actions and checks need to be carried out:

1. Check that the subcontractor is certified to an external standard such as BS5750; certainly, if the subcontractor has achieved BS5750, then there should be little need to carry out further checks on technical capability. There is still a need, however, to carry out financial checks. If no certification has been achieved, then further questions need to be asked. These are detailed below.

2. Check that any of our projects which have used the subcontractor have been happy with performance. Details can be found in the project debrief file for each project. This file should contain a completed questionnaire on subcontractor performance.

3. Ask the software contractor for the names of at least two companies who you can approach to ask about performance. A subcontractor's reluctance to give such names should be regarded seriously. However, you should recognize that there may be circumstances which prevent the subcontractor from giving this information; for example, it may need clearance from an agency such as the Ministry of Defence which is not forthcoming. If possible you should ask for the names of more than two companies and randomly nominate two of them.

4. Apply the checklist found in Appendix B.1 of the quality manual. This will normally require a day visit to the software developer's premises. This checklist contains 25 questions designed to probe a software developer's technical and managerial practices. Poor answers to more than ten of these questions should be regarded seriously.

5. If the subcontractor is carrying out a large proportion of work on a project—more than 25 per cent of the monetary worth—then a financial check should be carried out to ensure that the company is in good health. The body that carries out this check for us is *Information Systems and Intelligence*, who provide very accurate company financial profiles and are able to pronounce on the financial health of a wide variety of developers.

There is a reference to BS5750 in the extract. This is the British instantiation of the International Standard ISO 9001. Chapter 14 describes ISO 9001 in detail.

3.9 PROJECT COSTING

3.9.1 Conventional costing

A vital task during the planning stage is to produce a costing of the project. There are a number of techniques used to achieve this: some are based on project costing in other industries, while others are based on the modern technique of software metrication. This subsection will concentrate on the former. Probably the most popular method of costing a software project is based on an identification of the tasks in the project and a costing of the individual tasks based on historical data or experience. One of the most common means of expressing the breakdown of tasks in a project is the *work breakdown structure*. Figure 3.2 shows a very small fragment from such a structure. It is worth stressing that the extract shown is very small; often, a work breakdown structure for a substantial system will contain thousands of boxes.

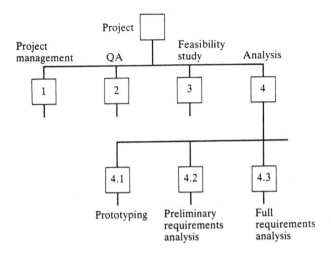

Figure 3.2 A fragment of a work breakdown structure.

There are three important things to notice about a work breakdown structure. First, it is hierarchical: tasks at a high level are expressed in terms of tasks at the next level, and so on. This reflects the hierarchical structure of the project. Second, each task in the work breakdown structure is prefixed with the number of the task which is its immediate superior. This allows a unique numbering to be maintained. This is required because a project will have a reporting standard which, when a task is completed, will result in a report generated and sent to the project manager; having unique numbering leaves no margin for ambiguity or error in the reporting. Third, a project manager, or any other member of staff on a project, given a task number, can trace back to the major tasks from which that task is derived. For example, a task 4.3.2.2 can be traced back to tasks 4.3.2, 4.3, and 4. This is an example of the traceability principle which I described in Chapter 1 applied to project planning.

The work breakdown structure is developed during project planning after an initial system design has been produced, and will be at a relatively abstract level; it may, for example, contain only three levels of task. However, during the initial developmental stages of the project it will gradually be refined until tasks are expressed at quite a low level; for example, the tasks might be specified at the module level.

The work breakdown structure is produced for a number of reasons. First, it produces a breakdown of a software project which is in discrete chunks whose completion can be monitored, and hence can be used for progress reporting and cost accounting. Second, it provides a major input into the costing process. One organized way of carrying out costing is to develop a work breakdown structure, assign costs to each element, and accumulate the costs as a total. To this total are added any elements not covered by task analysis, such as travelling costs, consultant costs, and overheads.

For small projects, work breakdown techniques often give acceptable results. However, for many projects, this cost is often on the low side. There are two reasons for this: first, there seems to be a tendency for staff to underestimate the cost of tasks—this tendency seems particularly marked on medium-sized and larger projects; second, owing to a phenomenon known as *communicational complexity*. When staff work on a project their work can be split into two components: 'useful' work such as programming and designing, and communicational work, such as reading memos, attending meetings and inducting new staff onto a project. As a project increases in size the communicational complexity tends to rise exponentially, sometimes to the point where it dominates the real work. Work breakdown structures are unable to predict the communicational complexity part of a project.

In order to cost projects, a quality manual should provide a costing standard for expressing the costs of various parts of a project and a procedure for calculating the overall cost and the costs of each task in the project. Normally, these will contain instructions for forming a base cost from a work breakdown structure, and then adjusting it based on a number of approaches. The source of data for the adjustment can be varied. The developer may use a modern, metrics-based costing technique as a back-up and adjust the estimate based on what the metric-based technique produces. This technique uses past historical data to predict the future cost of a system. The estimate could also be adjusted by comparing similar sized projects, or by looking at the risk assessment of the project.

The important point is that the quality manual should offer guidance on the source of data and what should be done with it. As well as this macro level of comparison, the quality system should provide directives about micro-level cost comparison, such as similarities and differences comparisons. The former involves the comparison of a component of a system, such as a subsystem, with a similar component of the system or a similar component of another system. The latter involves looking at dissimilar components and seeing whether the costs reflect the dissimilarity

Nowhere is the need for uniform adherence to a quality system clearer than in project costing. A wise developer who was once very cynical about quality systems—until he became a project manager—told me that as long as everybody adhered to the quality system instructions on costing he was happy, even if the results were not particularly accurate. At least, he told me, the error in costing would be consistent and the trend in errors could be discerned and allowed for.

Self Assessment Question 3.6 If a company used a historical method for costing what would be the managerial implications?

Solution The main implication is that the actual cost of projects should be monitored accurately, together with data such as the staff hours devoted to project tasks such as requirements analysis.

3.9.2 Advanced costing and estimation techniques

This chapter would not be complete without briefly describing two advanced methods of software costing which are based on the idea of measurement and the use of software metrics: numbers extracted from the products and processes of the software project. Software metrics are described in more detail in Chapter 11.

There are two main methods for costing and estimating based on software metrication: COCOMO (Boehm, 1981) and Function Point Analysis (Symons, 1991). COCOMO is a method developed by the American computer scientist Barry Boehm. Boehm postulated that a software project cost is determined by a number of factors he called *cost drivers*. Typical cost drivers are the degree of use of tools on a project and the capability of the staff on a project. Boehm identified 15 cost drivers and suggested that, for each project a company undertakes, the project manager estimates each of the cost drivers on a five point scale together with the size of the system in lines of code. This information, for all completed projects, is then stored in a historical database. When a project manager wishes to calculate the resources required for a new project all that he or she has to do is to estimate the number of lines of code and the values of the cost drivers. This information is then processed by a software tool which then examines the historical cost database and predicts the resources of the project.

The second technique, Function Point Analysis, is similar to COCOMO in that a historical database is used. However, the database contains different information. It contains attributes extracted from a requirements specification. In the first version of Function Point Analysis, developed by the IBM manager Allen Albrecht (Albrecht and Gaffney, 1993), the attributes extracted from a requirements specification included the number of master files, the number of transaction files and the number of enquiries. More modern versions of Function Point Analysis, oriented towards database technology and fourth-generation languages, collect other information such as the number of bubbles in a data flow diagram.

The factors that are counted are inserted into an algebraic expression known as a *function point count*. This represents the functional size of a system. For each completed project the company stores the eventual cost of the project and its function point count. When a new project is started the project manager extracts the counts of attributes in the requirements specification, calculates the function point count and then uses a tool which processes the historical database and, based on previous values of function point count and cost, produces a resource estimate.

3.10 TASK IDENTIFICATION

This is the process whereby the tasks that make up a project are identified, specified, their resources estimated and their timing decided upon. The previous section has already described much of this work in connection with estimating. The work breakdown structure described there provides a good starting point for the remainder of the work. Costing of each task is normally based on staff experience, for example that a subsystem estimated to be 1500 lines of code normally requires 40 person-days. Once each task has been identified and a resource estimate for the task specified, the process of timing the tasks is carried out. Here the project manager decides when each task is to be carried out

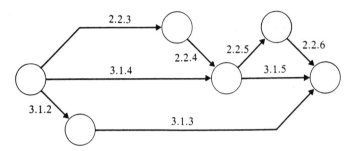

2.2.3 Develop simulator
2.2.4 Test simulator
2.2.5 Install simulator
2.2.6 Produce simulator report
3.1.2 Review system test suite
3.1.3 Apply system test suite
3.1.4 Produce acceptance test suite
3.1.5 Review acceptance test suite

Figure 3.3 An extract from an activity network.

and often specifies data such as the earliest start date, the latest start date, the earliest and latest completion date, and so on.

The project manager will also specify which tasks have to be carried out serially and which are to be carried out in parallel. There are a number of graphical devices for specifying the time sequencing of tasks. Almost certainly the most popular is the *activity network.* In an activity network, tasks are represented by lines which join specific points in a software project. A short fragment from an activity network is shown in Fig. 3.3. The diagram shows tasks which have to be carried out serially such as tasks 3.1.4 and 3.1.5, together with tasks which can be carried out in parallel, such as tasks 3.1.3 and 2.2.3. This is quite a simple version of an activity network; more complex versions normally include resource information for a task, earliest start, latest start, earliest finish and latest finish information. Many quality systems specify that the tasks on the activity network use the same numbering as the work breakdown structure, so that there is traceability between the activity network and the rest of the project plan.

Many software developers use automated tools for the processing of such activity networks. Such tools enable the project manager to examine resource expenditure across the duration of a project and identify, for each task, a time interval known as a *float.* If an activity had a float of n days then the project manager knows that the activity has n days' slack in which carrying out no progress on that activity will not delay the project.

Another important piece of information which such tools provide is the *critical path* of a project. This is a set of tasks which form a path through a project such that if any of the tasks were delayed by n days, the whole project would also be delayed by n days. Such tasks will require extensive monitoring by the project manager. Because of the increasing use of tools to process activity networks many software developers specify their task identification standards in the format demanded by a particular tool.

It is important to point out that both the activity network and the work breakdown structure will be developed in outline at the beginning of a project and will subsequently be refined as developmental activities occur. For example, on completion of the system design, the project manager is able to provide much more detailed information about the various detailed design and programming tasks that occur later in the project.

3.11 THE PROJECT PLAN

The overall document which describes the process of project planning is the *project plan*. A good project plan should have at least five sections which correspond to the following headings: introduction, project organization, managerial aspects, the technical process, and task aspects.

The introduction should give a brief description of how the project came about; for example, it should describe the process whereby the project was contracted for. This part of the introduction should briefly describe the system that is to be developed—usually no more than a page of text is required for this. The reason for brevity is that this part of the project plan will be read by senior management who have very little time to consider project documents, and are more concerned with high-level concerns such as whether a project fits in with the business objectives of their company.

The introduction should also describe the project deliverables: not only software deliverables which comprise the final system, but also any subsidiary software, documentation, services and training that are required. Subsidiary software usually includes tools which may have been developed to help produce the software, for example a tool which generated large files of test data. Normally, subsidiary software will only be specified as a deliverable if the customer or a third party are to maintain a system.

In addition, the introduction should describe any important documents which are relevant to the project. This section will always contain a reference to documentation initially provided by the customer, such as a statement of requirements, but will also refer to documents such as the project contract, and external and internal standards used by the software developer. The introduction should also include a section which describes any definitions and acronyms used in the plan.

The second section of the project plan should describe how the software project is to be organized: which life-cycle model is to be adopted, and the developmental tasks which are to be carried out, and how they are to be validated. This section should include how the project is organized: which tasks are to be carried out by developmental staff, customers and subcontractors; the managerial relationship between staff within the project; the boundaries and relationship between the project and internal agencies such as the quality assurance department; the boundaries and relationship between the development team and the customer; and the boundaries and relationship between the developmental team and any subcontractors.

The third section of the project plan should include details of how the project is to be managed. It should contain the results of the risk analysis, and how likely risks are to be managed. It is important that this part of the plan should record any assumptions made by the developer; for example, that the customer will return documents sent for comment within a specified time period.

Self Assessment Question 3.7 What is the role of assumptions in this part of the project plan?

Solution It tells the customer under what conditions the project will be successfully completed. A major reason for describing these assumptions is to inform the customer what his or her acceptable behaviour is in terms of project success. For example, one assumption might be that the customer does not substitute any staff in important technical meetings. Customers who do this usually add time to a project when their staff disagree with each other.

An important part of this section is a list of dependencies: tasks or activities which cannot be started until other tasks are completed; for example, the task of system design cannot be completed unless the requirements specification has been signed off by the customer.

This section should also describe how the project is to be staffed: what staff will be required, what skills are needed and when staff are to be assigned to the project. It should include a description of how work carried out on the project will be monitored and how reports on project progress will be presented—not only to the software developer's high-level management but also to the customer.

The fourth section of the project plan should describe the technical solution that will be adopted to create the software. This will include any development methods, notations and software tools which will be used in the project. Often, software developers will include descriptions of the documentation that will be used during the various stages of the project. This section will also normally contain a description of the services provided by other parts of the software developer's organization. For example, if the software developer has an independent test department, then its role within the project will be described here.

The final section—and usually the longest—will be a description of the individual costed tasks in the project; when they occur; the dependencies with other tasks, such as whether they are to be carried out serially or in parallel; and the capabilities of staff who are to carry out the tasks. The resource requirements for the project should be detailed here, not only on a task-by-task but also on a phase-by-phase basis. The budget for the project should also be listed in this section of the project plan, together with the budget expenditure on a week-by-week or month-by-month basis.

Finally, the schedule for the project should be specified. This should be organized around milestones. A *milestone* is an event which is easy to recognize and provides the tick of a clock which indicates that a project is progressing. A popular milestone is one which is associated with the delivery or signing-off of an important project document such as a system design. Two types of milestone will be specified: internal and external. The former are used by the project team to judge progress and are usually based on events of medium importance, such as the completion of coding of a subsystem; the latter are major events, such as the completion of the requirements specification, which are used by the customer to judge progress.

It is worth stating that the final part of the project plan will evolve and become more refined as a project progresses. During project planning only an outline requirements analysis and design will have been carried out, and hence tasks will, perhaps, only be specified at the subsystem level. However, as a project proceeds and the nature of the system to be developed unwinds, more and more detail should be added to this part of the project plan. Before leaving this chapter it is worth while stressing an important point: that the specification of the detailed organization of a project plan presented in this section is not prescriptive; there is considerable leeway in the way such a plan is organized. However, whatever form of project plan organization you adopt it should, according to Rook (1990), be judged by the main requirements for such a plan:

- that it provides the project manager with a basis for allocating resources during a project and for predicting, monitoring and reporting on progress and cost;
- that it provides high-level management with a summary of a project and a means by which they can monitor its progress;
- that it provides the customer with the same insight and progress monitoring capability as the developer.

If a project plan does not satisfy these three demands, then it has failed.

3.12 SUMMARY

Project planning is one of the most important tasks carried out on a software project. Project planning tasks which fail usually give rise to very serious problems on a software project. Because of this, the software developer should have standards, procedures and guidelines which address activities such as risk analysis, the development of the quality plan, the development of the project plan, cost estimating, and project organization.

3.13 FURTHER READING

Rook (1990) is an excellent short tutorial on project management which could be read in two nights. Brookes (1975) is the classic book on software project management. Technically, it is a little out-of-date, but it still contains some of the wisest and most relevant advice on how to manage large software projects. Charette (1989) is the best treatment of risk within a software project environment that I have read. The best treatment of modern process-oriented project management that I know of is Humphrey (1989). If you are interested in costing, the standard work is Boehm (1981); a good review can also be found in Monanty (1981). A description of Funtion Point Analysis can be found in Symons (1991).

PROBLEMS

3.1 Write down the type of questions that you would include in a risk questionnaire which deals with the risks inherent in the application area.

3.2 You have discovered that the customer for a software system is hesitant, does not know the application area and is prone to changing his mind. How would you organize a project to take account of these factors?

3.3 You have received a memo from your boss which expresses some degree of cynicism about the need for a configuration management system on the project for which you are responsible for quality. Write a memo explaining why the project needs a good configuration management system.

3.4 If you adopt a modern costing technique such as COCOMO what are the implications for your quality system?

3.5 Why does each project require a quality plan? Surely you could use a single quality plan for each project?

3.6 The statement: 'The system should keep an up-to-date set of data which contains details of staff sales' is not a verification requirement. Explain why.

4

REQUIREMENTS ANALYSIS

AIMS

- To describe the main features of the requirements specification.
- To show what the features of a good requirements specification are and describe the standards and procedures required to encourage the development of these documents.
- To outline some of the techniques for validating requirements specifications that should be part of a quality system.
- To describe how verification requirements, used for the derivation of system and acceptance tests, are generated at an early stage of the software project.
- To list the standards and procedures which are normally associated with the requirements specification process.

4.1 INTRODUCTION

One of the sobering facts about the processes of requirements analysis and requirements specification is that not only are they error-prone, but that an error committed during these parts of the software project, if not detected until a later stage, can have a serious effect on the success of the project, both in terms of budget and time overruns. Some of the main problems that are encountered are:

- The requirements specification is expressed at too high a level of abstraction. There is not enough detail in it for the system designer to produce an adequate design.
- Poor communication channels exist between the developer and the customer. This might occur for a number of reasons; for example, ignorance of information technology concepts by the customer, multiple substitution of customer representatives during the analysis process, and the novelty of the application.

- A poor expression of requirements, due to factors such as ambiguity or just plain poor writing style.
- An inadequate specification of the data that is to be manipulated by a system. Increasingly, companies seem to be getting better at specifying the functions of a system—what it does—but still fall down on the process of data specification.
- Poor organization of the requirements specification. This is often manifested by functions being randomly expressed, with no structure which brings together associated functions.
- Changes in requirements being generated by the customer. A software system is a reflection of the real world. Unfortunately, the real world changes from day to day and this gives rise to changes in requirements, not only during the process of requirements analysis and requirements specification, but at later stages of the project. For example, a developer producing a financial package will often need to carry out extensive changes if a government announces new financial laws.

4.2 THE REQUIREMENTS SPECIFICATION

The key document on any software project is the requirements specification. It is this document which forms the basis for much of the development that follows the processes of requirements analysis and requirements specification: detailed costing; the development of the system design; the construction of the system and acceptance tests; and the production of documentation such as user manuals. The first document that the software developer receives from a customer is a statement of requirements. Usually this document will be at a very high level of abstraction and contain many problems, some of which are described below.

Ambiguities. These are statements which are capable of being interpreted in a number of ways.

Design directives. These are statements which instruct the developer to carry out design in a particular way, for example by splitting a system into a number of subsystems. Normally, design directives should be discouraged, and the software developer should urge the customer to remove them from the system requirements. Sometimes, however, there are good reasons for a design directive. For example, a customer may request an addition to an existing software system which already has a well established process and data architecture and requires the developer to structure the addition in a way that fits in with this architecture.

Contradictions. These are statements which are in direct variance with each other. Statements of requirements usually contain many contradictions. If these were close to each other, then their detection would be easy; however, they are often separated by many pages of text.

Platitudes. A platitude is a section of text which everybody agrees on, but which has no exact meaning. An example of a platitude is the sentence which, time and time again, occurs in statements of requirements: 'The system must be user-friendly'. Platitudes are usually easy to detect; however, what is difficult is deciding on the hidden meaning beneath them.

Mixed levels of abstraction. A statement of requirements will contain instructions which are at different levels of detail. For example, it might contain the sentence:

> The system should provide reports on the functioning of the chemical reactors currently operating.

together with the sentences:

> When the valve report command is initiated a list of valves and their malfunctions will be displayed on the originating VDU. Only the last ten malfunctions will be displayed.

Now, both these statements are important: the first represents a high-level view of a system which might be read by the customer's senior management, while the second represents a more detailed view which might be read by engineers concerned with controlling the chemical plant. The major problem with these statements is that they are not organized and structured, but spread almost randomly throughout the statement of requirements.

The two most important components of a statement of requirements are *functions* and *constraints*. A function is a statement which describes what a system is to do. For example, the statement:

> The system should produce data on the pressure experienced by a model plane in a wind tunnel.

is a function, albeit at a high level of abstraction.

A constraint is something which constrains the developer in some way. It can be a product constraint or a process constraint. A product constraint is a constraint on some characteristic of the software system. The most frequently occurring constraints are those which specify a performance threshold or maximum memory occupation.

A process constraint is a statement which constrains the way in which a particular software process or collection of processes are carried out; for example, a customer may ask that all calls to a computer's file subsystem be routed via the operating system, or specify that a certain standard be used for a technical activity such as system design.

Self Assessment Question 4.1 Is the statement: 'The developer should use the programming language C' a function, a constraint or a process constraint?

Solution It is a process constraint: it constrains the way a project is carried out.

The main aim of a requirements specification is to identify the various categories of information in a statement of requirements and then structure the requirements specification in such a way that it can be easily accessed by staff carrying out developmental activities. Any requirements specification which does not address this is seriously lacking.

4.3 SPECIFYING FUNCTIONALITY

The most important point about the specification of systems functions is that it should be hierarchic: functions should be split into subfunctions, these should then be further decomposed into sub-subfunctions, and so on. This should be reflected in the standards used for requirements specification.

There are a number of ways of documenting this hierarchy. One way is via numbered paragraphs. An example of this is shown below for part of a system for monitoring the working of a chemical plant which consists of a number of reactors:

3 The system should produce data on the functioning of valves.

3.1 The system should produce data on the functioning of outlet valves.

3.1.1 The malfunction command will produce data on the degree of malfunctioning associated with a specific outlet valve on a particular reactor. Staff who use this command should provide a valid valve name together with a valid reactor name. The system will respond with the name of the valve, the name of the reactor and a list of malfunctions over the current operating period. Each malfunction should be detailed according to its type, when it occurred and the date on which the malfunction was cleared.

3.1.2 The current state command will produce data on the current state of a particular outlet valve. The staff who use this command should provide a valid valve name together with a valid reactor name. The system will respond with the current state: this will either be open or closed.

3.2 The system should produce data on the functioning of inlet valves.

3.2.1 The malfunction command will produce data on the degree of malfunctioning associated with a specific inlet valve on a particular reactor. Staff who use this command should provide a valid valve name together with a valid reactor name. The system will respond with the name of the valve, the name of the reactor and a list of malfunctions over the current operating period. Each malfunction should be detailed according to its type, when it occurred and the date on which the malfunction was cleared.

3.2.2 The current state command will produce data on the current state of a particular inlet valve. The staff who use this command should provide a valid valve name together with a valid reactor name. The system will respond with the current state: this will either be open or closed.

There are a number of reasons why the functional part of the requirements specification should be structured in such a way and a standard encourage this. The first reason is that it provides a description which is neatly partitioned into levels of detail which enable different staff, in both the customer's and the developer's organization, to read as much as is necessary for them to do. For example, with the chemical plant specification shown above, the manager of the plant will want to read only the top level of the document, while his or her engineers will want to see a much more detailed description of what functional facilities will be provided.

Another reason for having this form of hierarchy is that different staff in both the development team and the customer's organization may want to access a number of levels, but may only want to look at part of the document. For example, with the chemical plant requirements specification, engineers who are only concerned with plant optimization may wish to read only that part of the specification which deals with the management information necessary for them to perform their tasks; while engineers concerned with the day-to-day functioning of a plant will be interested in that part of the requirements specification which deals with monitoring and control. The same argument holds for the developer—especially when the software project is a large one. Normally in such projects an analyst, for example, is only allocated a part of the system to be specified— usually a functionally related part—and will want to concentrate only on that part of the requirements specification concerned with the part of the system with which he or she is dealing.

In summary, a hierarchical organization of the functional section of the requirements specification enables both customer and developer staff to concentrate on those parts of a system which are of concern to them, without having to read descriptions of parts of the specification which do not concern them. The numbered indented form of functional description described above is a very popular form of organization. However, an increasing number of developers are adopting graphical notations. The most popular graphical notation is the data flow diagram. For a good introduction to this form of specification see Page-Jones (1988). An important point which is worth reiterating here is that the functional requirements part of the requirements specification should not contain any design or implementation details. For example, in the fragment of requirements specification for the chemical plant system there is no indication whether commands are to be implemented via a menu, a windows interface, or whether line-based commands are to be used. This is something which is normally decided during design. Nevertheless, you will sometimes be faced with a customer who will insist on a particular implementation. The ideal solution is to persuade the customer not to insist on an implementation; however, if he or she persists then a separate section of the requirements specification should contain these details.

The requirements specification standard should insist that in a hierarchical form of specification a unique number is assigned to each function. These functions should be referenced in another part of the system specification concerned with grouping the functions into various categories. A list of some of these categories is shown below for both information systems and real-time systems (Redmill, 1988):

Monitoring	Control
Query processing	Report generation
System start-up	System shutdown
Exception handling	Critical condition
Security	Database integrity checking
Data validation	Error monitoring
Recovery after abnormal termination	Database update
Optimization	Adjustment of system parameters

Self Assessment Question 4.2 Which of the sixteen categories above does the sentence 'When a catastrophic error is detected the system should shut down and start up in monitoring mode'.

Solution It can be regarded as being in the start-up, system shut down, error monitoring and critical condition categories.

Thus, the reader of the requirements specification who wishes to find out what functions are concerned with security can examine this part of the requirements specification, look in the subsection marked *security*, and extract the unique identifiers of the functions which are concerned with this functional area.

4.4 DATA SPECIFICATION

Another important component of any requirements specification is a section which describes the data that forms part of the application. A good standard for requirements specification should devote a considerable amount of space to this feature.

This specification should, in common with the functional specification, not contain any implementation details; for example, terms such as *indexed sequential file*, *direct file*, and *6 bit field* should not be included.

A good standard to adopt is to insist that the developer specify data in the form of entities, attributes and relations. This is becoming standard practice in information system development where a number of development methods insist that such data is specified graphically. However, other application areas, such as military command and control, are becoming so data rich that I suspect any project which does not specify data in such a way will become the exception during the coming decade.

An *entity* is an object which is of major interest to the customer. In an air-traffic control application typical entities might be a plane, a flight plan, and a radar; in a stock-control application typical entities are a warehouse, a product, a product order, and a queue of product orders which, as yet, cannot be satisfied because the product is out of stock. Eventually entities become implemented, usually in some form of collection of records: in a file, an array, or some form of dynamic data structure such as a linked list.

An *attribute* is a property of an entity. Typical attributes for a plane entity in an air-traffic control system are: the plane identifier, its current position, its estimated landing time, the type of plane, its destination, and the location from which it started its journey. Again, there is no need to specify any physical details. An important attribute or set of attributes is known as a *key*. This is a collection of attributes which uniquely identify a particular occurrence of an entity. For example, in the air-traffic control system the key would be the plane identifier.

The final component of the data specification should be a description of the relationships between the entities. These relationships will be either *one-to-one* or *one-to-n*. With the former, a single occurrence of an entity is associated with a single occurrence of another entity. For example, in a staff management system the fact that an employee is allowed to drive only one company car would be modelled using a one-to-one relation. A one-to-n relation models the association between one entity occurrence and one or more other entities. For example, in a chemical plant application the fact that a computer monitors the state of a number of reactors would be modelled by means of a one-to-n relation.

Relations are vital for a designer who might, for example, be designing a part of a system which produces reports and wishes to know how many subsidiary items to access after an occurrence of an entity has been processed. Entities, attributes and relations represent a logical view of a system which is uncluttered with design and implementation details and, hence, represents a view which can be easily read, by both the developer and the customer. Every quality system should have a standard which describes how such information is to be documented. An extract from such a standard is shown below:

> Normally on our projects the first process that is carried out is to determine the entities, attributes and relations inherent in a system. This process is carried out by interrogating the customer, and by reading any documentation such as a statement of requirements which is provided by the customer.
>
> An entity is an object which will be implemented in data; an attribute is information which is associated with an entity and is normally implemented as a field in a record.
>
> A relation describes how many occurrences of one entity are associated with a single occurrence of another entity. A one-to-one relation means one occurrence is associated, while a one-to-n relation means that a number of occurrences are associated. For examples of such relations see section 14.5 of the Sample Project Documentation Manual. In documenting relations, entities and attributes two forms of layout are specified.
>
> The first is known as an E-R diagram. This is normally used for projects which use the SSADM development method. For other projects a strict textual form of layout is used. This layout first lists each entity followed by a colon, followed by the attributes listed in alphabetical order. Attributes which form a key and which uniquely identify an entity occurrence are displayed in bold. The entities are listed in alphabetic order. Relations are also listed in alphabetic order. Each relation is displayed on a line. Its name is displayed first, followed by the first entity together with the second entity and terminated by the relation type: whether it is one-to-one or one-to-n. A sample listing of this data is shown below.

> ENTITIES
>   Location: **Name**, TelNo
>   StaffMember: **WorksId**, CurrentBonus, Dept, Name, Salary,
>
>   ⋮
>
> RELATIONS
>   AttendedTrainingCourse: Employee, Course, 1-to-n
>   Manages: Manager, Employee, 1-to-n
>
>   ⋮

Some software developers include data information in the functional part of their requirements specification. An example of this form of combined specification is shown below, with the data items italicized:

> When the OutOfStock command is initiated the user provides a *ProductId*. The system will then scan the system data and will produce a list of *ProductName* of those products for which there is no stock available. When the update command is initiated the system will process a sequence of *ProductOrder*s. Each *ProductOrder* will contain a *ProductId* and a *DeliveredAmount*: an integer

which represents the quantity of product delivered. Each order will result in the increase in the *NumberStocked* of each product.

Self Assessment Question 4.3 Does the fragment above involve the traceability concept outlined in Chapter 1?

Solution Yes, it represents traceability between the functional parts of the requirements specification and the data specification.

It is important to point out that although this is a useful way of connecting together system functions and system data it does not absolve the analyst from specifying data using a notation such as an E-R diagram—this information is still needed. The advantage of this form of linking description is that it leads to easy validation. For example, when the system is designed, and the entities and attributes are specified in computer terms, staff can check that the design specification actually meets the functional part of the requirements specification; for example, someone checking for the correct implementation of the first function shown above can read the design documentation in order to check that a data element corresponding to a product identifier is read, a database of product details is scanned, and the product names listed.

It is worth deviating slightly to point out that the example of incorporating data details within a functional specification helps support the important feature of traceability described in Chapter 1. By structuring the functional part of the requirements specification in this way the developer is able to start the process whereby system functions can be traced to a system design and, eventually, to the program code which implements the design.

4.5 MODES OF OPERATION

As well as functional and data components, the requirements specification should also contain details of the modes of operation which the system can be in. There are a large number of these modes; some examples are emergency operation, when a potentially catastrophic result occurs, or is about to occur; shutdown operation, when the system is to be closed down; error recovery operation, when the system is trying to return from an error back to its normal state; and self-test, when the system is checking its own operation for correctness. This section of the requirements specification should detail these modes of operation and should describe when it enters and leaves these modes. An example of such a description is shown below:

Emergency state
The system will enter an emergency state when functions 3.4, 3.5, 3.9, 5.2, 5.4, 5.5 and 5.6 are executed. In general this state is entered when a problem is experienced with the inlet and outlet valves which leads to the system's inability to close or open these valves. When in this state functions 13.2 and 13.3 are initiated and depending on the results of these functions the system will either return to the normal operation state or move to manual state where operator intervention can occur.

This describes what happens when inlet and outlet valves of a chemical reactor stick. When they do, functions 13.2 and 13.3, which are concerned with checking the state of the valves and attempting to open them, are invoked. If these functions are successful the system moves to its normal operating state; if not the system enters the manual state where intervention in the operation of the chemical reactors is taken over by process workers. There are a number of states which systems can find themselves in (Redmill, 1988):

System generation	Installation
Start-up	Self-test
Normal operation	Emergency
Degraded	Automatic
Semi-automatic	Manual
On-line	Batch
Periodic	Housekeeping
Shutdown	Error recovery
Error isolation	Back-up

4.6 INTERFACES

A section of the requirements specification should describe the interface between the proposed system and entities which are beyond the scope of the system. This would include external hardware, users, and any external software. The description of the external hardware should include information such as: the structure of files which are intended for processing by other systems; the rate at which signals from an interface will arrive; the length of time that data is available at an interface before they disappear; the transmission rate associated with a particular interface; the nature of errors associated with an interface and the electrical characteristics of an interface.

The description of the human interface should include a description of the staff who interact with the computer: for example, what their technical capabilities are; whether help facilities are needed; what form of interface (line, menu or window) is needed; any requirements for reaction time; whether certain functions in the requirements specification need easily recognizable signals such as emergency displays; and any security requirements.

The external software interface part of the requirements specification should include details of data formats, file formats, protocols and subroutine calls associated with any software to be interfaced with the system that is being developed. For example, if a spreadsheet is to be used to display results from a file produced by a system, then this part of the requirements specification should include the format of the data required by the spreadsheet and also how to invoke the spreadsheet for the particular functions that it is intended to carry out.

4.7 CUSTOMER–ANALYST INTERACTION

A good quality system should provide standards and procedures which would enable the interaction between the customer and the developer to be documented as closely as possible. One of the problems that many software developers face during requirements analysis is that of a statement of requirements which is at far too abstract a level. During the early stages of a software project the statement of requirements will become the main focus of debate. A considerable amount of discussion will ensue at the end of which a requirements specification will emerge. If the developer does not keep track of additions, deletions and clarifications that a customer has made, then he or she has no defence from the customer who might claim that, for example, the company has misrepresented a functional set of features in the requirements specification. The production of some form of audit trail which points out that the features were confirmed by the customer would, at worst, lead to some form of moral ascendancy over the customer and at best demonstrate to the customer that care is being taken over the project.

Since the statement of requirements is a poor place to begin such an audit trail, many companies adopt the strategy that a first draft of the requirements specification is produced, and that both the developer and the customer regard the draft as a starting point in the process of developing the final requirements specification, which could then be used by staff such as system designers.

This first draft, which would be expressed using the requirements specification standard, and would hence feature uniquely identified functions, could be used as the final destination of any audit trail. Any negotiations over the requirements specification would then refer back to entities such as functions which could be easily identified, rather than the abstract wish lists that many statements of requirements seem to be. There is no reason why this first draft should not go through a series of cycles; indeed, a serious software developer will plan for this, and assume that because requirements analysis is such a difficult task, evolution is the only way to deal with the development of the requirements specification.

A procedure for documenting the interaction between the developer and the customer is shown below:

> One of the items that our company takes very seriously is the process of requirements analysis. We have had a number of problems in the past when customers, at a very late stage in the requirements analysis process, have changed their minds over major requirements and have attempted to convince us that the change of mind was communicated to us at a very early stage of the project. It is hence important that we keep a diary of interactions between the customer and the analysts working on the project.
>
> When a change to a draft of the requirements specification is suggested the analyst must enter the details of the change in the requirements log. Each entry in the log contains a brief description of the change, how the change came about, the number(s) of the functions that were changed or, if the change was to a non-functional part of the system, the section and paragraph number in the requirements specification. Each entry should also describe how the proposed change was communicated; for example, whether it was via telephone or via a written memo. If the change was in a written form then any identification of the change such as a reference number should be included. Use the keywords DETAIL, FUNCTIONS AFFECTED, REFERENCE and SEVERITY to mark the components of an entry.
>
> The final part of the entry should be an indication of its severity; we have decided on five levels of severity: from 0 (trivial) to 4 (very serious). A very serious change is one which would have a

substantial effect on the project in resource terms. If an analyst encounters a change at level 3 or 4 then either the staff member he reports to, or the project manager, must be informed, as these types of changes often lead to budget overruns and late delivery.

It is important that as many of the interactions as possible between the analysts and the customer should be accompanied by paper documentation. We recognize that there will be rare occasions when a telephone call is the medium of communication. If it is, then do attempt to get a memo from the customer following up the change. If this proves impossible you should at least note the time of the call and the customer representative that you spoke to and write a confirmation letter.

All changes which lead from one version of the requirements specification to the next should be documented and the change sent to the customer for approval and, after approval, to the project library for archiving. In our project planning standard PP 1/5 Section 3.4.2 you will see that all our projects should write in an assumption that certain documents such as notification of requirements changes should be read by the customer and turned around within a specific time. Analysts should look at the project plan for their project, see what the time limit is for requirements changes and add a sentence to the effect that the developer is expecting comments back in n weeks and the non-receipt of comments will be taken as agreement.

An example of an entry for a change is shown below:

Change 17
DETAIL This change was initiated by the customer who asked for all malfunctions of the system to be written to a log file.

FUNCTIONS AFFECTED 12.1-12.22, 13.4-13.18, 14.1, 14.3.

REFERENCE. Confirmed in letter to D Aspinall dated 12/3/90, reference number bpt 56/Aww12.

SEVERITY 2.

4.8 THE REQUIREMENTS SPECIFICATION AND THE STATEMENT OF REQUIREMENTS

One major problem that the customer has when reading and checking a requirements specification is that of relating the contents of that document to the statement of requirements that he or she has produced. It is a good idea to reproduce the statement of requirements in the requirements specification—usually as an appendix—with the items in the statement of requirements cross-referenced to items in the requirements specification. For example, functional requirements in the statement of requirements would be annotated with the function numbers from the requirements specification and non-functional requirements would be annotated with section and paragraph numbers. Any new requirements which have been discovered and which are not contained in the statement of requirements should be referenced in this section.

Self Assessment Question 4.4 What is the cross-referencing described in the previous paragraph an example of?

Solution It is an example of traceability.

It is worth issuing a warning here: that often this will prove a very difficult task—if not an impossible one. Many statements of requirements tend to be too abstract, often resembling a vague wish list. In this case the labour involved in cross-referencing the statement of requirements to the requirements specification would be wasted.

However, increasingly, there are customers—usually those with a large amount of experience of dealing with software developers—who produce relatively well structured statements of requirements, and it is these customers who most welcome cross-referencing in order to help them check that a requirements specification correlates with their needs. For this reason, a quality system should at least offer the project manager the option of producing this section of the requirements specification and standards and procedures for the process of cross-referencing.

4.9 VALIDATING THE REQUIREMENTS SPECIFICATION

At the end of the requirements analysis phase both the developer and the customer will need a high degree of confidence that the requirements specification is a correct reflection of the needs of the customer. The role of validation is to check that those needs have been catered for, and that the requirements specification is an adequate basis for further activities such as system design; procedures should be provided by the quality system for validation. Currently there are a number of techniques for validation of a requirements specification: prototyping, simulation, and technical reviews are the three main ones. *Simulation* is the process of modelling a system in order to determine whether non-functional requirements—usually response times—can be implemented. *Prototyping* is the process of producing an early version of a system in order to check with the customer that the developer has a correct view of what is needed from a system. *Technical reviews* are meetings of staff who examine a project document, such as a requirements specification, system design or project plan, for correctness.

Reviews have been found exceptionally useful for two reasons: first, they constitute a collective process whereby a number of staff take a dispassionate look at a software document; and second, they can be held early on in the software project, in order to detect errors that, if undiscovered, are capable of causing a catastrophe. Pressman (1994) has described a number of principles and guidelines for the organization and conduct of technical reviews.

Ideally, between three and five staff should be involved in a technical review. In the review of the requirements specification, this would typically be a chairperson, usually a senior member of staff from the project; the analyst who prepared the part of the requirements specification being reviewed; an analyst from another project; a customer representative; and whoever is to produce the system and acceptance tests. The last member is an important participant: he or she is able to probe any weaknesses in the system design by asking searching questions about how particular combinations of operations would be tested.

A point which should be made about the chairperson—or, as he or she is sometimes called, the *moderator*—is that the project manager should not chair such reviews, or even attend them. There are two reasons for this. First, project managers have other pressures on them which they often see as being much more important than software quality. These will concern issues such as the number of days to the date of release of the software and the amount of budget remaining for their projects. Consequently, there will be a subconscious tendency for managers to skimp on the task of chairing the reviews in order to sweep problems under the carpet. Second, a review is a bruising experience for the member of staff whose work is being reviewed. Often such work is torn to pieces. If the manager is in attendance there will be a tendency for staff whose work is being examined to regard the presence as some sort of personnel evaluation exercise, and to become exceptionally defensive, rather than have the very open attitude to errors that is a prerequisite for the successful review.

Standards for review meetings should insist that they last no more than two hours. When properly run, reviews are intensive and exhausting and most people's span of attention lasts for no longer than two hours. After this time they tend to lose interest in the topic of a review very quickly.

It is also important to point out that guidelines for reviews should specify the amount of time that should be devoted to preparing for a review. What the participants who attend a review are doing is debugging; this is not something that can be done in a few seconds, but requires time for reflective thought. Pressman advises that advance preparation should take no more than two hours per person.

It should be remembered that it is the document which is the subject of a review, not the person who developed the document. This is an important point, because a review can be quite a harrowing experience for the staff whose document or program code is being reviewed. Nobody likes criticism, and at a review the staff involved have to take two hours of implied criticism. The role of the moderator is key in a review: he or she has to organize and run the meeting in such a way that the product is decoupled from the person that produced it.

There are a number of strategies aimed at depersonalizing a review. A simple one is never to refer to errors as errors, but as problems. One particularly good moderator that I know of announces, at the beginning of the review, that the document or program code being reviewed is the collective responsibility of the attendees in the review. The blame for any errors that remain after the review has been completed is divided equally among the participants. Another moderator of my acquaintance always tries to encourage positive remarks about a program, e.g. that it is well structured or easy to read, as well as encouraging the error-detection process.

Another guideline is to set an agenda and stick to it. Reviews can meander quite a bit, with a solution to a problem being aired, followed by a discussion of similar problems encountered on other projects, followed by a discussion of an old project that some of the participants worked on, and eventually ending up with a general free-for-all about office politics, sexual politics, and the quality of the eating houses in the area.

An important point related to keeping to an agenda is that the moderator should not allow the review to be taken up with discussions about how an error should be rectified. A review is an extremely useful validation and verification technique for detecting errors; it is less good at remedying them. The only person who is really capable of removing an error is the person who produced the document under review. It is, of course, impractical to ban all discussion about how an error can be eradicated. However, this should be brief and along the lines of: 'We had that problem with one of our programs: ring Geoff up and he'll tell you how he coped with it.'

The agenda for a review should be quite simple. Normally, the first item that should be dealt with is any general points about the item for review. Next, the participants should work through a checklist of overall points about the product. This should be followed by a detailed reading of the item. The amount of time that is devoted to each of these activities will depend on the item that is being reviewed. However, the final activity—i.e. reading the item line-by-line—will take up most of the time.

It is important that the moderator or a secretary takes written notes during a review and that a standard should specify the structure of these notes. In particular, a list of errors—or rather problems—should be produced, for two reasons: first, attendees will forget what went on in a review. It may be days before the member of staff who produced the item reviewed gets around to changing it. Second, quality assurance staff will be required to ensure that reviews are being carried out correctly, and any actions outstanding have been dealt with. They usually do this via formal audits and spot-checks. A set of minutes, together with a list of outstanding problems, is essential for them to do their jobs efficiently.

A final point to be made about reviews is that each type of product being reviewed should have a checklist associated with it—provided by the quality system. For example, programs or subroutines would have a checklist that contains instructions about detecting unsafe programming constructs, non-initialized variables, non-conformance to coding standards, over-complex interfaces, and convoluted program code.

The review process is shown in Fig. 4.1 which is an extract from an existing procedure. First, the item to be reviewed is produced and the member of staff who produced it considers that it is near to being correct. This is often an iterative process, whereby whoever produced the item checks specifics with colleagues. The staff member then informs whoever is to chair the review that the item being reviewed is ready. It is sent to the moderator, who then evaluates whether it is in fact ready. If it is, the review is organized: the room booked, participants informed, and copies of the review item, together with current guidelines for the item type, are circulated.

Finally, shortly before the day of the meeting the agenda is sent to all participants. The review is then held, and a list of problems produced, together with the minutes of the review. Copies of these are sent to each of the participants and at least one copy is filed in the project library.

The procedure for holding a review should specify a number of outcomes. First, the review may have been totally successful. In this case the item is passed and stored in the project library. Eventually, it will be frozen, along with all the other similar items that have been reviewed. For example, the requirements specification will be reviewed a chunk at a time, and when the whole of the requirements specification is deemed to have been satisfactorily reviewed it is frozen, and any further changes are rigorously monitored and controlled. Second, there may be some small errors associated with the item that is being reviewed. In this case the item is regarded as having passed the review. The member of staff who produced the item then makes any amendments, and shows them to the moderator of the review who signs the item off as fully passing the review. Third, there may be major problems with the item. In this case it is then modified and has to be re-reviewed, preferably with the same members of the original review being present.

A number of review formats have been devised. The most popular are Fagan Inspections developed by Michael Fagan (1986), which has an emphasis on not only detecting errors, but also using error data to improve software processes such as requirements analysis. Part of a procedure for running a review is shown below:

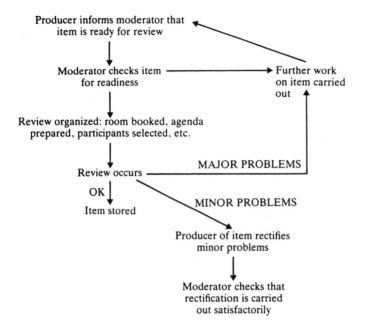

Figure 4.1 The review process.

7 Technical reviews

One of the main techniques that we use to implement quality control is the technical review. This is just a meeting of staff who examine a critical project document for correctness and who issue a report on the problems that have been encountered during the review. The process of organizing a review is shown below.

The member of staff responsible for an item that is to be reviewed informs the chair of the review that the item is ready. The chair checks that the item is in a fit state for review. If it is not then it is returned to the originator for reworking. If the item is ready for review the chair books a room, selects the participants for the review (usually between three and five members of staff), arranges for the review material and any supporting material to be duplicated and sent to the participants, and informs each participant of the date and place of the review. Who the chair invites to the review depends on the material to be reviewed, as does the nature of the supporting material. These details can be found in sections 7.1 to 7.8.

For many of our reviews there will be checklists which describe the particular problems that review participants should be looking for. Copies of the checklists should also be sent to each participant. The review is held. One of the participants is nominated as a recorder. The chair will normally ask any of the participants whether there are any general problems with the item that is being reviewed. After this the document is processed serially, item by item; for example, if it is a requirements specification this will be done on a paragraph-by-paragraph basis, if it is program code then it will be done on a module-by-module basis. Each time a problem is discovered it is noted down on the review report form. This form contains sections which describe the nature of the problem, where it occurs, the staff member responsible, and the severity of the error. For further details of this form see section 8.1.

At the end of the review the chair will decide whether the item has passed the review, has passed subject to minor revision, or has not passed. In the first case the chair signs off the object on the review report form. In the second case the originator of the item rectifies the minor problem and the chair of the review checks the changes and signs off the review report form. In the third case a re-review is needed.

Once an item has been reviewed it should be consigned to the project library, accompanied by the review report form. The remainder of this section describes information specific to each review type that our quality manual supports.

7.1 The requirements specification review

There should normally be either four or five participants at this review, one of whom should not be the project manager or the manager to which the producer of the item to be reviewed reports. For this review a selection of the following staff should be invited: the producer of the section of requirements specification that is to be reviewed; an analyst from another project; one of the system design team; a customer representative; and any staff responsible for the derivation of the system tests.

The documentation items that are provided with this review are: the section of requirements specification that is to be reviewed, any verification requirements and the customer statement of requirements. These items should be circulated to the participants. A document that should also be made available for reference during the review is the journal which records the interaction with the customer; the bulk of this document precludes it being copied and circulated to the participants of the review. If a scenario analysis has been carried out then any scenarios should be made available to the participants.

The checklist which is relevant to this review is checklist RR 1.2 and all participants should be provided with it.

The description of the requirements specification review includes a reference to *scenario analysis*. This is a process whereby the customer and the analyst describe a series of interlinked actions which should be dealt with by the system which is being specified. For example, in a stock control system a series of interlinked actions would be: a customer ringing in to purchase a product, the salesperson discovering that the item is out of stock, the salesperson placing an order on a back-order queue, and a sales confirmation document being issued to the customer. These scenarios are useful for checking that a requirements specification is complete and the interrelation between functions has been properly documented.

4.10 DEVELOPING THE VERIFICATION REQUIREMENTS

Another area of activity occurring during requirements analysis which a quality manual should address via standards and procedures is the generation of the verification requirements. Chapter 4 has already described the nature of verification requirements: that they are requirements which are of direct interest to the customer, rather than those which are concerned with the internal functioning of the system.

At the end of the requirements analysis task staff responsible for testing will read the requirements specification and derive the verification requirements. It is important that this process is begun at an early stage in the project, for the following reasons:

- Staff who are to carry out the testing of a system may have a requirement for special-purpose testing tools or hardware. It is important that these requirements are known as early in a project as possible, so that if there is a need for the tools to be produced by a subcontractor, or by another part of the developer's organization, then as long a lead-time as possible is available: subcontracted software is a major problem in many projects, and a project manager often likes to see as much slack in the subcontracting process as it is possible to achieve.

- The project manager will need to know, as early as possible, the extent of the system testing that needs to be carried out in order to resource this part of the project.
- A good tester who is attempting to extract verification requirements from a requirements specification will ask searching questions about any ambiguities and contradictions that occur. This is a major aid in the validation of the requirements specification.

The last of these three points is the most important: a good tester who continually asks the question: 'But how do I test this?' soon gets to the heart of some very serious problems with a requirements specification. As an example, assume that the analysts in a software project have let through the sentence: 'The system should be user-friendly', which occurred in the statement of requirements and the requirements specification. A good tester would look at the sentence and ask some demanding questions about how to specify the tests which check this. What would normally happen would be that the analysts would be asked to clarify the sentence. They may come back with a number of interpretations:

- That the phrase means that the customer wants a help facility which provides on-line guidance that staff using the system can refer to during operation. Now the analyst and the tester may disagree that this interpretation actually leads to a user-friendly system. Nevertheless, it provides the tester and the analyst with a much clearer view of what is required by the user, and enables the tester to devise some tests: a test to see whether the help facility can be properly invoked, and a series of tests to check whether the text associated with a particular help message is in fact a help facility rather than a hindrance facility.
- That the phrase means that the customer wants a command-based system with long and short commands. Again, the analyst and tester may be sceptical about whether this is, in fact, a manifestation of user-friendliness. However, it has clarified the requirements specification to the point where tests can be derived to check that both long and short commands are recognized by the system.
- That the customer, when he or she uses the phrase 'user-friendly', wants a windows interface. Now there isn't really a test for having a windows interface: you've either got it or you haven't. Nevertheless, by asking the question: 'How do I test this?', the tester has uncovered a major problem with the requirements specification.
- That the customer, instead of having any facilities in mind, is more concerned with the behaviour of the system in that he or she does not want a high error rate when staff interact with a system. This is mainly a preoccupation of customers who have contracted for safety-critical systems, but also concerns those who have systems which require large amounts of data entry and who may have to spend large amounts of resources in ensuring the accuracy of the data that is keyed in. In this case the developer would be allowed to devise an adequate interface, and the tester would then develop some tests to check that a particular error rate was sustainable; for example, tests could be run with real users of the system, which monitored the number of errors

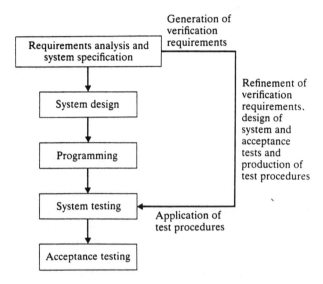

Figure 4.2 Verification requirements and development.

per hour that they made, and checked that a numerical threshold specified by the customer was not exceeded.

At this point it is worth describing the relationship between the verification requirements and the other development activities which occur on a project. Figure 4.2 describes this relationship. The verification requirements are produced during the process of requirements specification. They are then expanded during system design so that it becomes more obvious how they are going to be tested. For example, the verification requirement:

V3.4 When the back-orders command is initiated with the important order parameter, the system will display the back-order queue in decreasing order of customer importance.

will give rise to the refinement:

V3.4-D The back-orders command will be checked by initiating the command with at least three test databases consisting of varying lengths of queue. The tester will check that the command has been implemented correctly by running a utility which prints the queue entries on a printer, and then checking that the screen displays tally with the printed output.

The next stage for the testers is to expand this description into a *test procedure*. This is a detailed description of how the test is to be carried out: it will include details on how the

Table 4.1 Tabular representation of verification requirements

Command typed in ok	1	1	1	0
Date ok	1		0	
Shop ok	1	0		
Results displayed	1			
Date error			1	
Shop location error		1		
Command error				1
	17.1	17.2	17.3	17.4

test is to be started, terminated, aborted, the location of test databases, how to operate the utility mentioned in the test design above, and what to look for on the screens that will be generated.

This is just an introduction to the process of testing; Chapter 7 contains far more detail on the topic. The important point worth making here is that a quality manual should offer specific guidance on how to generate the verification requirements, how to document them, and how to interact with the analysts on a project if problems in interpretation occur during this process.

This chapter has included an extract from a quality manual describing what a verification requirement is. Normally, such requirements are documented using natural language. However, for many systems, especially commercial data processing systems, where many of the functions are transaction-based, a tabular form is a useful way of displaying collections of verification requirements which correspond to a particular feature.

An example of this tabular display is shown in Table 4.1. It describes the verification requirements for a command which displays the number of customers processed on a particular day by a particular shop in a large retail chain. The user of this command specifies the command name, the name of a shop, and a date; if these have been correctly communicated to the system, then data is displayed. However, if there has been an error in the date or the name of the shop an error message is displayed. A 1 entry stands for a condition being true, while a 0 entry stands for falsity. The first column shows what happens if the command has been invoked correctly: the command name is correct, the date is of the correct format and the shop name is correct. A correct initiation of the command leads to correct results being displayed. The second column stands for what happens when the command has been invoked, but an incorrect shop name has been typed in. Notice that the entry for *Date OK* has no 1 or 0 entry. This means that it is irrelevant as to whether the user has typed in a correct or incorrect date. The numbers on the bottom row represent the numbers of the functions associated with the verification requirements. These numbers are the unique identification of each function in the requirements specification.

This form of documentation is extremely useful. It enables staff responsible for checking the verification requirements to check for completeness and consistency. Companies that I know of who have employed this form of documentation always tell me that it enables them to have a high degree of confidence that their requirements specification is correct. It also has the advantage that it is automatable via a spreadsheet.

There are a number of places where verification requirements can be documented. Many companies place them in their quality plan. Some add them as an appendix to the system specification. One or two companies that I have worked for have even put them as an appendix to their project plan.

4.11 THE STRUCTURE OF THE REQUIREMENTS SPECIFICATION

This section details all the components which form part of the standard for a requirements specification. The structure of the requirements specification outlined below is partially based on the one presented in Redmill (1988). For a much more detailed description of the contents of a requirements specification the reader is referred to this work:

1. Title
2. Contents
3. Introduction
4. About this document
5. Glossary
6. System requirements
7. Target system environment
8. Customer-imposed constraints.

An important point that should be made before outlining the contents of each section is that staff carrying out activities such as system testing or system design will be continually referring to this document, and a numbering system should be adopted which uniquely identifies every requirement which is to be validated.

The introduction should be brief (no more than a single page), it should describe the system and outline any unusual features both in the development of the system and also in the system itself. The section headed *About this document* should describe any naming conventions; the scope of the document; the main topics in the document; the intended audience; any legal and contractual issues associated with the document; any relevant standards, both local and external; how the requirements specification is to be maintained and issued; and, finally, the distribution list for the requirements specification.

The glossary should contain a list of terms and their definitions. It is well worth dividing this part of the requirements specification into two sections: terms specific to the application and technical terms specific to hardware and software details.

The major part of the requirements specification will be the system requirements. These are normally divided into a number of sections. One section will detail the functional requirements; this should be structured hierarchically. Another will describe non-functional requirements, e.g. those concerned with performance, availability, adaptability, reliability, memory occupancy, file size, and so on. A subsection should be devoted to each category of non-functional requirement.

The seventh section—target system environment—should describe the environment into which the system is to be placed. This section should not only contain a description of the hardware on which the system is to be mounted, but also any other hardware interfaces such as communication lines. It should also describe the interface to other software systems and the human interface: the capabilities of the staff who are to use the system and what they will use the system for.

The final section is a list of any constraints insisted on by the customer. This section should be divided into two parts: design, validation and implementation constraints, which constrain the developer in the way that the system is developed and checked; and project constraints, which constrain the way that the project is managed.

Self Assessment Question 4.5 Where in the requirements section should the fact that a project involves a trans-national collaboration be specified?

Solution It should be in the introduction if this is outside the norm for the company.

4.12 QUALITY MANUAL REQUIREMENTS

The following documents or sections should form part of the quality manual for a software development organization:

1. Functional requirements specification standard
2. Non-functional requirements specification standard
3. Data requirements specification standard
4. System environment specification standard
5. Customer–developer interaction standard
6. Customer–developer interaction procedure
7. Statement of requirements traceability standard
8. Requirements specification checklist
9. Prototyping procedure
10. Prototyping standard
11. Requirements review procedure
12. Requirements review standard
13. Requirements review checklist
14. Verification requirements standard
15. Verification requirements procedure.

Normally items 1 to 4 are included in an overall requirements specification standard and procedure, which often also includes items 5 to 8. Items 9 and 10 are often collected together as one document, as are items 11, 12 and 13, and items 14 and 15.

4.13 SUMMARY

Next to the project plan the requirements specification is the most important document generated during a software project. Because it is used by a large number of staff, ranging from the project manager to technical writers, it is vitally important that a company has good standards, procedures and guidelines which describe the process of developing a requirements specification, its validation and its structure.

4.14 FURTHER READING

There are few good works that have been published on requirements analysis and specification. However, Stokes (1990) is an excellent tutorial introduction to these topics, Boehm (1984) is an invaluable introduction to the techniques used for validating requirements, and Davis (1990) is a good book-length introduction to requirements analysis. Easteal and Davies (1989) is a good, short introduction to both design and requirements analysis.

5

SYSTEM DESIGN

AIMS

- To describe the main documentation used for system design.
- To describe some important techniques and documentation used to validate a system design against a requirements specification.
- To outline the structure of the system design specification.
- To describe how the system design process is quality assured.

5.1 INTRODUCTION

System design is the process which gives rise to an architecture of a system. The aim of system design is to produce a modular description of a system which will satisfy the requirements described in the requirements specification—both functional and non-functional—at the same time respecting the customer's design and implementation directives and the constraints specified in the requirements specification. Indeed, one of the ways in which to judge the quality of a requirements specification is to see whether it contains enough information for the designer to carry out his or her job efficiently.

The units or modules which a design is expressed in depends on the application area and the implementation media. For third-generation languages such as C, Pascal or FORTRAN, the units will be subroutines and procedures, for fourth-generation languages the units will be programs, and for languages which are object-oriented or contain some object-oriented facilities, the units will be packages or classes: collections of procedures or subroutines which are associated with a particular collection of data.

As well as the design being expressed in terms of processing units it should also be expressed in terms of the underlying data. In a third-generation language this data will either be in-memory data such as arrays or linked lists, or file-based data such as indexed sequential files or direct files. For fourth-generation languages the data will be specified in terms of tables.

The main problem that developers face during the design process is checking that the system design which has been produced actually meets the requirements detailed in the requirements specification. There are two aspects to this difficulty. The first is technical: for some requirements such as response time there is little theory around which enables the developer to feel confident that a requirement has been satisfied. The second aspect, which is less of a problem, is that in projects with poor quality assurance there is either very little or very poor documentation, which hinders the developer in checking that, for example, functional requirements are being satisfied. In the previous chapter great stress was placed on the fact that the requirements specification should detail as clearly as possible all the user requirements for a system. The aim of this chapter is to show how, in a number of ways, validation can be made an easier process. This requires both the accurate specification of a design and the construction of linking documents which trace from a requirements specification to a system design and vice versa.

5.2 DESIGN DOCUMENTATION

A major quality concern in system design is the expression of the design—either textually or in terms of graphics. Any standard for system design should identify the individual modules in a system: packages, subroutines or programs, and also identify the relationship between the modules, i.e. how each uses facilities provided by another. Normally, this means that the calling structure of the system should be documented. As well as the calling structure, the system design should also specify the interface between modules, i.e. what the parameters of each module are, and what global data areas are to be read from or written to. The functionality of each module should be specified in enough detail so that the programmer responsible for coding the module should be able to take the specification, the description of the interface and the list of calls to other modules, and produce program code without querying the design. An example of a specification for a module expressed in a third-generation language is shown below:

MODULE CheckupMain(DataArea: [1:30] of Real)
CALLS BringSensor
READS SensorFile: File of Real
WRITES Malfunction
FUNCTION
This module brings in the last 30 items of sensor data read by the main sensor and held in *SensorFile* and places the values in *DataArea*. It then checks whether the data contained in *DataArea* is in ascending order. If it is, then the boolean variable *Malfunction* is set to true; it is set to false otherwise.

It is relatively easy to specify a system design notation which could be processed by a software tool and which would set up a code skeleton corresponding to the module, with information such as the function of the module copied in as a comment.

This form of documentation could be modified for any target programming language; a language which implements packages would have a system design notation which, for each subroutine in the package, would contain details such as those shown above, together with a specification of the data that the package manipulates. For a fourth-generation language accessing a relational database the format would again be similar, except that instead of global variables, tables would normally be referenced. An example of a module specification for a fourth-generation language is shown below.

> PROGRAM FindNills (Monthlist: Table of months)
> READS EmployeeDetails, Sales
> This program displays a list of employees who have achieved no sales for *Monthlist*. The list of employees numbers will be displayed in decreasing order of total sales over the last five years.
> SCREEN Emplist

An extra feature here is that of the name of a screen. In systems which are based on transactions it is important that the design notation used contains details of any input and output.

A quality manual can take one of two attitudes towards a system design notation: either to have a single notation, or a number of notations, each of which are oriented towards a particular programming language. The decision as to which to adopt depends on local circumstances and trade-offs.

Self Assessment Question 5.1 Can you think of an advantage and a disadvantage of using a single system design notation?

Solution Adopting one system design notation has the advantage that it leads to lower training and familiarization costs, but for a software developer who uses a wide variety of programming languages the disadvantage is that this could lead to an awkward fit with a number of languages and could result in error-prone validation of a programmed module with respect to its design.

The normal solution adopted by developers who have a wide spread of applications, both third-generation language- and fourth-generation language-specific, is to have two notations: one biased towards the former, the other towards the latter.

5.3 DATA SPECIFICATION

A quality system should also provide standards for the specification of the underlying data to be manipulated by a system. This is vitally important not only for data-rich systems such as commercial data processing systems, but also for those systems which are not traditionally associated with large amounts of data, for example, system software and telecommunications systems. There are two ways of specifying data depending on the technology used. The extract shown below is part of a standard for the description of the data in a third-generation language such as C or Pascal:

> **9.1 Data specification**
> It is vitally important that the data manipulated by our systems is adequately documented.

Data manipulated by programs will consist of simple types such as integers, characters and reals together with composite types which are records containing fields which have a certain type. There will also be types which will be collections of objects such as strings, arrays or sequences. The final type are collections of objects where some ordering criterion applies.

The data specification for a third-generation target language is simple. It consists of the names of any simple types followed by definitions of array and sequence types. Arrays are introduced by means of the keyword *array* followed by square brackets into which are inserted the bounds of the array, sequences are identified by the keyword *sequence* followed by the keyword *of* and the type of the objects in the sequence. The types are then followed by the list of global variables with their associated types. Finally a narrative describes the types and the global variables. Any reference to types and globals will be italicized. The keyword *Types* introduces the types, *Globals* introduces the global variables and *Narrative* introduces a description of the types and global variables. An example of this form of specification is shown below:

Types
Salesman : record
      SalesPersonName: String
      Salary: Integer
      WorksId: Integer
      CurrentSales: Integer
SalesForce: array [1..CurrentSalestot] of Salesman
SalesOrder = sequence of Salesman.

Globals
HighestSales:Salesman
EmployedSalesmen: SalesForce
SalesQueue: SalesOrder

Narrative
Salesman represents data on a salesman currently employed by the company.

Salesforce is the collection of salesmen employed by the company.

SalesOrder is a queue of salesmen which is ordered on descending CurrentSales.

HighestSales is a variable which contains the details of the salesman who currently has the highest sales. This salesman should currently be at the head of the queue of salesmen.

EmployedSalesmen is a variable which holds the current employees of the company who are involved in sales.

SalesQueue is a variable which holds the queue of salesmen in decreasing order of sales.

The important point about this form of specification is that it should roughly correspond to the data definition facilities in a programming language so that programming staff can easily implement it. This is shown above where the target language is Pascal-like. When the language is a fourth-generation language, the data definition standard will be oriented towards expressing data as tables.

5.4 DESIGN PROCEDURE

Another component of the design process which the quality manual must address is the process of carrying out the design. This should include instructions on how the design is carried out in a step-by-step fashion, what documents should be examined when carrying out a design, and the mechanisms which enable the system designer to check a design. If the developer uses a standard development methodology such as the American Yourdon Structured Development (Yourdon and Constantine, 1979) or the British SSADM (Ashworth and Goodland, 1990), then much of this information can be found in the manuals for this method. However, if the developer does not use such methodologies, then the quality manual should provide a detailed description of what should occur. An excerpt from a design procedure is shown below:

8.1 System design procedure

Our software systems are normally designed in a top-down fashion, unless a customer insists that a standard development methodology is employed.

The technique that we use is known as functional decomposition. This involves writing down an outline design using natural language, and then splitting up that description into less abstract descriptions. For example, the outline design for a system which processes a stream of monitor readings and produces a summary report is shown below:

1 Open monitor file
2 Process data in the monitor file
3 Produce reports

This represents the first level of the design, with each part of the design sequentially numbered. It is important to stress that this specification of processes occurs after the data architecture of the system has been defined. The next stage in the design process is to decompose this description further. For example, the second statement above can be expanded to:

2.1 Produce error data
2.2 Produce summary data

The third step might be expanded to:

3.1 Produce error report
3.2 Produce average readings report
3.3 Produce unusual readings report

Notice that each decomposition is numbered sequentially, and is traced back to the design statement from which it originates. The process of decomposition stops when the designer feels that he or she has reached a module (function, procedure or subroutine) and no further decomposition is required. These modules are then documented according to the standard contained in section 8.2 of this document. There are a number of things to be borne in mind when carrying out the design process.

1. Modules should be designed so that they only carry out one function. We have found that such modules are easy to maintain. Modules which are multi-functional tend to require major rework when requirements changes occur.

2. If some aspect of the system to be developed has a high probability of change, then that aspect should be hidden away in a module. For example, if you are developing a system for processing a queue of orders from customers with the queue ordered on the time that items join the queue and you know that, in the future, the customer may change the ordering criterion, then the details of how the queue is represented should be hidden away in the small number of modules which add an item to the queue, remove an item from the queue, check whether the queue is empty, and count the number of items on the queue. It is important that such details should not be placed throughout the system design, but hidden in a relatively small number of modules. Section 7.1 of a requirements specification generated by any of our projects will contain a list of likely changes which may

Table 5.1 A verification matrix

	A	B	C	D	E	F
1.1	x					
1.2		x	x	x		
1.3			x			
2.1		x		x	x	
2.2				x		x
2.3			x			
2.4			x	x		
2.5		x				
3.1	x		x	x	x	x
3.2	x	x	x	x	x	

be occasioned by factors such as the customer's environment, working practices, and business policy.

3. If you suspect that some part of the system that you are designing is going to give response time problems, then that part of the system should be designed using the information hiding principle described in the previous point. Normally, problems with response time will have been identified during the risk analysis part of project planning, and the project manager will have allowed some extra development time which is intertwined with system testing. This time is normally used for tuning: changing the system to speed it up. Hence there is a need to localize design details of those parts of the system which may require modification to meet performance requirements.

4. In carrying out the design process the designer should always bear in mind that the design is to satisfy a set of quality attributes. These are either functional or non-functional. Our standards insist that the former are documented in appendix A.1 and that the latter should be placed in appendix A.2 of the requirements specification.

5.5 DESIGN VALIDATION

An important part of the design stage is the process of providing evidence that a design actually meets a requirements specification. In Chapter 1 I explained that the requirements specification gives rise to a number of quality attributes. During a software project a system and its documentation will be examined or executed in order to check whether these quality attributes are present.

It is important that during design as many of these checks are carried out as possible. By doing this the developer is saved the embarrassment and increased resource expenditure of discovering major problems late in a project. The major validation task during design is that of determining whether the system design represents a system that meets its functional requirements. There are a number of ways of doing this. The first is by constructing a document known as the *verification matrix*. This is a two-dimensional table which lists both the functions of a system and the modules contained in it. An example of such a matrix is shown in Table 5.1. At the top of the matrix is a row containing the names of the modules in the system. The first column contains the numbers of the functions specified in the requirements specification. An x in a cell of the matrix indicates that a particular module is executed when the function is exercised. For example, the second row shows that modules B, C and D are exercised when function 1.2 is invoked. This matrix would be produced by the designer after the design has been completed. It provides a form of validation that, as a minimum, the design meets all the functional quality attributes which have been identified during requirements analysis.

Self Assessment Question 5.2 Can you think how a verification matrix is of help in identifying whether the designer has included any extra functions in the system which are not in the requirements specification?

Solution These are often manifested in modules which do not have any x entries in their columns.

It is worth issuing a warning that, although the verification matrix is of great help in determining whether redundant functions are present, it does not provide 100 per cent assurance. For example, the designer may have structured the system in such a way that extra functions which are not required are supported by modules which also support the real functions of the system. However, this would usually be manifested in multi-functional modules that would normally be discouraged by the quality system.

For a large system the verification matrix will be big and take a considerable time to produce. There are two solutions to this problem: first, the matrix can be automated by using a spreadsheet; and second, the size of the matrix (the number of cells) can be substantially reduced by splitting it up into a number of smaller matrices which would correspond to functional subsets of the requirements specification.

The verification matrix is also of help during testing. For example, the functional quality attributes described above will give rise to system tests and acceptance tests. If a module in the matrix has a small number of x entries, then that module is not going to be thoroughly exercised by system test data. The staff concerned with testing the system may decide that they would like that module to be rigorously tested. There are, then, a number of options that could be adopted:

- Obsessively test the small number of functions that the module implements during system testing.
- Ask the programmer who is to produce the module to test it more rigorously than usual.
- Ask the integration testers to exercise the module thoroughly during integration testing.
- Make the module the subject of a code review.

The verification matrix implements a form of traceability which is vital in a software project, as it relates functions to the code which implements them. In order to see why this is, consider what happens during the process of acceptance testing when an acceptance test fails. Assume that acceptance test 5000 fails. The professional software developer will then modify the system after the cause of the error has been determined. He or she will then run the acceptance test to confirm that the modification has been applied correctly. Most developers will then move on to test 5001. This is not the correct action to take.

Self Assessment Question 5.3 Why is this not the correct action to take?

Solution The change to the system which was applied to make acceptance test 5000 work may have inserted other errors into the system—errors which would only be detected by acceptance tests prior to test 5000. If a developer does not have traceability built into his or her documentation, then all the acceptance tests previous to test 5000 will need to be re-executed. If the developer used the verification matrix the testing effort is substantially reduced. All that is required is for the tester to examine which modules have been changed and then rerun all those acceptance tests which involve those modules.

Many software engineering textbooks stress functional checking. However, many software systems give rise to quality attributes which are non-functional in nature (many of these were discussed in Chapter 1). It is important that the software designer provide some evidence that these quality attributes are implemented in the design produced. This evidence is usually provided by a separate document sometimes known as the *non-functional quality attribute validation document*, but sometimes implemented as a subsection in the system design specification.

Some examples of these quality attributes are shown below:

Changes to the staff details in the system should not involve any changes to the program code of the system.

The system should produce staff summary data records which can be transferred directly to a row on a Lotus 1-2-3 spreadsheet.

The system should occupy no more than 20k of main memory storage.

The maximum response time for any Staff Retrieval command is 2 sec.

The first quality attribute is associated with the maintainability quality factor. A designer would demonstrate that the system design met this attribute by explaining that staff details are held in a table on a file which is separate from the program code.

The second attribute is associated with the interoperability quality factor. The designer would demonstrate that this attribute has been satisfied by showing that the section of the data architecture which describes the records emitted by the system has the same format as that expected by the spreadsheet.

The third attribute is associated with the performance quality factor. A designer would demonstrate that the design meets this requirement by estimating the code size of each module in the system and comparing it with that specified in the description of the quality attribute.

The fourth attribute is again associated with the performance quality factor. For a simple system, the designer would calculate the algorithmic complexity of each module and make a rough estimate of the execution time of each command. For more complex systems, the project may call for advanced techniques, such as simulation, to be used.

So far we have described the fact that the production of documentation is able to provide a framework in which quality controls for design can be implemented. The controls themselves can be implemented in a number of ways: a senior member of staff could sign off the documentation produced by the designer, or a formal review of a design could take place.

This review would not be attended by the customer.

Self Assessment Question 5.4 Why wouldn't the customer be invited to a design review?

Solution Because they are highly technical and solely involve the developer's solution.

Normally a design review would be attended by the designer of the system, or the member of the design team who produced the design; staff responsible for testing the system; a designer from another project; and the senior programmer responsible for implementing the system. The documents given to the members of the review team would be the requirements specification, the quality plan, and descriptions of external interfaces such as communication lines. Normally, design reviews only have enough time to deal with a small section of a design at a time.

A design review has a number of aims. The first is to check that the standards and procedures adopted by the project have not been violated. Normally this is detected by staff preparing for a review who notify the chair at the beginning of the review of any non-compliances that they have found.

The second aim is to ensure that any non-functional quality attribute specified for the system has been implemented. For example, the customer may have specified that he wants high maintainability in a system. A major task of the review meeting is then to look at the design and point out any areas of the system which are difficult to change.

The third aim of the design review is to ensure that the functional characteristics specified in the requirements specification have been met in the design. This is often done by the designer of the system talking through these functions and detailing which parts of the design are executed when a particular function is exercised.

The nature of a design review really depends on the amount of documentation that has been produced by the designer. For example, if the quality plan has insisted that the designer produces a verification matrix, then a consideration of whether the system actually meets its functional requirements can either be skipped, or the designer could talk through a small number of functions with the review team. If not, then a large amount of time spent in the review would involve examining each functional quality attribute with the designer explaining how the design implemented the quality attribute and the members of the review team pointing out problems or pronouncing themselves satisfied.

It is important to provide a checklist for staff carrying out the design review process. This enables them to be clear about what is being examined in a review.

A fragment from an example review checklist is shown below. It contains major questions about third-generation language designs which should be on the agenda of every design review. It must be stressed that only a selection from a real checklist is shown:

3.4 System Design Checklist

Does the system implement its functional requirements as detailed in the functional quality attributes section of the quality plan?

Does the system meet its non-functional requirements as detailed in the non-functional quality attributes section of the quality plan?

Is the interface with entities outside the system adequately defined? For example, are the specifications of modules which interact with hardware correct and do they provide the right level of detail for the implementation team?

Are the interfaces of modules correct?

Can a programmer take the functional description of a module and implement it in the chosen programming language?

Are objects described in the requirements specification documented in the data design?

Is the architecture of the system sufficiently modular? Does it, for example, contain modules with small interfaces which carry out only one function?

Is there a missing level of abstraction in the design? This is often indicated by a module calling more than six or seven modules.

Self Assessment Question 5.5 Which of the first two questions above would be the easiest to answer?

Solution Generally it is easier to check functional correctness: a designer can talk through what a system does quite easily. On the other side of the coin, some non-functional requirements are awfully difficult to check from a design, for example response time and memory occupancy; however, there tends to be fewer of these to check than functional requirements. The answer really depends on the system—I would adjudge a dead-heat normally.

5.6 THE STRUCTURE OF THE SYSTEM DESIGN SPECIFICATION

The document which is finally produced by the designer is the system design specification. Many of the components of this document have already been discussed in this chapter and are now summarized in this section. The headings of the specification should be:

1. Title
2. Contents
3. Introduction
4. About this document
5. Glossary
6. Module architecture

7. Data architecture
8. Interface to entities outside the system
9. Quality attributes and the system architecture.

The introduction should be brief, and describe the main inputs into the design process. For example, if security was the overriding concern in the requirements specification this should be stated here. Any unusual features of the document should also be described here; for example, the first use of a design notation which was insisted upon by the customer should be mentioned. An example of part of an introduction is shown below:

> The design described in this document details a system which controls the injection of drugs into a hospital patient who is normally in a critical condition. The system is a safety-critical one in which a design or programming error could cause the death of the patient. Consequently a large amount of resource is to be spent on the validation of the system; in particular the validation of the design against the requirements specification.
>
> Another feature of the system is that it needs to fit into a relatively small amount of memory and has well defined response rates which are critical: if a drug is not injected at specific times then the patient will suffer and could even die.
>
> A novel aspect of the system is that the pump used for the injection of drugs is new and this is the first time that we have produced a system for this type of device.

The section *About this document* should describe any naming conventions; the scope of the document; the main items in the document; the intended readership; any legal and contractual issues associated with the document; any relevant standards, both internal and external; how the system design is to be maintained and issued; and, finally, the distribution list for the system design.

The *Glossary* should contain a list of design terms and their definitions. An example is shown below:

> **Global data**. This is data which is accessible by all the modules in a system.

Module architecture describes the chunks of software into which the system has been partitioned, together with the interfaces between the chunks. *Data architecture* contains the specification of the data manipulated by the modules in the system. *Interface to entities outside the system* describes the way in which the system interfaces with the remainder of the system: hardware, other software, and users.

For users, this section will contain details of the screens and outputs produced by the system, for hardware it will describe the format of data passed to the hardware and a description of the modules which carry out interaction with the hardware—either modules provided by the hardware manufacturer, or modules which are to be written by the developer. For software, it will describe the format of records passed to any software outside the scope of the system and a specification of the modules which may interact with this software.

The final section, *Quality attributes and the system architecture*, should include documentation which demonstrates that the designer has, in fact, considered and implemented the quality attributes which have been identified during the early stages of the project. This documentation may include a verification matrix, but will also contain outline descriptions of why the designer feels the architecture meets the non-functional quality attributes.

5.7 QUALITY MANUAL REQUIREMENTS

1. Functional design standard
2. Data design standard
3. System design procedure
4. Design validation procedure
5. System design review procedure
6. System design review standard
7. System design review checklist.

Items 1 to 3 are usually subsumed under a single system design standards and procedures document. Also, items 5 to 7 are normally grouped together in a system design review standards and procedures document.

5.8 SUMMARY

The process of design involves members of a development team deriving a system architecture which consists of discrete chunks known as modules. There are two aspects to the quality processes concerned with system design. The first is that they should encourage specifications which reflect the requirements contained in the requirements specification: there should be good traceability back to functional and non-functional quality factors. The second is that the system design should be an adequate basis for tasks which are to be carried out later; for example, programmers who read the functional specification of a module should, ideally, be able to program that module without reference back to the system designer.

5.9 FURTHER READING

Pressman (1994) contains an excellent chapter on software design that describes a number of popular design methods. Parnas and Clements (1986) is an excellent article which points out that although system design documentation describes a linear process from the receipt of requirements analysis to the completion of system design, this is just faking it: the design process is quite non-linear and involves a large amount of backtracking and discarding of alternatives. This is an antidote to the views of a large number of QA practitioners of my acquaintance, who imagine that a project progresses linearly, and attempt to develop quality management systems which have this model of development at their heart. Yourdon and Constantine (1979) is quite an old book but still contains a lot of wisdom about the design process. Easteal and Davies (1989) is a good, short introduction to modern design ideas while Page-Jones (1988) is a much longer treatment which also includes material on requirements analysis.

PROBLEMS

5.1 How would you use a system design review to check that the interoperability quality factor was present in a design?

5.2 An error which is often made by system designers is to develop a design which implements functions that are not specified in the requirements specification. How would you check a design to ensure that this does not happen?

5.3 Write down ten items that you would include in a system design checklist for a system design which will eventually be implemented in a third-generation programming language such as COBOL or Pascal.

5.4 Develop a standard for a system design notation for your favourite programming language.

5.5 Write a brief case which proposes that your company's design documentation should be augmented by the use of a verification matrix.

DETAILED DESIGN AND PROGRAMMING

AIMS

- To describe the nature of a detailed design notation.
- To describe the nature of a programming standard.

6.1 INTRODUCTION

At this stage in the software development process the development team will have produced a system design and a requirements specification. The remaining developmental tasks involve converting the system design into program code. This can be carried out in either one or two stages. If two stages are involved they are normally called *detailed design* and *programming*. The former involves specifying the detailed flow of control in a system in a form which can be easily translated into program code, while the latter simply involves the conversion of the individual module specifications. A two-stage process is usually implemented by developers who have adopted portability as an important quality attribute for *all* their projects—including across a range of programming languages.

> **Self Assessment Question 6.1** How does a detailed design notation help portability?
>
> **Solution** Modules expressed in a detailed design notation should, provided the notation is good, be translated easily into a wide variety of programming languages.

Detailed design is also used by developers who employ programming languages which are not very readable, or which do not provide adequate structuring facilities. Probably the best example of a family of languages which come into this category are the assembler languages.

It is important to point out that this chapter concentrates on third-generation technology. The quality assurance aspects of fourth-generation technology are dealt with in Chapter 9.

6.2 DETAILED DESIGN

A good detailed design standard should be able to be easily translated into program code, and also be able to express a wide variety of control structures such as *while, for, repeat, if,* and *case* constructs. An example of a fragment taken from a detailed design language which the author has used is shown below:

```
Clear RangeFlag
Add CurrentCount to MonthCount
Repeat
    Call MonitorRead(Reading)
    Check whether Reading is between 10 and 100
    If the Reading is between these limits then
        Add the Reading to CurrentCount
        Set RangeFlag
    EndIf
    Call CheckStatus(StatusFlag)
    Case StatusFlag of
        violation: Call ViolationHandler
        normal: Continue
        OutOfRange: Call RangeHandler
    EndCase
Until Call MonitorHang(CurrentMonitor)
```

Here the keywords which introduce the constructs are in bold. The individual detailed design fragments of each module in a system can easily be inserted as comments into the source code of a system. However, it is worth issuing a word of warning about this practice. For high-level languages it can actually make the program text less readable. For example, consider the source code which implements the first few detailed design statements above, with the statements inserted as comments:

```
(* Clear RangeFlag *)
RangeFlag:= 0;
(*Add CurrentCount to MonthCount *)
MonthCount := MonthCount + CurrentCount;
```

This level of commenting is far too high, and actually detracts from readability in that it can hide the structure of a module. Most developers who employ a detailed design notation express their designs at a higher level where a single line of detailed design may be equivalent to four or five lines of program code and where in-code commenting is not too intrusive; or, if they use a detailed design notation of the level shown above, then they keep the documentation containing the notation separate from the program code.

The one example where annotation of the source code is useful is if the code is expressed in an assembler language. Most assembler languages allow the programmer to write comments side by side with the program code as shown below:

```
CLS rflg    ; Clear RangeFlag
LD cc
ADD mc
ST cc       ; Add MonthCount to CurrentCount
```

The many programming limitations of assembler languages can be greatly mitigated by copying a detailed design into a file, adding the symbols which mark a comment, and then programming the assembler code into the file.

Normally, the notation used for data design that is employed during system design is carried through to detailed design. The procedure for detailed design should describe the process of receipt of a system design; the actions that should be carried out when the designer detects a problem with the detailed design; and the process of checking the detailed design against the system design. There are three ways in which this checking can be carried out: in a full review similar to a system design review; as a structured walkthrough in which the producer of the detailed design takes a meeting of peers through the detailed design, executing it as if he or she were the computer; or as a simple meeting between the detailed designer and the member of staff designated to sign off the design as being correct. The third course is usually adopted. The quality manual should contain procedures for all three methods.

Self Assessment Question 6.2 Why do you think that most developers do not use full technical reviews to validate program code, but usually stick to the signing off of modules by a single member of staff?

Solution The reason is that if you review every item of code in a technical review an immense amount of resource would be used up. Programming errors are less serious than requirements or design errors, so a company that uses technical reviews will concentrate their effort on reviews of the requirements specification or the system design.

6.3 PROGRAMMING

The testing aspects of unit programming are dealt with in Chapter 7. Also, Chapter 13 describes the process of writing a programming standard within the context of the practice of standards and procedure development. However, for the sake of completeness it is worth describing the main components of a programming standard:

- *Bureaucratic comments.* There is a need for each module in a system to be annotated with comments which include the name of the programmer; his or her telephone extension; the date that the module was completed; the version number if the module has undergone a series of changes since it was first programmed; and the function of the module. Normally, the function will be expressed in terms of how the parameters of the module or any accessed global variables are used to change other parameters, global variables or files. It is also a good idea to write the names of the modules which call the module as comments. A good standard should also instruct programmers to comment code which is difficult to understand, for example program code which uses an arcane feature of the programming language to achieve a speed-up.

- *Unsafe programming constructs.* This mainly concerns the *goto* statement; however, some programming languages also have escape facilities which are, in effect, disguised *gotos*. The standard should direct the programmer to avoid these constructs, or only to use them within very specific contexts such as when a module of a safety-critical system discovers an emergency condition. An example of such a condition is when a chemical monitoring system discovers the fact that a reactor has all its inlet valves open and its outlet valves shut, with reactants being poured into a potentially explosive reactor. In this case, the programmer does not want to carry out a graceful exit from the module. What is required is a fast *goto* to some program code which handles the emergency condition. However, it is worth stressing that such examples are rare, and the norm should be to avoid constructs which make the program code unreadable.

- *Layout conventions.* A good programming standard should describe how a module should be physically displayed on the page. This not only describes the use of indentation of control constructs, but also the display of all non-loop initializations at the head of a module; the initialization of loop variables just before the loop starts; any naming conventions for identifiers and the names of modules; the declaration of constants; and the incorporation of fragments of detailed design as comments into the program code.

- *Defensive programming conventions.* A programming standard should describe the mandatory elements of a defensive programming strategy; for example, it should describe the layout conventions for code which detects error conditions, and allowable associated actions such as transferring to an error printing routine. It should also describe what defensive code is not allowed. For example, for many real-time systems, the inclusion of defensive programming code during development, which is then removed during operation, can lead to subtle timing changes which may force errors during operation.

- *Limits on conditions.* An important source of error during maintenance occurs when staff have to read and understand complex boolean conditions which contain a large number of boolean *and* and *or* operators.

- *Limits on the functionality of a module.* As has been mentioned in Chapter 5: one of the important features of a well designed system is that the modules in the system normally carry out only one function. If a programmer is given responsibility for producing a chunk of code which contains a number of modules, then part of the programming standard should insist that each module has functional cohesion. This feature was rather unsubtly enforced in the early programming standards by the insistence that a module had a maximum line length—usually no more than the line length of one sheet of line printer listing paper.

- *Limits on global variables.* This is another important feature of a programming standard. Programmers should limit the amount of access they make to global variables. A system which contains modules that have a number of both read and write references to global variables is exceptionally difficult to maintain. Often, during maintenance, a requirements change gives rise to a change to a global variable; for example, if the variable was a record, then the change might give rise to some extra fields in the record. This means that the change will usually impinge on the modules which refer to the global variables that have been modified. If there are a lot of references, then this can give rise to substantial browsing and modification.
- *Indentation limits.* Modules which have a large number of control structures nested within each other are terribly difficult to understand and debug. Many programming standards insist on an upper limit to the depth. This usually means that the programmer has either to recode a module to eliminate the extra nesting, or replace the offending control structures that make a call to a module. Both solutions lead to more readable code.

Self Assessment Question 6.3 Why do you think that a well designed system should contain modules which carry out one function?

Solution If you have multi-functional modules, then you will find that a change to one of the functions in the module will normally affect the other functions in the module, thus necessitating further reprogramming. Hence, multi-functional modules tend to consume more effort during activities such as maintenance.

These, then, are a selection of the major components of a programming standard. They are usually intended to make software more readable and also more maintainable. One other topic remains: that of ensuring that a module or chunk of code is correct—that it meets its design specification.

There are two options available to the software developer. The first is unit testing (this is described in Chapter 7). The second is to have a full technical review to which the following members of staff are invited; the programmer; another programmer on the same project; a programmer from another project; and the designer of the module or system. The general form of a technical review which examines program code is that the participants are asked to point out any poor programming practices or any violations of programming standards. The programmer then describes the design specification that he or she was given, and then walks through the program showing how it would be executed by the computer. The programmer will describe how other modules were called, what results were expected from these calls, how global variables were updated, how data was obtained from the environment in which the module was embedded, and give a description of the detailed calculations that were performed. As this description proceeds, the review participants will detect errors in the program meeting its design specification. As with any technical review, any problems which occurred would be documented, and a decision about the outcome of the review—whether it was completely satisfactory, largely satisfactory (with some minor problems), or unsatisfactory—made by the chairman.

An important point to be made about this form of review is that if all the program code in a system were reviewed in such a way, then the developer would be committing a large amount of resources to validation at a late stage in the project. Reviews are more productive at the front-end of a project where major errors are often discovered, and it is often a good idea to commit most of your validation resources to the validation of the requirements specification or system design. There are a number of ways to reduce expenditure on code reviews. The first is to review only modules which are potentially error-prone. The criteria used for this will depend on the company. Companies that I have dealt with have reviewed large modules, modules with complicated control structures, and modules which are produced either by new staff or by staff who have a history of developing error-prone modules.

An alternative to a selective review is to have informal walkthroughs on all the program code that only involves two or three programmers. In such a walkthrough, a module is executed and problems notified to the programmer who then rectifies them. It is assumed that after these reviews the programmer carries out any necessary rework.

6.4 QUALITY MANUAL REQUIREMENTS

1. Detailed design standard
2. Detailed design procedure
3. Detailed design review procedure
4. Detailed design review standard
5. Programming standard
6. Programming procedure
7. Code review standard
8. Code review procedure.

If the developer uses a number of programming languages, then there will be a programming standard for each language. If the developer uses walkthroughs or informal meetings, then there will be standards and procedures for these. Items 1 and 2, 3 and 4, 5 and 6, and 7 and 8 are normally combined into four separate documents.

6.5 SUMMARY

The main components of a quality system which deal with detailed design and programming are standards for the layout of the detailed design notation used by the developer and of any programming languages used. It is also important that procedures are specified which deal with the process of producing detailed designs and coded modules, and the process of querying poor module specifications which have been produced by designers.

PROBLEMS

6.1 Write down the part of a programming standard for your favourite third-generation programming language which deals with the bureaucratic information required at the front of a module.

6.2 Write down the headings and subheadings for a programming standard for your favourite third-generation programming language.

6.3 If your company decided to have detailed design reviews what do you think would happen in these meetings?

7

TESTING

AIMS

- To describe the nature of software testing.
- To outline the relationship between software testing and quality assurance.
- To describe the quality documentation required to support the testing process.
- To describe the main testing activities.

7.1 INTRODUCTION

Without a doubt testing is one of the most widely used quality controls. Indeed, many quality assurance practitioners point out that, in the past, an over-emphasis on system and acceptance testing as a quality control led to serious errors such as requirements errors being detected at too late a stage in the software project, after a large amount of resources for the project had been committed.

There are a number of testing activities which are employed on a project. These were described in detail in Chapter 2; however, it is worth outlining them here before examining the relationship between testing and quality assurance.

First, a definition: testing is the application of a quality control which involves the execution of a system or part of a system. There are a number of testing activities: these can be categorized as either *white box* or *black box*. A white box activity is one which relies on a knowledge of the structure of the program code that is being tested. A black box activity is one which does not require this knowledge.

Self Assessment Question 7.1 Do you think that unit testing, sometimes known as module testing, should be a black box activity, a white box activity or both?

Solution It should be both. The tester will check out the functions of a module with test data (black box) and then check that these tests have achieved some structural metric such as 100 per cent of statements have been executed. If the metric has not been reached, then further data is created which exercises the parts of the module which have not been executed (white box).

There are five main testing activities: unit testing, package testing, integration testing, system testing, and acceptance testing. *Unit testing* is the testing of a module in isolation. For a fourth-generation language a module will be a program, and for a third-generation language a module will be a subroutine. A programmer tests a module against a specification which can be found in the system design. Normally, test data is chosen which thoroughly explores the function of the module and, as a final check, the programmer confirms that the tests have achieved an adequate coverage of some structural metric. The structural metric that is almost invariably chosen is the statement, with many software developers insisting that unit tests cover 100 per cent of all the statements in a module.

Package testing is a technique used in systems which are structured into units known as *packages*. A package is a collection of modules together with a data area. For example, a package which implements a queue would contain a data structure that implemented the queue—perhaps an array—together with modules which access this queue; for example, modules which add an item to a queue, remove an item from a queue, count the number of items in a queue, and initialize a queue.

Once a package has been put together it can then be used by programmers who are implementing the functionality of a system. They use the package by calling the modules associated with the package; they do not access the data structure of the package directly, because this leads to a poorly maintained system: a system which contains references to the data structure throughout its code is a maintenance nightmare. When a change to that data structure occurred a programmer would then have to examine large segments of code and modify the references. However, a package-based organization means that all changes to the underlying data are localized to the package itself, saving a large amount of effort.

Packages are a facility of a number of modern programming languages such as Ada and Modula 2, where, if a programmer did try to directly reference the data in a package, a compiler error would result. Developers with less modern languages such as C can ensure that their programmers follow a package discipline by instructing them not to directly access data structures by means of a programming standard such as the one described in Chapter 6.

Package testing is a form of testing which ensures that the modules in a package work correctly in conjunction with each other. For example, testing the queue package described above would involve a number of tests, one of which would check that when a queue had an item added and then removed the queue remained the same. Package testing is a black box activity, as no knowledge of program code is required. An extract from a procedure which describes package testing is shown below:

2.3 Package testing

We normally develop systems as collections of packages. These contain data definitions and the code for the modules which access these data definitions. We currently use Ada for many projects and this language offers a facility whereby packages can be defined and syntactically checked. All our Ada projects make extensive use of this facility and a form of testing known as package testing is always to be applied.

This form of testing involves the programmer compiling the package and writing test cases which check that the package modules work in conjunction with each other; top-level (scaffold) software will be required to be written in order to invoke the modules. For example, a module which enters a name into a table would be executed and then a module which checks that that name has been correctly entered would then be executed after this. Guidelines for the selection of package tests and details of possible combinations of modules can be found in section 2.3.4.

The tests that have to be carried out have to be documented on the form shown in section 2.3.1. For each test the programmer has to describe what the test is intended to achieve and the results expected. The test data, the test outcome and the source code for the test should all be stored in files described in the naming convention section of this manual (section 1.4).

Integration testing is the process of testing a system as it is being integrated: when modules are added to it a few at a time. Normally, an integration test occurs when a number of modules have been added; the main aim of the integration test is to check that the interface between the system that has been built up, and the modules that have been integrated, is correct. However, integration testing is also an opportunity for early functional testing: a developer may have discovered that after a particular integration, enough modules now reside in the partial system that has been built up to implement one of the system functions. Therefore, a subsidiary testing task often carried out after an integration is to execute a preliminary test of some system functions.

System testing is the process of checking that the system constructed matches user requirements. For this, the functional quality attributes and non-functional attributes which are of concern to the customer are tested by executing the system. Normally this execution is of the whole system, but not necessarily in its target environment. For example, if the system was to process data from a nuclear reactor, or from a large number of transaction clerks, the input data from these sources would be simulated, either by hardware or software. System testing is a black box activity.

Acceptance testing is the demonstration to the customer that the customer-related quality attributes have been properly implemented. To do this, a subset of the system tests is agreed on by the developer and the customer, and is then executed on the system within its target environment, with the customer witnessing and signing off the tests. Acceptance testing, like system testing, is a black box activity.

7.2 TESTING AND QUALITY ASSURANCE

There is a commonly held belief that quality assurance and testing are synonymous. I remember asking a student who had recently completed a degree course in software engineering whether he had been taught anything about software quality assurance. He said that, yes, he had attended a lecture on the topic, and that the lecturer had devoted the hour to giving them hints and tips on the selection of program test data.

Testing is a large component of quality assurance, but to place it in context it is worth restating the nature of quality assurance: that it is the definition of quality attributes which are either customer-related or developer-related, and the definition of quality controls which provide explicit evidence that those attributes are present, either in the whole system that has been developed, a part of the system, or in the documentation that has been produced for it.

Testing is a quality control which addresses many of the quality attributes that are functional in nature, together with some which are non-functional. Unit testing checks that a module carries out the function that is specified for it in the system design, for example functional correctness of the module: a developer-related attribute. Package testing verifies that the functions of the modules in a package are correct by checking their execution in conjunction with each other: again, a developer-related attribute. Integration testing checks that interfaces are correct and that functions implemented in the partial system that has been constructed are correctly implemented. The former is a developer-related quality attribute; the latter a customer-related attribute. System and acceptance testing checks that the functions and constraints in a system have been correctly implemented: these are also customer-specific quality attributes.

It is worth pointing out that not all testing involves functional attributes. Some examples of testing which involve non-functional attributes are:

- Executing a module to check on its execution speed in order to ensure that the final response time of a system is acceptable.
- Executing commands in a system to provide confirmation that the quality attribute of response time has been met.
- Keeping data on failures that occurred during system testing in order to predict the reliability of a system.
- Running a whole series of tests with the real users of a system and, at the same time, keeping data on the number of errors that they made in invoking system functions. This would be carried out in order to check that a quality attribute related to usability was present.

This is just a small selection of non-functional quality attributes which can be validated as a result of testing. However, it is certainly true that the vast majority of testing activities on a software project are aimed at implementing controls on quality attributes which are functional—both customer-related and developer-related.

7.3 UNIT TESTING

Unit testing is mainly oriented towards the checking of the function of a module, although a quality plan will call for response time testing of modules for systems which are time-critical. The standards and procedures for testing will govern how test data is to be selected, how tests are to be documented, and how to resolve any problems should the input to the testing process—the module specification—be poorly expressed.

The main medium for holding testing information is the *unit folder* or *programmer's notebook*. The main testing details that should be included in this document are:

- The rationale for the test data that was chosen.
- The location of the test data for the module.
- The location of the test outcomes that were generated for the module.
- Documentation of the test coverage.
- Bureaucratic information such as the name of the programmer and the date of the tests.

An example of part of a procedure for unit testing is shown below:

7.5 Subroutine testing

COBOL subroutines are always tested singly. We call this testing *subroutine testing*; it is performed by the programmer who developed the subroutine. It involves the programmer enclosing the subroutine with program code which: calls it, transfers test data to the subroutine and displays any test results. In this quality manual this extra code is known as *scaffold software*. The tests that are carried out are known as *functional tests*. They check that the subroutine is functionally correct. The only documentation which is used to develop these tests is the subroutine specification produced by the member of staff who acts as the design authority. This documentation will be given to the programmer before the detailed coding of the subroutine is carried out and is incorporated as a comment in the header of the subroutine.

Detailed guidelines for the generation of test data can be found in section 8.8 of this quality manual. Examples of test data can be found in appendix C of the same manual.

When the programmer has felt that he or she has fully functionally tested the subroutine an item of documentation known as the unit folder is completed. This contains information such as descriptions of test carried out. Full details of the information that has to be entered into this document can be found in section 7.7 of this quality manual. When this documentation has been completed the unit folder is submitted to a designated member of staff for checking. This will normally be the senior programmer who has been attached to the project. However, for small projects this could be the team leader. If this member of staff signs off the unit folder it is submitted to the project library and comes under configuration control. Full details of this process can be found in section 11.8 of this quality manual.

The rationale for test data selection is a description of why certain items of data were chosen to test the unit. This should not be too long: usually between 100 and 200 words describing the strategy adopted. There are a number of strategies which can be used.

The first is very simple: all it involves is writing down a tabular representation of the individual data items that are processed by a module and deriving tests based on combinations of these data items. As a simple example, consider the testing of a table module. Assume that the table associates an integer key that lies between 1000 and 2000 with an employee record. The aim of the module is to check that a particular employee with a particular key is in the table. If a key that lies outside the range is given, then an error is displayed. Table 7.1 shows the different outcomes. Here the various conditions that affect the module are displayed and all the possible combinations of conditions are combined. For example, the third row states that when a valid key is provided, and the key is not in the table, then it will not be found. The first and second rows of the table contain a blank; this is a 'don't care' condition, for which it is irrelevant whether the key is in the table; indeed we can be certain that it is not, since the key for these two rows

Table 7.1 A tabular representation of data values

Key value	Key in table	Result
< 1000		error message
> 2000		error message
valid key	no	not found
valid key	yes	found

Table 7.2 Test data for a sort problem

n	Result
1	sorted
$maxint/2$	sorted
$maxint$	sorted

will be out of the range of the table. Table 7.2 gives another example. It represents the tests for a module which has two arguments: *arr*, an array of integers which contains up to a maximum of *maxint* items, and an integer n. The module sorts the first n items in the array. The first column of Table 7.2 details the values of n and the second column details the outcome which occurs. Such tables are useful for exploring combinations of data values and are normally used to develop an initial data set. There are, however, two further methods for deriving data that tend to be more revealing when it comes to discovering errors.

The first is known as *error guessing*. Here, the tester derives test data which supposedly contains an error. In the sorting example above, error guessing data for n would be a negative integer, zero, and an integer greater than *maxint*.

Self Assessment Question 7.2 A module processes an integer representing the number of a record in a file and then prints out all the records from that point. If the tester selects an integer greater than the number of integers in the file would this be an example of error guessing?

Solution Yes it would: the data represents an error.

The second is based on a technique known as *equivalence partitioning*. In order to understand this technique, consider Fig. 7.1. This shows the data space for a particular module, which represents all the possible data values that can be processed by a module or a program. The data space is partitioned into three subspaces. Each subspace represents data which is processed in the same way, e.g. one of the subspaces may represent the processing of a particular type of error data. Test data generation, based on equivalence partitioning, involves the tester generating data which either lies on, or is close to, the boundary of the subspaces. Test data generated in this way is capable of detecting common programming errors, such as a loop that executes one too many times, or one too few times, or a condition in which a < operator has been written rather than a ≤ operator. As you will recognize, these are all common errors committed by programmers.

Table 7.3 The initial test set

arr	n	num	result
num in table	$n = maxint$		found
num not in table	$n = maxint$		not found
num in table	$n = maxint/2$		found
num not in table	$n < maxint$		not found
num in table	$n = 1$		found
num not in table	$n = 1$		not found

As an example of the three techniques in action, consider the testing of a module that has three parameters: the first, *arr*, is an array of integers which contains no more than *maxint* integers; the second, *n*, is an integer; and the third, *num*, is another integer. The module searches for *num* in the first *n* locations of *arr*. If it is contained there, then a 1 is returned, otherwise a 0 is returned. The initial test set might look like that in Table 7.3. This is quite a good test set as it explores the behaviour of the table over its full size. Notice that the value of *num* has been marked as 'don't care'. A number of further tests can be generated from error guessing. The table can now be supplemented with the data which represents an empty array and an over-large array, as shown in Table 7.4. The table can be further added to by data generated from equivalence partitioning. A number of tests can be generated: the first would involve the data being positioned at location $n+1$, just off the boundary of the array; the next would involve it being positioned at location *n*, just on the boundary; and the final test would involve it being positioned at location $n - 1$, just within the array.

Table 7.5 shows the final result of this deletion of data. Such a table, supplemented with an explanation of the reasons for each row, could be used for the first part of the unit test documentation.

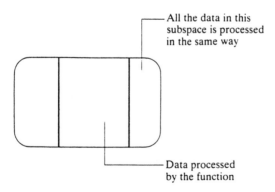

Figure 7.1 A data space and subspaces.

Table 7.4 The initial test set supplemented by error data

arr	n	num	result
num in table	$n = maxint$		found
num not in table	$n = maxint$		not found
num in table	$n = maxint/2$		found
num not in table	$n < maxint$		not found
num in table	$n = 1$		found
num not in table	$n = 1$		not found
	$n = 0$		error
	$n > maxint$		error

Table 7.5 The initial test set supplemented with boundary data

arr	n	num	result
num in table	$n = maxint$		found
num not in table	$n = maxint$		not found
num in table	$n = maxint/2$		found
num not in table	$n < maxint$		not found
num in table	$n = 1$		found
num not in table	$n = 1$		not found
	$n = 0$		error
	$n > maxint$		error
num at position $n + 1$	$n < maxint$		not found
num at position n	$n \leq maxint$		found
num at position $n - 1$	$n \leq maxint$		found

7.4 INTEGRATION TESTING

There are a number of distinct forms of integration strategy. Top-down integration, as the name suggests, builds up a system from the top-level modules downwards. Bottom-up integration starts with the lowest level modules and works upwards. Middle-out integration starts in the middle of the design of a system, and either integrates upwards or downwards. Normally, systems developed as packages are integrated in this way: packages are integrated top-down, and the system is then integrated from the interfaces to the packages upwards.

There are a number of reasons why software projects carry out integration testing:

- When a module is integrated and tested and an error is discovered the process of detecting the error is efficient as, normally, the error is in the module that has been integrated. The tester need look no further. This is in contrast to system testing whereby if an error is discovered, it could be contained in one of many thousands of modules.
- Top-down integration in particular allows the customer to get an early view of a system. Normally the top-level modules in a system are those dealing with the human–computer interface. Since these are integrated first, the customer or the user can get a good view of the functionality of the software at a relatively early point in the project and is able to point out potential problems to the developer.
- During integration some of the system tests which are to be carried out can be executed. There is a maxim for software development that the earlier a test can be

carried out the better because rectification is cheaper the earlier it occurs in the software project.

Self Assessment Question 7.3 Can you think how integration testing can be used to give early warning of serious response time problems with a system?

Solution During integration the staff carrying out integration testing would measure the response time as part of the testing process. If it looks like the response time is going to be exceeded well before the integration phase is complete, then this is an indication that serious problems have occurred.

A quality system should offer a number of facilities to staff who wish to carry out integration testing: it should provide guidance to staff on the best strategy to adopt, and also give advice on how the process should be planned on an integration-by-integration basis. An example of this, in the form of an extract from an integration procedure, is found below:

5.4 Integration procedure

5.4.1 Integration

Unless there is a very good reason for not doing it, all our projects should integrate subroutines which have been produced by programmers. If a project manager decides not to integrate he or she should contact his or her technical manager and give good reason before deciding on this course of action.

Integration is planned after the overall system design has been frozen and comes under configuration control. There are a number of decisions that a project manager or designer has to make regarding integration:

1. What form of integration to adopt. There are essentially three strategies which we use. The pros and cons of each strategy are detailed below in sections 5.4.2 to 5.4.4.

2. The order in which integration is to occur. Given that a project manager has chosen the strategy there is still considerable leeway as to the order in which subroutines are inserted.

3. The number of subroutines which are to be added at a time.

A number of inputs have to be considered before addressing the last two points. First, it is necessary to determine the information needed which drives a consideration of the number of modules to be integrated at a time. Normally, an integration strategy should not involve the integration of more than 10 modules at a time. Integration over that limit often means that errors in some of the subroutines which are integrated may interact with each other to produce subtle effects that reduce the effectiveness of debugging.

There are two ways of carrying out integration. The first is by assuming that each integration will always involve n modules. The value of n will be determined by the overall complexity of the subroutines in the system. For a system with a large number of modules with complex processing code and big interfaces n will be low. For a system consisting, in the main, of single function subroutines n will tend towards a high level.

The second option which can be adopted is to specify that the normal number of modules which will be integrated will usually be n, but that very complex modules, identified by the designer, will be integrated singly or with a small number of other modules. This strategy is suitable for a system with a large number of not very complex subroutines, but with a few large ones.

The second point—the order in which the subroutines are integrated—may be constrained by programmer availability: for example, you may know that some subroutines will be produced by a programmer who is joining the project late. However, if planning is carried out well there should be quite a degree of leeway for the order of integration.

In considering the order of integration the designer or project manager should bear in mind two criteria: the criticality of the functions that are contained in the system and also the importance of the functions. For example, we normally integrate our systems in a top-down fashion. Also, the systems we produce tend to have the human–computer interface embedded in the top-level modules. If there is a feeling that the customer has not quite correctly communicated some of the functions, then the top-level modules which implement the interface for these functions should be integrated first.

The second criterion is that of importance of functions. As part of the project planning procedure the project manager will have carried out a risk analysis of the project (see Project Procedures, section 13.3). If the project is a high-risk one, then a good strategy to adopt is to integrate the system in such a way that the important functions of the system are integrated first, followed by the next most important functions, and so on. In this way, if the project starts to look as if it is heading for trouble in terms of lateness the project manager can ask the customer whether he or she wishes to take delivery of the software that has so far been integrated, after some acceptance testing has, of course, taken place.

As part of the analysis (see Analysis Procedures, section 11.1), analysts for a high-risk project will have ordered the system functions in decreasing order of importance; these details can be found in section 7.3 of the requirements specification.

5.4.2 Top-down integration

There are a large number of reasons for adopting top-down integration.

1. The system does not require any extra software to hold it together. The system is, in effect, its own test-bed. In the past, with bottom-up integration, we have found that we have had to produce scaffold software which has been as large as 40 per cent of the final system size.

2. It enables us to demonstrate the human–computer interface to the customer at a relatively early stage of the project. The vast majority of our systems have this interface embedded in top-level modules.

3. You have a working version of the system from the moment that the first integration has been correctly tested.

4. It provides an extra fillip to a project. If a project is particularly long you will find staff morale dropping somewhere during the middle of the project because of the perceived lack of progress in terms of executable code. The news that the first version of the system—albeit the first few modules which form the initial integration—is working, has a surprising effect on staff morale.

5. It is able to detect top-level control and sequencing errors better than the other forms of integration that our quality manual describes.

$\vdots$

In the extract above, the term *scaffold software* is used. This is software which holds a system together while it is being integrated.

As well as providing advice on how to plan integration, a quality assurance system should also specify detailed standards which describe the form of documentation that is to be produced during integration testing. The main document that should be produced is the *integration plan*. The structure of this document is simple; it usually consists of an introduction which describes the integration strategy that was adopted and includes a rationale for the strategy. The remainder of the document contains a page devoted to each integration. Each integration should be given a unique identifier, which is usually the name of a system or subsystem, followed by the number of the integration. It should describe the modules which make up the system to which further modules are to be added, and the names of the modules to be added. There should also be a description in each case of the tests that are to be carried out—both tests on the interfaces between the integrated modules and the partial system into which they are to be inserted, and also early functional tests which act as a preliminary check on user functions.

An example of such documentation is shown below:

Integration: TransSys23
System to be integrated into: MIS, TransUp, TransDown, TransValid:: NewUp, LongID; Tax-Upd, RecArchive
Modules to be added: TaxDed, OldVals, NewVals
Interface tests:

1. This should check that when an update record is written to the receivables database, the database is correctly updated.

2. This should check that when the tax deduction command has been initiated, the staff member who is to have his or her tax record amended has his or her financial record correctly retrieved.

3. This should check that when information on a new member of staff is inserted into the employment database the correct record details are entered into the database.

4. This should check that when the new values table and the old values table are merged then the resulting table contains the correctly merged data.

Functional tests: 12.3, 12.4, 12.5

There are a number of things to notice about this example document. First, the system into which modules are to be integrated is specified in terms of subsystems. If a subsystem is only partially present, the modules are then listed, preceded by a double colon which follows a module name and terminated by a semi-colon. Second, the most important point to notice is that the tests are not specified in very much detail. This assumes that the staff who are going to carry out the tests are familiar with the system and its interface. If not, then a lot more detail needs to be included: the sort of detail that you will find in the documentation for system and acceptance testing, described in the next section. The final point to make is that the functional tests are uniquely identified by their number in the requirements specification.

7.5 SYSTEM AND ACCEPTANCE TESTING

The process of deriving system and acceptance tests is driven by the quality attributes which are specified in the quality plan as verification requirements. There will be a wide variety of controls which are used to ensure that these quality attributes are implemented correctly; however, the main control will arise from system testing and acceptance. You will remember that acceptance testing is the process of demonstrating to the customer that the software system developed contains quality attributes which are relevant to the customer. System testing is a preliminary set of tests which ensure that the acceptance testing phase will be relatively trouble-free. System and acceptance tests will usually demonstrate that certain functions have been implemented; however, there will also be a number of non-functional tests which have to be carried out, for example tests which check on response time. There are a number of documents which are used to describe and document the system and acceptance test process. They are:

- The test design specification
- The test case specification
- The test procedure
- The test log
- The test problem report form
- The test summary.

The test design specification describes the design of a test which confirms that a particular quality attribute is present. The test case specification describes each of the individual tests which make up the test design. Test procedures are detailed step-by-step instructions on how a particular test is to be carried out. The test log is a description of what happened during a particular set of tests described by a test design specification. The test problem report form describes what happened when a test failed.

7.5.1 Test design specification

This document is one which describes how a feature or related group of features is to be tested. It does not specify any test cases, but describes in general terms the test philosophy that is to be adopted. The following are normally found in a test design specification.

A unique identifier. This identifies the document and should contain some reference to the quality attribute to be tested. For example, if the attribute was a function, then the number should include a reference to the function in the quality plan.

Test item. This describes what is being tested. Normally, test design specifications are only written for system and acceptance tests, although some companies who develop large systems which require a complex integration phase develop these documents for integration tests. Therefore, this section would state that the test was either a functional system test, functional acceptance test, constraint system test, constraint acceptance test or integration test. If it is an integration test, this section may also specify the version of the system which is being tested.

Test description. This will give an outline description of the test and the test methods that are to be used. For example, if boundary analysis is to be applied it will specify the range of data values which will be used and, hence, describe the boundaries. A typical description is shown below:

> This test will check that when the out-of-stock command is invoked, then a correct result will be displayed on the VDU which originates the command. A correct result will be a message which says whether a particular product typed in is out of stock. The tester will execute the command by providing correct and incorrect product identifiers. These identifiers will be ten-character strings, and the tester will test correct product identifiers ranging from the alphabetically earliest to the alphabetically latest, including the end-point identifiers. The tester will also choose incorrect identifiers ranging from single-letter identifiers to ten-letter identifiers. Each test will use the same test database.

Tests applied. These are the test identifiers of the individual tests which are applied. These tests are described by unique identifiers, as described in the next section.

Pass/fail criteria. This is a description of how a series of tests would be judged to have passed or failed. For the test description above, it would tell the tester that the test would have passed if the tester had chosen a product which has no stock associated with it in the test database.

7.5.2 Test case specification

This document describes the individual tests which make up a test design. Each test case will be uniquely numbered, and will contain a number of different items of data.

Test input. This lists the data which is applied for the test. If the data is stored in a file, then all that would be required would be to name the file that stores the data.

Test output. This should describe the output expected from the test.

Software and hardware requirements. This describes the hardware and software required for the test and includes not only any testing tools and scaffold software but also the version of the operating system that is to be used, and version numbers of any other supporting software.

Special instructions. If the test requires any special actions from the tester, for example, to disconnect the computer from some peripherals, then this section would list these actions.

Inter-case dependencies. If any other tests are required to precede a test then these are described here; for example, one test may check that the process of writing an item to a database has been correctly implemented and another might check that the item added is still in the database. If a test depends on a previous test and that previous test fails, then this part of the document will describe what the tester should do.

An example of this documentation is shown below for a system which carries out image processing:

Test 3.36

Test input. This system test checks that a picture is displayed at the right resolution. A test database containing a large sample of pictures can be found in file TestPic.sys.

Test output. Each test which involves comparing a picture with a defined resolution will be passed if the characters 'yes' are displayed in the top left hand corner of the screen. Anything else will be regarded as a test failure.

Hardware and software. No special software is required. The system can be found in the project library as Sys.obj. There will be a number of versions of this so, before extracting the system from the project library, check with the library administrator what the current project version is. The hardware used will be the standard 486 configuration asked for by the customer with a Tixuy 33 screen.

Special instructions None.

Inter-case dependencies. None.

Self Assessment Question 7.4 What is the difference between the test design specification and the test case specification?

Solution The former is a high-level design document which describes how a set of features are to be tested. The latter contains much more detailed descriptions of tests; for example, it will contain the software and hardware requirements for a test.

7.5.3 Test procedure

This document describes the step-by-step process whereby a test is executed and also how a series of similar test cases are to be carried out. It will list all the steps needed to set up and start a test, make any measurements such as response time, shut down a test, restart a test after a failure and stop a test. The test procedure will also contain details about where the item to be tested can be found; what sort of item it is—a module, a system or a partially integrated version of a system; and what sort of test is to be carried out.

Normally, test procedures are written in considerable detail when the staff who are to carry out a test are not familiar with the software being tested, for example an independent test group. When the developers are the staff who carry out testing, the quality system should provide guidance on how the requirements for test procedure documentation can be relaxed.

7.5.4 Test log

This is a description of what happens when a particular test is carried out. It should describe what is being tested; what test procedure is being used; what happened during the test; what hardware or software was used; a description of any events which were not expected; and if the test failed there should be references to the problem reports that were generated when a test did not behave as expected.

7.5.5 Test problem report form

A test problem report form is generated when a test procedure gives rise to an event which was not expected by the tester. This document will contain information about the event; what hardware and software environment was used; whether any attempt to repeat the test took place; when the error was detected; and who carried out the test.

7.5.6 Test summary

This is a summary of a series of tests. It is usually issued after a subsystem, or even a whole system, has been tested. It should describe what has been tested; evaluate the success of the series of tests described; give details of any outstanding errors that were discovered by testing; and provide summary information such as the length of time taken for testing.

Self Assessment Question 7.5 During development how do you think test problem report forms are processed by a software project?

Solution They are normally given to a member of staff who determines whether the form describes a real error or whether the tester has misinterpreted the test documentation. If the report form describes a real error, then the source of the error is determined and the system is modified. For example, if the error was a design error, then the system design, detailed design and code are changed.

7.6 QUALITY MANUAL REQUIREMENTS

1. Unit folder standard
2. Unit testing procedure
3. Integration test standard
4. Integration test procedure
5. Test design specification standard
6. Test case specification standard
7. Test log standard
8. Test problem report standard
9. System testing procedure
10. Acceptance testing procedure.

Normally, all these documents would be subsumed within a testing standards and procedures document.

7.7 SUMMARY

Testing is the most popular quality control used on software projects. There are four main testing activities: system testing, acceptance testing, unit testing, and integration testing. A quality manual should have standards and procedures which govern all these activities. They should describe the tests which are to be carried out and the results of those tests. It is also important that procedures governing testing describe what should happen when a test fails.

7.8 FURTHER READING

There are few good books published on testing. My two favourites are Myers (1979) and Kaner (1989). The former is excellent on topics such as test design but somewhat out-of-date technically, while the latter is excellent on tools and test documentation. Together they form an ideal pair of works which should adorn every software developer's bookshelf. Heitzel (1985) is a good companion to both the above books.

PROBLEMS

7.1 Describe the relationship between the elements of test documentation described in Section 7.5 of this chapter.

7.2 One of the guiding principles of quality assurance is that validation activities should be as independent as possible of the staff who have produced an item that is to be validated. How would you implement this principle with regard to testing?

7.3 Can you think of any circumstances when a unit testing standard and procedure can be relaxed?

7.4 Explain how traceability can be maintained between the functions in a requirements specification and the system tests which check that these functions have been implemented correctly.

7.5 Can you think of the advantages and disadvantages of top-down and bottom-up integration testing?

8

CONFIGURATION MANAGEMENT

AIMS

- To describe the role of configuration management within a software project.
- To describe the various components that make up configuration management.
- To outline the steps that take place when a change is applied to a document or program code.

8.1 INTRODUCTION

There is a myth that change to a software product and its associated documentation only occurs during maintenance: that after a system is handed over to a customer, then new requirements which arise during the lifetime of a software product will require that product to be modified. While change during maintenance is a major resource consumer, change during development is also a widespread phenomenon. During development there are two major reasons for change. The first has already been alluded to in previous chapters: the fact that customer requirements will change during a project—particularly a long project. For example, a project to deliver a financial information system may need to be extensively redesigned when new financial laws or instruments are unexpectedly brought in by a government which is responding to a crisis; or a defence system may be changed in mid-project when the customer for a military air-based command and control system discovers that a potentially unfriendly country has recently received advanced airborne warning technology.

A second reason for change is the fact that developing a software system is a very complicated business and is error-prone; often the errors that have been committed in one phase are only discovered during a later stage. This not only requires reworking of the system code, but also the modification of earlier project documents such as the system design specification.

The last 15 years have seen many projects get into trouble because they have been unable to cope with change. A typical instance of this problem is where different staff have received different versions of system documentation, with each version corresponding to different states of the system during its lifetime. I recently visited one project where the design did not match the specification, the program code did not match the design, and the system test specification documented tests which checked out an out-of-date system specification, all because changes were applied to project documentation in an undisciplined way. It is the role of configuration management to control change in such a way that major problems with modifications do not occur.

It is important to point out that although the previous paragraphs have stressed change *during* a project as being a major reason for the existence of a configuration management system, for some categories of software developer a configuration management system is vital for other reasons. These are developers who produce multi-versions of software which are tailored to a particular customer's needs; for example, accounting packages which can be modified according to the financial practices of the customer. For developers of such systems adequate configuration management is almost an obsession. Without such a discipline the developer is helpless when, for example, an error report is transmitted by the customer. If the developer does not know what version of the software was sent to the customer, then discovering the cause of the error becomes immensely time-consuming.

A good configuration management system should be able to provide data which answers questions such as:

- How many proposed changes to the system remain to be applied?
- What changes were applied to version n of the system specification in order to derive version $n + 1$ of that document?
- What versions of a system are in existence?
- How many faults have we cleared that have been notified against the current version of the system?
- Have the changes which have been applied to version n of the program code been validated? That is, that the changes applied have been checked, and that a check has been carried out which ensures that other non-sanctioned changes have not been applied.
- What versions of modules make up version n of our current system?

Self Assessment Question 8.1 Would a configuration management system normally be able to answer a question about who initially produced a document or some code?

Solution No, the name of staff who carried out the initial development of a requirements specification, design or program code would normally be placed somewhere in the document that they developed. For example, the programmer who developed a module would have his or her name as a comment in the module header.

Configuration management is a discipline which:

- Provides information about the various configurations or versions of a system at points in time.
- Keeps information about changes to all system components—including both software and documentation.
- Provides methods and tools for controlling changes.
- Provides facilities for the validation of changes throughout the life of a system.

The remainder of this chapter describes the components of such a system.

8.2 THE PROCESS OF CONFIGURATION MANAGEMENT

Fig. 8.1 shows the main configuration management activities that occur within a software project. First, a change request is generated. This may originate from two sources: from the customer who wants a new requirement implemented or has discovered an error, or from the development team in response to the discovery of major problems with the system during validation. The change is communicated to the configuration management system via a change request note; details of what should appear in this form can be found later in this chapter. The change is then submitted to a part of the software project known as the *Change Control Board*. This sounds as if it contains a large number of staff; however, in practice the duties of a Change Control Board are often discharged by one person. This will often be the project manager or another senior member of the project; sometimes it is a function carried out by quality assurance staff.

An excerpt from a quality manual detailing the role of a change control board is shown below:

2.3 The Change Control Board

Each project that we carry out will have a configuration management plan. Details of what should be in this plan can be found in section 2.5. An important part of the configuration management process is the Change Control Board. The staff who carry out this function will vary from project to project. On small projects this function will be taken by the project manager. On large projects we often have this function exercised by the project manager and the member of the quality department assigned to the project.

At periods during the project the Change Control Board will consider requests for changes to documentation and code which has been frozen. The frequency of this process will depend on the project and also at what point the project is at. At the beginning of an innovative project, where a requirements specification has just been frozen, you may find it useful to have relatively frequent consideration of changes; during acceptance testing, when the system should be as near to what the customer requires, the frequency will normally be much less.

If one person is carrying out the functions of the Change Control Board there is no need for a formal meeting. However, no matter what form the Change Control Board takes there will always be a need to fill in and file the decision documentation described in section 2.6.

Normally, some form of analysis of the change has been carried out by project staff and information about the severity of the change is provided, as well as a description. The

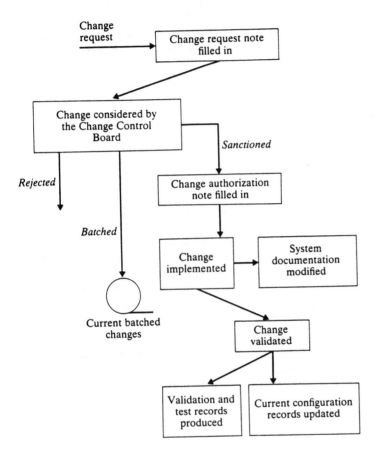

Figure 8.1 The process of configuration management.

reason why severity is specified is so that the Change Control Board can decide what is to happen to a change. The Board looks at a number of factors in deciding what is to happen to a change, the main ones being the impact of the change on the software project and also whether the change is necessary in order to satisfy the requirements specification generated at the beginning of the project. There are three decisions that can be made:

- *Allowed*: the change is to be applied as soon as possible.
- *Disallowed*: the change will not take place.
- *Batched*: the change will take place sometime in the future.

Changes which are allowed are normally those changes which the project regards as important, or which are relatively trivial. For example, a change in response to a serious error which would result in the non-implementation of an important function would come under this category, as would a minor change to the display of data requested by the customer.

Changes which are disallowed are those which the Change Control Board agree are not necessary, have a serious impact on the project, or fall outside the remit of the project. For example, a change request by a customer which would result in the addition of a function not initially documented in the requirements specification would come into this category. If a customer request has been disallowed, then the configuration management system should allow the option of the customer re-requesting the change. In this case the change is costed, the impact on the project in terms of extended delivery time is specified, and the customer is asked whether he or she wishes to re-present the change, with of course the eventual outcome being delay of the project and an increase in the cost of the system. If the customer agrees, then the change is normally re-presented and allowed.

Changes which are delayed are those changes which the software developer thinks are a good idea, but which, for one reason or another, cannot be immediately implemented. An example is a change to a financial package requested by a customer who claims that the package does not do what the manual says it should. The developer may discover that the customer has misread the manual, but that the proposed change would actually make sense in marketing the package: that it provides some extra functionality which may sell more copies of the package. In this case, the proposed change is turned down as not immediately implementable, but it is placed on a queue of changes to be implemented during the development of the next version of the package.

Once a positive change decision has been arrived at, two events occur. First, the change is added to the configuration management system documentation. Second, the change is communicated to the staff who have been nominated as responsible for its implementation.

Self Assessment Question 8.2 Assume that a module has been changed in response to an error being discovered and this change occurred during system testing. What validation should a configuration management system insist on?

Solution First, the module should be checked for functional correctness. Second, all the system tests which the module participated in should be rerun. Third, staff should check that no extra changes have been made to the module.

The change is carried out, and all documentation associated with the change is modified and new versions of the documentation produced. For example, if a requirements change has been authorized, then a wide variety of documents will need to be changed, including the requirements specification, the system design, detailed design, program code, and all the associated test documentation. Once the change has taken place, it is validated. This validation could take a number of forms, depending on the severity of the change. A small change—for example, a modification to the program code of a single module—would only require the generation of some module test data and the rerunning of any affected system tests; while a large requirements change would require a number of reviews to take place, together with the generation of module, integration, system, and acceptance test data.

An important point to be made about configuration management is that it requires the definition of what is known as a *baseline*. A baseline represents a well defined point in the development of a system. Normally, the point is associated with the delivery or freezing of an important item of documentation or a version of the program code of a system. For example, there will always be a baseline associated with the delivery of the requirements specification. Up to the point that a baseline is declared, the documents associated with that baseline can be changed at will. However, after that point, any change to these documents have to go through the configuration management process detailed above.

Self Assessment Question 8.3 Would the system design be a document that is baselined?

Solution Yes, all important documents associated with a system are baselined and the design is a crucial one.

8.3 CONFIGURATION MANAGEMENT ACTIVITIES

There are a number of activities which make up the process of configuration management. They will be explored here within the context described in the previous section. The activities of this section make up the configuration management system to be used by a project. This will normally be documented in the quality plan.

8.3.1 Configuration identification

The process of configuration identification involves the specification of those components in the software project which will be formally placed under configuration control. These components are known as *configuration items*. Normally, configuration items for early documents in the software project will be associated with subsystems; for example, subsystem requirements specifications and designs in the case of large projects. For smaller systems, the full requirements specification and system design will be specified as configuration items. The identification of configuration items from program code will depend on the nature of the application, but often each module will be designated as a configuration item and will come under configuration control when it is finally tested by the programmer who produced it.

Configuration items are often defined in terms of other configuration items. The code of a subsystem will be a configuration item, as could be the individual modules which make up the subsystem. Hence, a change proposed to a particular configuration item will often imply that its component configuration items will be changed; for example, a functional change to a subsystem will be recorded as a requirements change to that subsystem, and also a change to all those modules in the subsystem which require modification.

A configuration item will be identified by a version number. All changes to a configuration item will normally be applied to the latest version. In larger projects, as well as version numbers some items will have variant numbers. These numbers represent a collection of configuration items which are gathered together by virtue of the fact that they implement different functions or they may be tailored to the customer's local circumstances. For example, a subsystem may exist in a number of variants, each variant corresponding to a particular operating system on which the system containing the subsystem is implemented.

Normally, a numbering standard is adopted: each configuration item is given a version number and a variant number. When a change is carried out to an item, that change is applied to its variants. A configuration is a collection of configuration items.

Many of the configuration items will be identified early in the project. These will, almost invariably, be standard documentation items, such as the requirements specification, system design, system test specification, etc. However, when system design has been completed code-related configuration items will be added to the list.

8.3.2 Configuration control

This is the process whereby a change is communicated to a project and then carried out. A quality manual should provide direction to those staff setting up a configuration management system for a project, as follows:

- Procedures which detail the actions required and the route taken when changes are communicated to those members of staff responsible for evaluating and sanctioning changes.
- Standards for the documentation used to communicate a proposed change, and the result of the deliberations of the Change Control Board.
- Guidelines to be used when evaluating whether or not a change is to be allowed.
- Procedures to be used for informing staff about changes and the effect on the configuration items they are dealing with.

8.3.3 Status accounting

Status accounting is the recording and storage of data required for configuration management. This involves keeping data on which parts of a software system have been identified as configuration items; details of the configuration items which a particular part may consist of; the existing versions of configuration items and their variants; the configurations which are currently being maintained; and the list of changes which have been applied to a version in order to create another version.

Status accounting also involves the recording and storage of data about changes: those which have been proposed but not yet considered; those under consideration, those which have been allowed or refused; and those which have been delayed for incorporation into subsequent versions of a configuration item.

8.3.4 Configuration auditing

This process is often carried out by quality assurance staff. It involves checking that standards and procedures associated with configuration management have not been violated. This means that staff responsible for this function should be able to trace a path through from a successful change proposal to the final tests and checks on all the configuration items which have been affected by that change: that there is an audit trail which involves change notes; minutes of the deliberations of the Change Control Board; a directive informing staff to carry out the change; evidence that the version numbers of affected configuration items have been updated; and evidence that reviews or tests which check that the change has been implemented correctly without affecting the other parts of the system have been carried out. The last item is vitally important as it is often highly likely that a change to a system, for example to modify a function, will affect some functions of the system which should remain unaffected.

8.4 DOCUMENTATION FOR CONFIGURATION MANAGEMENT

The documentation associated with configuration management is as follows:

- Change request note
- Control board minute
- Change authorization note
- Change validation report
- Configuration item change trail
- Configuration bulletin.

The remainder of this section looks in a little more detail at the contents of this documentation.

8.4.1 Change request note

The change request note should contain the following information: a unique change number, the date of request, page number, name of project, and a brief identifier for the change.

The form should also contain the reason for the change, a description of the change, a prediction of the amount of effort required for the change, and the configuration items which will be affected by the change. The form should also have some space for comments which expand on the reason for change.

The final part of the form should be used to record the Change Control Board's decision: whether the change is to be allowed, forbidden or batched. It should also contain information such as the date of the Change Control Board decision, and the name of the person who was responsible for evaluating the change. This final part of the change request note would also include space for the Change Control Board to explain why they took a particular decision. This would normally only be filled in when a decision is made to forbid the change or to batch it in the next version of the system.

Self Assessment Question 8.4 Can you think of any reasons why a change request would be turned down?

Solution There are two main reasons. First, the request is for a requirements change which is not in the original requirements specification and the customer will not pay for the change. Second, the change is in response to an error which is not really an error. For example it occurred because the customer misread the user manual or a member of the developer's staff misread some specification.

8.4.2 Control Board minute

This is essentially a linking document which will contain details of the changes that were considered at one sitting of the Change Control Board. When the Change Control Board consists of a number of staff, it makes sense for the Board to meet regularly to consider non-urgent changes. The Control Board minute details, in summary form, the change request notes that were processed by the board at one meeting and the outcome of the requests. This document will mainly consist of change request note identifiers and brief descriptions of the outcome of the Change Control Board's deliberations. When the change control function is delegated to one person, a software developer will omit completing Control Board minutes and will rely on the configuration bulletin to provide information to staff. This item is discussed below.

8.4.3 Change authorization note

This document authorizes a particular change or set of changes which have arisen from a change request note and a decision by the Change Control Board to allow the changes. It will consist of information such as a reference to the change request note, date of issue, page number, name of project, and the name of the change. It will also detail the changes that need to be carried out. Often these will be the same as those on the corresponding change request note; however, where a company uses change notes which specify a number of changes, the change authorization note will only contain the subset of the changes which were allowed.

The change authorization note will also contain a list of configuration items which are affected by the changes and how their version numbering is to be changed.

8.4.4 Change validation report

This is a report which is issued after a change or set of changes associated with a change request note has been implemented. It details the testing and validation that has occurred. This testing and validation will be in two forms: checks that the change has been applied correctly and checks which ensure that remaining functions and other quality factors in the system have not been affected by the change. The report will detail the tests and reviews which have been carried out to this end, and will usually contain a list of each test and review identifiers. These identifiers can be used to look up the detailed documentation dealing with these activities in the project library.

8.4.5 Configuration item change trail

This is a set of documents, one per configuration item, which detail the evolution of the item from the moment it was baselined. It consists of a series of change identifiers followed by a brief synopsis of the reason for a change. It will also detail the change in numbering which occurred from version to version as a result of the changes.

8.4.6 Configuration bulletin

This document contains the current configuration of the system, expressed in terms of configuration identifiers, current version numbers, and variant numbers. It is used by staff to check that they are currently processing the right version of a configuration item.

8.5 QUALITY MANUAL REQUIREMENTS

1. Configuration management system set-up guidelines
2. Change control procedure
3. Change request note standard
4. Control board minute standard
5. Change authorization standard
6. Change notification note standard
7. Change validation procedure
8. Change validation report standard
9. Configuration item change trail standard.

Normally, all these documents will be subsumed under a configuration management and control standard and procedure.

8.6 SUMMARY

Change occurs throughout a software project as well as during operation. A configuration management system is a set of standards, procedures and guidelines which ensure that the process of change is as smooth as it should be. Collectively, a configuration management system should govern the processes of notifying change, appraising, specifying, and validating changes and the documentation of the state of a system in terms of baselines and changes. A software developer who does not have detailed standards and procedures which describe configuration activities is destined to waste a large amount of resources and commit a large number of errors.

8.7 FURTHER READING

The problem which faces the author who wishes to write about configuration management is that, while it is an important topic, there is not quite enough information on it to fill a book. Consequently, there is a distinct lack of good texts. The best book that I can recommend is Babich (1986) and a good, short article on the subject is Bersoff (1984).

PROBLEMS

8.1 What sort of events do you think would give rise to a change request being submitted to the Change Control Board?

8.2 Write down a standard for a change request note.

8.3 Write down all the documents which you think would be baselined on a large software project.

8.4 Give an example of a change to a baselined document which would affect a large number of other baselined documents.

QA AND THE NEW TECHNOLOGIES

AIMS

- To outline the effect of new technology on a quality system.
- To describe in some detail the effect that four specific new technologies have on quality in the software project.

9.1 INTRODUCTION

The aim of this chapter is to examine four of the more popular software advances which are transforming the way we develop software, and their impact on the QA practices in a company. In each case the use of the technology described in this chapter requires extra components to the quality system. One of the most serious problems I find with software developers is that although many of them are keen to advance in terms of adopting new technology, little effort is put into adapting the quality system to cope with this new technology. In some cases some major modifications are needed. For example, the use of a new programming language might require large changes to programming standards and the standards and procedures used for module testing.

9.2 PROTOTYPING

9.2.1 What is prototyping?

Prototyping is the process of developing a working model of a system early on in a project. Such a working model can be shown to the customer, who suggests improvements. These improvements are incorporated in the prototype and it is shown again to the customer, and so on. Prototyping is a valuable technique, both for the customer and the developer. All too often I have met customers, faced with an inadequate implementation, who have said during acceptance testing: 'If only you had shown me the system earlier in the project I could have told you exactly what I wanted.' Prototyping has a number of advantages:

- It enables the customer to preview the system well before major development work starts.
- It enables the developers to know exactly what they need to deliver. Previously, developers have attempted to deliver the system that reflects the requirements specification. Unfortunately, since this specification is written in natural language there is always considerable scope for misunderstanding. By asking the customer to sign off the prototype, the developers are able to have an exact reference point from which to judge their implementation.
- It enables early customer training to take place. Customer training is often rushed and inadequate, and a prototype can be used to integrate training properly in the development project. It also has the allied advantage of enabling the developer to meet the staff who are actually going to use the prototype. A common feature of many software projects is that the customer representative has rarely encountered or been part of the application that is to be developed and is, consequently, not the ideal person to talk to about system requirements.
- It can act as a test oracle during the later stages of system development. A test oracle is a version of a system that will always deliver the right results when executed. A prototype can be used as an oracle by feeding its output, together with the output of the final developed system, through a file comparator. This means that the tester has very little work to do when examining test output during system testing and acceptance testing. All that needs to be done is to examine the output of the file comparator in order to see whether the developed system has given a different result to the oracle.

Self Assessment Question 9.1 Why do you think prototyping is·effective?

Solution The main reason is that it provides a validation of the requirements specification early in a project. Error rectification during prototyping costs much less than if it occurred during an activity such as system testing.

9.2.2 Techniques to achieve prototyping

A number of techniques are available to the developer who wishes to produce an early version of a system. They range from rather simple techniques, such as showing the customer some sample screens, to using sophisticated programming languages which are capable of packing a lot of functionality punch into a small amount of program code. The main prototyping techniques are as follows:

- Relax the quality assurance standards of the project. Tolerate errors in the prototype in an attempt to get out a rough working version of the system quickly. This could mean a whole variety of tactics could be applied: skimping on the requirements specification, omitting the system design stage, carrying out perfunctory system tests, and omitting many of the reviews that would normally be scheduled.

- Implement only those parts of a system whose requirements are felt to be ill-expressed or fuzzy. This might mean the developer deciding on an incremental development strategy, with subsystems that have a high amount of risk attached to them being implemented first.
- Use a table-driven processor approach to development. This relies on a set of tools that are table-driven and have a clean interface between them. The ideal candidate for this approach is UNIX, which contains table-driven processors such as YACC that enable software to be produced very quickly.
- Employ a programming language that enables the developer to implement a large amount of functionality in a physically small amount of program code. Probably the best example of this is the fourth-generation programming language. Such languages are usually interfaced to relational database systems, and allow very complex commercial data processing to be implemented in very short sections of program code. However, fourth-generation languages are not the only medium for this form of prototyping—programming languages such as PROLOG, SETL, LISP, and APL have all been successfully employed to produce prototypes.
- Use an application-oriented programming language. Such languages are aimed at one particular application area, and contain data types which are used continually in that area. For example, an application-oriented language for a warehousing application would use data types for warehouses, stock bins and picking lists.

These, then, are some of the ways in which prototypes can be generated. Object-oriented programming languages are also an excellent medium for prototyping. Such languages contain a facility for defining the entities that were identified in the previous chapter using a facility known as a *class*. In terms of prototyping, an important facility of a class is *inheritance*. In order to explain what inheritance is, it is worth quoting an example: that of an invoice in a commercial data processing application.

Such an invoice will always contain the same details, irrespective of the application. It will contain the following information: the name of the supplier who has provided the services or goods that the invoice describes; the supplier's address; the name of the customer; the customer's address; a list of items supplied; their price; and the total price. In a purchasing application an invoice would, almost certainly, be the first entity discovered by an analyst.

In the first application in which the software developer uses an invoice, it would be defined using a class description of the components of the invoice, together with the functions which manipulate the invoice, e.g. creating an invoice. The application would then be implemented, and the class stored in a company-wide library.

The next time an application is developed that requires an invoice, the designer responsible would look in the library for any classes that described an implementation of an invoice. Let us assume that the system requires a slightly different form of invoice from the one contained in the library; for example, it might be for an overseas customer, where the tax deduction part of the invoice would be different.

The designer of the new system would define a new type of invoice which contained this element but which was mostly made up of the invoice class stored in the project library. This is inheritance—the new invoice class inherits many of the properties and operations of the stored invoice in the project library. This reduces the work required from the designer: all that has to be done is to write down the new components of the invoice, any new operations associated with this component, and then bring in the invoice class from the project library.

If a developer has built up an extensive library of classes, then prototyping can be effectively carried out. All it involves is for the analyst or designer responsible to call down pre-written classes from a project library, and join them together with some processing code. The following section will examine object-oriented languages in more detail and look at their QA implications.

9.2.3 Models of prototyping

There are a number of ways of implementing prototyping. The choice is really dependent on the type of software that is being developed, and project-specific factors such as the duration and size of the project. There are three popular prototyping models: throw-away prototyping, evolutionary prototyping, and incremental prototyping.

Throw-away prototyping corresponds to the popular idea of prototyping: the developer produces a prototype and then initiates the iterative process of showing the prototype to the customer and modifying it in response to the customer's wishes. When the prototyping phase has finished, the prototype is, in effect, thrown away: it is placed in an archive and conventional software development is started, based on a requirements specification that has been written by examining the detailed functionality of the prototype.

Throw-away prototyping is effective for short projects of a few months' duration. Unfortunately, for large projects it tends to be less than ideal. The reason, of course, is change. When conventional software development begins, the developer is almost invariably bombarded with changes of requirements from the customer. In the end, the conventional software part of a prototyping project can suffer from the same problems as a project which did not use prototyping.

Evolutionary prototyping is the complete antithesis to throw-away prototyping. Here, the developer aims to keep the prototype alive. The first stage of the evolutionary prototyping project involves the development of a prototype using the same activities and techniques that would be used for throw-away prototyping. However, after the customer has decided that everything is satisfactory, the developer then bases the remainder of the development work on the prototype that has been generated.

In the case of a prototype that has been generated using a fourth-generation programming language, this involves a process of optimization, whereby the initial prototype is modified to make it run faster and use less memory and file space. The important point about this form of evolutionary prototyping—and evolutionary prototyping in general—is that throughout the project a working prototype that matches current customer requirements is always available.

The final form of prototyping is known as *incremental prototyping*. This can be used in a project where the requirements can be neatly partitioned into functionally separate areas. For example, developing a system for a chemical plant involves the following functional areas: monitoring, control, the human–computer interface, and management information. If one of these functional areas is fuzzy, or the customer has difficulty expressing requirements, then a process of incremental development can be adopted. Here the system is developed as a series of small subsystems, each of which implements a subset of the functions. The early subsystems can then be used as prototypes.

QA AND THE NEW TECHNOLOGIES **137**

Self Assessment Question 9.2 Isn't prototyping the same as hacking and should be discouraged by a quality system?

Solution The technical process of prototyping looks very much like hacking. However, prototyping is normally controlled quite well by quality systems by the provision of standards and procedures; for example, a standard for reporting back on the progress of the evaluation of a prototype with a customer.

9.2.4 QA and prototyping

One of the myths about prototyping is that since it seems to be quite a flexible and free-ranging process very little quality assurance is needed. The reverse is true, in fact. I have come across a number of prototyping projects which have failed; the vast majority of these failures have arisen either because of a management failure or because the QA system did not contain facilities for monitoring, controlling, planning and costing the prototyping process. The discussion in this section will centre on throw-away prototyping as that is the form of prototype development often encountered in software projects. However, many of the points made are equally valid for both evolutionary and incremental prototyping. The first problem that is often found in quality systems is a lack of guidance about when to prototype and when not to prototype. There is an allied problem in that staff also carry out prototyping with only a hazy view of what the prototyping process is meant to achieve.

Thus, there is a need for a guideline document which describes the various reasons for prototyping and outlines the reasons why a decision to prototype may be taken. Such a document would ask questions about such project-specific factors as the volatility of customer requirements, changes in the customer's circumstances during the project, and whether there is a perception of an inability of the customer to convey requirements in written documents. Many of the questions in this guideline can be found in procedures which govern risk analysis. These are described in Chapter 3.

Another problem involves ignorance of what the prototyping process is meant to achieve. There are a number of useful ways in which prototyping can be used: for requirements elicitation, design evaluation, exploring the human–computer interface, and training; but, more often than not, we tend to associate prototyping solely with requirements-based activities.

Because of this fuzziness the project plan should have a section which describes why prototyping is to be used and what the deficiencies of the prototype will be. For example, in aiming to deliver a prototype rapidly, a developer may decide to tolerate quite a high number of errors which, although they would be serious if present in the final system, are no more than a slight irritant for staff carrying out prototyping. The section describing prototype deficiencies is an excellent remedy for one of the problems which afflict projects that use prototyping: that of the customer being so taken with the prototype that he or she asks for early delivery of a system which is a good prototype but a poor production system.

A major problem that has afflicted many prototyping-based projects is that of prototype evaluation. Typically, what might happen is that an analyst and customer may be so taken with prototyping that more and more time is spent on this process, with more and more functions being continually added, to the point where the prototype becomes impossible to implement within the hardware and response time constraints originally detailed in a requirements specification. There is a need for a quality system to provide standards and procedures for prototype evaluation which result in regular reports being sent to the project manager that describe the functional growth of the prototype.

> **Self Assessment Question 9.3** What do you think should be in these reports?
>
> **Solution** If the reports are used to just check the functional growth of a project, then they would contain a list of new functions added or deleted together with some estimate of the size of the functions.

Another problem found on prototyping projects is that analysts and programmers rush off and develop a prototype without thinking about whether they have perceived the conceptual architecture of the intended system correctly. What often happens is that a considerable amount of resources are then devoted to the production of an initial prototype which is highly defective. A good quality system should insist that before starting the prototyping process a software project carries out a very short paper and pencil specification exercise—taking no more than a few days—in order to check that the conceptual architecture of a proposed system is firmly established. Only then should staff begin prototyping.

Lack of proper documentation is another difficulty—particularly in the case of evolutionary prototyping. Once a prototype has been agreed with the customer, the prototyping standards and procedures should insist that the design and the requirements specification be documented. Such documentation is vital for staff who have to maintain the system.

A major problem, which has still not been solved satisfactorily, is that of costing and resourcing a prototyping-based project. For evolutionary prototyping it is still essentially a research problem. However, some guidelines can be given for costing throw-away prototyping-based projects. For example, prototyping guidelines should give directions to the developer to base the resources required for prototyping on a consideration of the risk factors on a project. Such guidelines should ask the project manager to examine previous resource figures from earlier prototyping-based projects, together with the results of their risk questionnaires. From these, a project manager should get a good idea of the amount of resources required for the prototyping part of the new project assuming, of course, that a risk questionnaire has been produced for that project.

9.3 OBJECT-ORIENTED PROGRAMMING LANGUAGES

9.3.1 What is an object-oriented programming language?

Object-oriented programming languages are languages in which objects can be implemented, together with facilities for ensuring that the implementation of objects can be hidden from the programmer, and facilities that enable a high degree of reusability to take place. This statement is rather platitudinous, and it is the aim of this section to explore this matter in a little more detail.

Objects are found in all applications—a plane in an air-traffic control system is an object; so is an invoice in a purchasing order system; and a student in an educational enrolment system is another example. Object-oriented programming languages implement objects as data structures and modules which access the data structures. They enable a programmer to produce an entity known as a *class*, which describes the data structures and the modules.

Figure 9.1 shows the structure of a typical class, in this instance a class that describes a queue. Associated with this class would be a description of the stored data that makes up the object, together with a description of the operations which allow access to the data—the operations being implemented as modules—and a mechanism for specifying which facilities of the class can be accessed by the programmer who employs the objects described by the class in an application.

This, then, is the base idea on which object-oriented programming languages are based. The facilities associated with objects in a language, the number of these facilities, and the quality of their implementation are a good guide to the object-orientedness of a programming language. The remainder of this section describes these facilities.

The first facility of an object-oriented programming language is that of providing a means whereby access to a data structure is restricted. For example, the designer of the queue object described above would, almost invariably, want to prevent a programmer from manipulating the base data structure that implements the queue. If such manipulation was allowed, it would lead to the development of a system where references to the underlying data structures are found scattered throughout the system. Such a system is a software maintenance headache, since a change to the underlying data requires, as a minimum, that the programmer implementing the change examines every module that references the data structure. In practice, it also leads to a vast amount of change necessitated by modifying each module that refers to the internal details of the data structure.

The facility that allows access to a system to be severely restricted is known as *information hiding*: the information about a data structure is hidden beneath a series of operations which only allow access to the data structure via parameters. For example, the operation of adding an item to a queue would be implemented as a module with two parameters: the first would be the item to be added, and the second would be the queue.

Another feature of an object-oriented programming language is *polymorphism* or, as it is sometimes called, *genericity*. This allows the software developer to define the data and operations that implement an object via the class mechanism, and instantiate the class for a variety of components in the data part of the class. For example, an object-oriented programming language would enable a developer to implement a queue class for, say, integers, and then use that class for a queue of messages in a communications

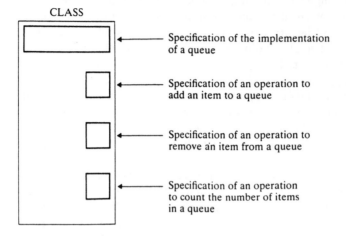

Figure 9.1 A class that specifies a queue.

system, a queue of spool files in an operating system, or a queue of back orders in a purchasing system. Moreover, this instantiation of a new instance of a class is usually a matter of writing a few extra lines of program code. Polymorphism allows a developer to build up a library of reusable objects, and contributes greatly towards the ability to develop reusable software.

A further feature of an object-oriented programming language is *inheritance* (described above). For example, a commercial data processing system developer may have already defined a class for purchase order objects which would describe an implementation in terms of a data structure that would hold information about the name of a customer making an order; the customer's address; the products being ordered; and a list of operations which communicate with data described by that class.

If another application came along, say, for a slightly different system which handles orders for dangerous chemicals, where the purchase order contains information about handling instructions for the items to be delivered, then the developer is able, using an object-oriented programming language, to define a new class which mainly consists of items from the old purchase order class, together with new extensions and operations which handle the new special case. In general, a good object-oriented programming language should allow a class to inherit properties from more than one class, and inherit properties more than once from the same class.

A final facility that should be provided by a class is *dynamic memory management*, where the underlying compiler software allows an object to be created when it is required, and deallocated when it is no longer needed.

The degree to which a programming language can be called object-oriented is dependent on how many of the above facilities have been implemented, and the degree of simplicity with which they have been implemented. There is a broad spectrum of languages which could be described as having object-oriented properties, ranging from those such as Ada, with a small number of facilities, up to the programming language Smalltalk which has the object as its base facility, and where every other facility of the language is integrated with this idea of an object. The language C^{++} lies in the top quarter of the object-oriented language spectrum: it is certainly nowhere near as sophisticated as Smalltalk, but it still contains a considerable amount of object-oriented facilities, albeit that some of them have been implemented in what might seem a slightly eccentric manner.

My suspicion is that of all the programming languages that have object-oriented facilities, it is C^{++} that will be the most popular and long-lived. This is not because it is an elegant language, but because it is built upon an existing popular programming language—C. The history of software engineering still only spans three and a half decades. However, this is long enough to show us that radical change does not occur in software development, but that change, dampened by the fact that we have a massive software maintenance mountain, is an evolutionary process which takes place in increments— increments which, more often than not, are based on an existing technology, programming language, or development method.

9.3.2 Object-oriented technology and software quality assurance

There are a number of ways in which object-oriented technology will affect the quality system of a company. The first is the model of software development adopted. The conventional life-cycle model involves a requirements specification being produced, followed by a system design and then program code. The requirements specification will mainly consist of functions; hence, from an early point in a conventional project, functionality will drive the development process.

Since object-oriented technology concentrates on data, a new life-cycle model needs to be adopted which identifies objects and operations during the requirements analysis phase. Although a functional specification is eventually produced, the standards and procedures for requirements analysis should direct the developer to produce an object model at an early stage. This means that a standard for a notation for expressing such models should be included in the quality system, together with a procedure which describes some means of validating the model.

Self Assessment Question 9.4 Is this a major change over the way that conventional projects are organised?

Solution It really depends on what you regard as a conventional project. For a conventional data processing project the answer is no, as these projects take the design of the data very seriously and it is almost one of the first tasks carried out. For a conventional real-time project, say, then there is a difference because such projects consider the functions of a system as the prime driver of development.

Another impact of object-oriented technology on the software project arises from the fact that classes are reusable. Software developers who employ object-oriented technology will increasingly find that they will have built up bigger and bigger class libraries, the contents of which can be reused in projects. There are a number of implications here for the software developer.

The first is that a tightening up of the quality controls associated with the validation of individual classes is usually needed. If a project manager is to incorporate a class into his or her software, then he or she needs to be reassured that the degree of validation that the class received is at least as good as that received by the system into which it is to be incorporated. This means that detailed records on such things as test cases and test coverage must be kept: more so than would normally be kept for conventional software development.

The second implication is that directives must be given, via standards and procedures, to system designers which specify that the first thing they should do is browse through a class library, and if they feel that components from the library are unsuitable for the system that they are designing, then they should produce some written explanation as part of the design documentation.

The third implication is that the quality system should normally impose some directions to the constructors of classes to include some extra bureaucratic information in the classes which enable staff who are going to browse through the class library to identify potential candidate classes for reusability. For example, a programming standard could insist on an exact description of the functionality of the individual components of a class.

The costing procedures for conventional project development should also be modified for object-oriented development. We saw in Chapter 3 that the main method for costing a project is to identify a list of tasks and then cost them on a historical basis. This normally takes place during the early stages of the requirements analysis and specification part of a project. However, the cost of an object-oriented system will depend on the degree of reusability that is to be employed. Therefore, the planning procedures of a company which uses object-oriented technology should be modified so that some preliminary assessment of the degree of reusability is carried out. Not only would this help to give rise to more accurate cost estimations, but it would enable project management to check out any claim from system designers that they were unable to reuse much of a class library: designers are notorious for adopting a not-invented-here syndrome.

Another impact of object-oriented technology is on the reviewing process, particularly if a company encourages new classes to be inserted into a class library. This means that standards and procedures should exist for class reviews rather than module reviews. Indeed, a developer who uses an object-oriented programming language should not really use module reviews since the vast majority of the validation that would occur in such reviews would be carried out in a class review.

One of the most difficult parts of object-oriented development is testing, particularly system and acceptance testing. When a failure occurs in a system or acceptance test it is often not clear where it occurs, particularly if a class is to be instantiated a number of times for different objects. Because of this, there should be standards and guidelines which direct the designers and constructors of classes to insert debugging information into the class which enables staff to identify the cause of a malfunctioning test.

9.4 FORMAL METHODS OF SOFTWARE DEVELOPMENT

9.4.1 What is a formal method of software development?

A formal method of software development makes use of mathematics for the specification and design of a system, together with mathematical proof as a validation method. A developer who uses a formal method first specifies the functionality of his or her system using discrete mathematics, and then reasons and proves properties of the system, for example that a specified security level in a secure communications system has been reached. When the developer is satisfied that the mathematical requirements specification is correct, it is then designed and specified in terms of mathematics. The mathematical design is then validated with respect to the specification. This mathematical specification of the design is then transformed into program code by staff responsible for implementation.

Formal methods of software development offer a great number of advantages to the developer. Because mathematics is an exact medium it means that ambiguities and contradictions can be detected more easily than in natural language documents. However, there is a cost: staff who use such mathematical methods of software development have to be highly trained, and inducting new staff into a project can take much longer than for staff who have been trained in more conventional methods. However, the gains can be considerable in terms of greatly reduced error rates and projects which do not exceed their budgets. Because of the cost in terms of implementing formal methods, they are currently used only for projects where there would be very large costs to the developer if an error occurred during operation. Such projects are mainly confined to the safety-critical and security areas.

Self Assessment Question 9.5 Would a formal methods project have the same life-cycle as a conventional project in the same application area but which used graphical notations?

Solution Yes, formal methods are purely a technical solution and the sequential mode of development where activities follow each other would be used.

9.4.2 Formal methods and software quality assurance

Both prototyping and object-oriented technology represent major divergences from conventional software development. Happily, formal methods do not, and require the same conventional development models that are employed by many software developers. The modifications to a quality system required for formal methods tend not to be too great.

The main impact concerns standards for specifying the mathematics used in requirements specifications and system designs, together with the procedures and standards used by staff who conduct reviews. The mathematical notations used in a formal method are, in a superficial sense, similar to programming languages, and hence require detailed standards for their layout: what indentation to use; how to separate the components of a formal specification; what conventions to use for the names of variables; and how to link together parts of a requirements specification or system design specification which are associated by virtue of the fact that they deal with connected sets of functions.

One of the major advantages of a formal notation is that reviewing becomes a more structured process. For example, a component of certain formal methods of software development is a statement known as a *data invariant*. This is a mathematical expression which remains true throughout the execution of a system, e.g. a data invariant may state that there will be no more than *MaxUs* users of a system.

One part of a review of a formal requirements specification can be structured around the process of discovering whether the operations detailed in it violate the data invariant, and staff responsible for developing the requirements specification have to convince the members of the review that this does not occur. Normally, the act of convincing uses rigorous argument rather than formal mathematical proof; but, nevertheless, there is still the option of using such proof if rigorous argument does not convince.

Because of the special nature of mathematics as a specification medium it is important that standards and procedures exist for the execution and documentation of reviews. Such reviews, as in conventional development, are normally confined to requirements specification, system design, and program code reviews.

It is worth pointing out that even though a developer may use a formal method, there is still a need for system and acceptance testing standards and procedures. Formality does not get rid of the need to demonstrate the correctness of a system to the customer—all it does is to reduce the levels of error discovered during this process.

9.5 STRUCTURED METHODS AND CASE TECHNOLOGY

Until the early eighties the vast majority of software developers used natural language for requirements specification and design. However, the early eighties saw an increase in use of the graphical notations associated with what are known as structured software development methods. The main advantage of these graphical notations was that they offered a high level of precision and a huge improvement over natural language. The disadvantage was that in order to be fully effective they required tool support. In 1981 I used a graphical notation to specify a large system; one of the things I noticed was that when I made a mistake I needed to carry out a very large amount of rework to recover from the error—even if it was a comparatively small one. Much of this rework could have been carried out in a semi-automatic fashion if tool support had been available. By the late eighties the tools were becoming available; they were implemented for high-end work stations or the more powerful PC configurations. Typically, these tools offered a number of facilities:

- The ability to create diagrams which describe the functions of a software system;
- The ability to create diagrams which describe the system design of both the processes and the data in a system.
- Error-checking facilities, such as the ability to point out errors in the flow of data in a requirements specification.
- The ability to process a graphical requirements specification and simulate its actions as a rudimentary prototype.

- The generation of code from a design.
- The storage and manipulation of project management information.

These tools, and their associated structured methods, have a potentially great influence on the quality management system of a company. The main influences are shown below:

- Many of the tools force the developer to produce requirements specifications and system designs to a fixed set of standards; for example, many Computer-Aided Software Engineering (CASE) tools which manipulate data flow diagrams insist on rigid conventions for the way in which such diagrams are displayed. In effect, these tools enforce their own requirements specification and system design standards, and obviate the need for the developer to specify his or her own standards.
- They relieve staff who attend requirements and system design reviews of many of the more bureaucratic checking activities. Since they are capable of detecting errors, such as the omission of an identifier in a module, they free staff who attend reviews to concentrate on important questions such as: does this system design actually implement the requirements specification?
- They relieve development staff of the need to construct and generate a large amount of useful but bureaucratic information.
- They increase the degree of traceability present in system documentation. For example, the documents produced by CASE tools enable staff to trace from a system's functions to the final code which implements the functions without expending very much effort.

9.6 SUMMARY

This chapter has described only a small number of new technologies. However, each case demonstrates an important point which is true for all new technologies: that to implement new advances in software development without considering their effect on the quality system will lead to the quality system becoming out-of-date, and giving rise to activities which are less than optimal in terms of the detection of errors.

9.7 FURTHER READING

Probably the best treatment of prototyping within a management information systems environment is Connell and Brice-Shaffer (1989). While the authors do not explicitly address quality assurance, they do provide enough technical details to enable quality assurance staff to write standards and procedures to govern the process. Ince (1991) describes the use of object-oriented technology within software engineering and touches on the testing and quality assurance aspects of the subject. Booch (1986) is a good book-length introduction to object-oriented development with an industrial bias, while an excellent new book (Sully, 1993) describes object-oriented development from a structured methods perspective.

A good introduction to formal methods of software development can be found as a chapter in Ince (1988). For the more mathematically inclined Cohen, Harwood and Jackson (1986) is probably the best book-level introduction. An excellent case study of the use of formal methods and statistical testing can be found in Cobb and Mills (1990). An easy-to-read introduction to structured development methods and associated tools technology is Martin and McClure (1987).

PROBLEMS

9.1 A dynamic analysis tool monitors the frequency of execution of the code in a system developed using a third-generation language. What modifications to a quality system do you think are needed to cope with the introduction of this tool?

9.2 A static analysis tool is a testing tool which detects errors in program code without executing that code. Typically the sort of errors that are detected by a modern static analysis tool are: uninitialized variables, program code that can never be executed and variables given a value which are never used before another value is given. They are also able to check that certain conditions holding between variables are true. What quality factors do you think this tool might improve?

9.3 What quality factors do you think prototyping addresses on a software project?

9.4 What areas of a quality manual do you think would need to be changed if a company adopts a new notation for the specification of functional requirements?

9.5 What areas of a quality manual do you think would need to be changed if a company adopts object-oriented technology?

QA AND THE HUMAN–COMPUTER INTERFACE

AIMS

- To outline the relationship between the human–computer interface and software quality assurance.
- To describe the various quality documents produced for the development of the human–computer interface.
- To examine the various tasks which are involved in the development of the human–computer interface.

10.1 INTRODUCTION

One of the most widespread weaknesses that I find in quality systems is the fact that they rarely, if ever, address important issues concerned with the human–computer interface. The result of this is that computer systems are still being developed which, although they meet the functionality described in their requirements specification, take no account of the capabilities of the user, the tasks that the user has to carry out, and the environment in which the system works. Some examples of systems I have come across where major problems have occurred are:

- The system which used auditory feedback to indicate that an error had been committed, or that the user was not allowed to carry out a particular operation. Auditory feedback is an excellent mechanism for this; however, this system was situated as part of a control house in a chemical plant which had not been soundproofed. The result was that the users of the system—staff responsible for operating the plant—were unable to hear the feedback, and on two occasions a serious accident was only narrowly averted. One of the operations staff who, quite reasonably, wanted to live until retirement, had taken the matter into his own hands and built an amplification system. This took the feedback from the computer and transmitted it to control staff via a rather old but large loudspeaker which he had kept in his garage.

- The data entry system which consisted of a number of transaction types that were initiated through a windows interface, where each transaction was designed in the same way, but with very small differences in aspects such as the shape of the window icons and their positions. It was almost as if the developers of the system had assigned the design of the interface to separate teams who never communicated with the other teams. Operators of this system were continually making errors and, even in times of recession, were leaving because of the awkward interactions that they were forced into by the system.
- The system intended for schoolchildren, that expected the users to use single line-by-line commands rather than menu commands. The system was aimed at very timid users, and the experience of continually making mistakes put many of them off using computers.
- The school records system where a careless use of two of the commands available to the teacher user resulted in the complete annihilation of the database.
- The system which purported to have a help system. In a sense it did, because the user was able to invoke a window which contained instructions on how to use the current command and the various options that were available. However, nobody had checked the text of the help messages. They were barely grammatical, and contained a large amount of technical jargon which some members of the development team later admitted to me that even they could not understand.
- The system where each command had quite a good interface, but where the user was asked to carry out a sort of digital acrobatics when combining a number of commands together to achieve some aim. The system was for foreign exchange dealers and, when in use, resulted in a number of mishaps which lost the bank using the system around £200 000 in two days. When the mishaps were notified to the user's management the system had to be withdrawn; the interface redesigned and implemented; and a large amount of expensive training material and courses had to be ditched and redeveloped.
- The system which provided facilities that enabled the user to navigate through quite a complex geographical database. Unfortunately, nobody really had much idea about how complex the navigation tasks were, and no facilities were provided which enabled the user to keep track of where he or she was in the database. Users continually gave up in frustration at being unable to return from a path through the database. The result was that the system, which was originally targeted for a population of around 200 users, was hardly used at all. By the time navigation facilities were tacked on after delivery, the system had got such a bad name that the user population was around 20 people.

Self Assessment Question 10.1 How would a QA system have avoided the problem detailed in the first bullet point above?

Solution There would normally be a checklist which detailed such environmentally important issues which the HCI designer would need to examine before doing very much work on the interface.

These, then, are examples of systems which, although they delivered the required functions, had such a poor interface with the user that they were virtually inoperable. I have deliberately chosen some poor systems; however, even in the more successful systems there are still annoying quirks which make them much less effective than they deserve to be. Normally, such poor interfaces arise from an inadequate perception of the characteristics of the user; a hazy idea of the tasks that the user has to carry out; and a neglect of the social, managerial and physical environments which the user works in. A good quality system should ensure that this will not happen.

10.2 THE USER/ENVIRONMENT QUESTIONNAIRE

The first important document necessary for HCI design that forms part of a quality system is a user/environment questionnaire. This is a document which contains questions about the users: their capabilities, the environment they work in, and the tasks which they carry out. The answers to this questionnaire, elicited during the early stages of the requirements analysis process, and often physically bound as part of the requirements specification, will be an important input into the process of designing a system's interface. Typical questions which would be asked in such a questionnaire are shown below:

- Who are the users of the system, i.e. who are the people that are to sit at a terminal or VDU and interact with the system?
- What are the current computer skills of the users? Are they first-time users; infrequent users who will remain infrequent; infrequent users who will be asked to become frequent users; or frequent and practised users?
- What is the nature of the tasks that they have to carry out? Do the users, for example, have to navigate through a complex database or produce a large number of drawings?
- Is the task repetitive or does it change from day to day?
- Are a number of users involved in the interaction with the computer? For example, might two or three users be sitting in front of the screen and talking to each other?
- Do a number of users interact together via the computer system; for example, as users of a system which simulates the conditions on the trading floor of a financial institution?
- If the system does consist of a number of interactive users who can affect the actions of other users by means of the computer, are there any other modes of communication involved, for example shouting?
- Is the time taken to carry out an operation critical?
- Is the environment in which the system is to be used poorly lit, noisy or dusty?

> **Self Assessment Question 10.2** How might the factor outlined in the fifth bullet point above affect the design of a system?
>
> **Solution** Usually it would affect basic design decisions which concern the size of screen to be provided and the possibility of having two keyboards or mice in tandem.

Self Assessment Question 10.3 How would information gathered from the question detailed in the eighth bullet point above be used?

Solution It would be used to design the interface such that fast response by the user is possible. It would also form an input into the system and acceptance testing process, whereby tests would be set up which involved real users and which monitored the speed of response by these users.

The answers to these questions and many others will determine the nature of the interface that is produced. For example, the interface to a military command and control system, where the users might be very experienced, where access is restricted, where noise is a problem and where lighting is weak, might be designed mainly as a touch screen system; where a system has a windows interface, the use of a mouse and auditory feedback would be totally inadequate.

Another useful HCI component in a quality system is a short document which describes how the HCI designer is going to respond to the information gathered by the questionnaire, a document sometimes called the *HCI Design Rationale*. At this stage in the project the process of requirements gathering is probably still proceeding, so that this rationale will still be a fairly succinct document. However, it should explain the general nature of the interface, based on factors such as the capabilities of the user and the physical environment in which the system is to be placed.

10.3 THE TASK SPECIFICATION

Another important part of a quality system is the task specification. There will be a task specification for each category of user of a system. The purpose of a task specification is to document the tasks which the user of a system carries out. The most useful notations for this tend to be graphical and hierarchical; an example is shown in Fig. 10.1. It describes one of the tasks carried out by the user of a library system. At the top level of the hierarchy is the overall task of responding to a returned book. At the next level of the diagram is a series of blocks which describe the various subtasks involved in this. The diagram shows some aspects which are not automated; for example, the insertion of an identification card into a reader. Those parts of the system which are not automatable are enclosed in dashed boxes. The subtasks specified at the second level of the diagram include entering book details; responding to an error in entering these details; and responding to the rather unlikely, but possible, error that the book has been previously returned and not logged out by the user when it has been borrowed.

An interesting feature of the notation is the use of boxes marked with a circle or an asterisk. The former indicates a task which has been split up into a number of alternative tasks (the diagram shows an example of this when normal processing or an error condition occurs). A task marked with an asterisk is repetitive; for example, the task of inputting book details is potentially a repetitive one since there is the possibility that an error will be committed during the process of inputting the data, thus leading to a potentially infinite application of the task of communicating book data.

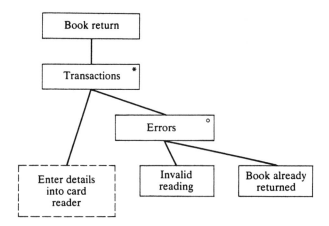

Figure 10.1 An example of a task specification notation.

The task specification is one of the most important documents produced in the early part of a software project. It should be completed by the time the requirements specification has been finished. It is often a good idea to either have a separate technical review of this document, or to have a review in which the user tasks are validated against those functions of the system to be carried out directly by the users. This is an exceptionally good check, not only on the completeness of both documents, but also on whether the HCI staff and those analysts responsible for producing the requirements specification have carried out their jobs correctly.

10.4 HCI DESIGN

Once task specification has been completed and reviewed, the next stage is to carry out a detailed design of the interface in terms of the interaction between the user and the system. The task specification should drive this design process. An important component of the process is an adequate notation for expressing the interaction. There are a number of notations, and Fig. 10.2 shows a particularly appealing one which illustrates how a user progresses through the facilities of a system. The diagram, which superficially looks like the type of graphical notation used in CASE technology, describes the flow of a system in terms of the actions taken by the user and the responses given by the system. Each bubble in the diagram represents a state that the system is in awaiting some response from a user. Each arc in the diagram represents the transition from one state to another. Every arc is labelled with a number which refers to an entry in a table. The arrows which do not point at any bubbles represent connections to other parts of the diagram which are not shown. Table 10.1 shows a fragment of such a table. The numbers which label arcs represent the event which caused the transition, the response of the system, and a

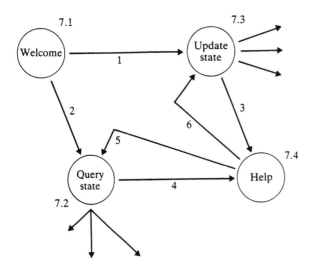

Figure 10.2 The documentation of user interaction.

Table 10.1 A fragment of a transition table

Transition	Action	Screen
1	Update command initiated	TOP-UPDATE
2	Query command initiated	TOP-QUERY
3	Help facility for update initiated	HELP-UPDATE
4	Help facility for query initiated	HELP-QUERY
5	Return from query help	TOP-QUERY
6	Return from update help	TOP-UPDATE

reference to any screens or windows which will be displayed when the transition occurs. These are written into the table displayed (shown as Table 10.1).

Normally, since screen and window design is generally left until a later stage of the project—usually programming—the final column of the table is left blank. In Table 10.1, the third entry describes the fact that the user has initiated a HELP facility which results in a transition from state 7.3 to 7.4, with the result that a help facility window is displayed, the screen associated with this facility being HELP-UPDATE. Another possible validation exercise that could be scheduled when such an HCI design is produced is an HCI design review. There would be three major documents that would form an input into this process: the task specification, the system design, and the HCI design specification itself. The aims of the review are twofold: first, review staff examine the task specification and check that each task has been implemented as part of the interface; then they examine the system design and the HCI design in order to check that there are modules in the design which invoke the HCI facilities and that they correspond to the functions being exercised by the user.

> **Self Assessment Question 10.4** Who would you invite to this review?
>
> **Solution** The member of staff who designed the interface would be invited; also, the designer of the overall system. The remainder of the participants would be free for the project manager to choose. I would invite an HCI designer from another project and a senior programmer who has responsibility for some implementation aspects of the project.

At this stage in the project, assuming that both the HCI design review and the task specification review are completed successfully, the architectural features of the design will be complete and the project will have started implementation of the system.

The role of the HCI staff at this stage of the project is to carry out the detailed design of the screens or windows that make up the human interface part of the system. There are two quality documents which are required for this. The first is a document which describes guidelines for screen and window design. Such a document would offer advice on screen layout, amount of information, use of tabular displays, the display of colours, and the use of effects such as flashing, inverse video and underlining.

The second is some form of standard for specifying the screens or windows that are to be designed. A good standard is normally very simple and contains a typical screen with the fields highlighted, together with bubbles which provide an explanation of the components of the screen. What is important about this notation is that it should be readily understandable by the programmer: that staff responsible for developing the modules which implement the interface can understand the meaning of each field, the data it is associated with, the format of the data, and the use of facilities such as inverse video.

10.5 HCI EVALUATION

Evaluation is the process of validating the HCI part of a system in order to check that it is usable by the group of users who will normally employ it. The evaluation process can occur at two points in the development process: at the beginning of development when system requirements are being elicited, or after implementation. If it occurs at the front-end of the software project, then it is normally used in conjunction with some form of prototyping: the development of an early flawed working version of a system. If it occurs at the back-end of a project, then it becomes part of the system testing and acceptance testing process. Prototyping and its QA implications were dealt with in Chapter 9; this section examines post-implementation evaluation. There are five ways of evaluating a system (Preece, Benyon *et al.*, 1993):

- The notation used to express the interface is analysed. Here, properties of the interface notation, such as the number of bubbles in a graphical diagram, are used as an input into the process of producing qualitative judgements about the effectiveness of the interface.
- The interface is evaluated by experts.

- Observational techniques, where users interacting with an interface are directly observed, and measurements such as the number of errors made, are used to judge the effectiveness of the interface.
- Questionnaires are used to evaluate users' perception of usefulness.
- Experimental methods are used to explore hypotheses about the interface.

This is not a book about HCI design, so I will not describe each of these techniques in detail. What I will do is to examine one technique, that based on observation, and look at the QA implications. In general these are the same as for any other technique. There are a number of ways of carrying out observational evaluation (Benyon, Preece *et al.,* 1993):

- *Direct observation.* Here an observer examines users interacting with a system.
- *Video recording.* Where a video camera is unobtrusively positioned in order to record the user's activity.
- *Software logging.* Where the system whose interface is to be evaluated is modified by inserting probes that record the interaction between the user and the system.
- *Interactive observation.* Here a human operator pretends to be the system. He or she intercepts user input and attempts to amend system output in order to reduce the problems with an interface.
- *Verbal protocols.* Here a user interacts with the system and, at the same time, voices his or her thoughts into a tape recorder.

The impacts of this form of evaluation on a QA system are various. First, the project plan should describe the evaluation method that is to be used, predict the resources needed, and outline when, during system or acceptance testing, it occurs. For example, for most projects customers are not too concerned about specifying acceptance criteria for the human–computer interface and simply state that it should be usable. Here, the developer would only employ evaluation during system testing in order to iron out any problems with an interface; resources should hence be specified only for the system testing phase. In some cases, however, the customer may be very keen to specify acceptance criteria. This occurs often with safety-critical systems, which have considerable human interaction and where the customer may specify that certain classes of error should never happen, certain classes occur at a certain rate, and so on. In this case the software developer may choose one method for system testing, such as direct observation,. and use the results from software logging, applied during acceptance testing, to provide evidence that it is highly likely that HCI acceptance criteria will be met during operation.

What is important is that if a technique such as direct observation is used, the resources, acceptance criteria and the reason for using the techniques should be described in the project plan. It is also important that if a combination of methods is used, the way in which they interact is specified. The project plan should also describe what data is to be extracted from observational studies: metrics such as the number of times a command was invoked, the frequency of errors, and the percentage of correct recovery from an error.

The project plan should also provide a rationale which describes why the chosen evaluation method has been selected. The choice of evaluation method is determined primarily by the results of a risk analysis; for example, observational evaluation is a very good way of rapidly pinpointing difficulties in an interface and provides an excellent, large quantity of qualitative data. However, it suffers from a major problem in that it requires quite a large amount of human resources and can also be very time-consuming. If the risk analysis pointed out problems such as the fact that the customer was not able to specify exactly the skills that users will have, that the system to be developed was critical in terms of operators not making many errors, that inexperienced staff are involved in developing the interface, and so on, then the resources required for observational evaluation would be fully justified.

Another important factor is the recording of the evaluation. Observational evaluation gives rise to a large amount of unstructured notes which are generated while observing human operators. This should be summarized in a document known as an *HCI Evaluation Report*, which forms part of the quality records for a project. This document should be divided into sections corresponding to each task, with the results of evaluations concerning each task summarized in some convenient form such as a table. For an evaluation technique which uses questionnaires, a table would summarize the attitudes of the users towards the interface. For observational evaluation, a table would summarize the tasks that were carried out, for example errors made, successful recoveries from an error carried out, any examples of the user taking a considerable time to carry out a task, and the number of times a help facility was invoked.

10.6 POSTSCRIPT

The important point to stress about the development of the human–computer interface is that it is an engineering task, and the same principles which govern other engineering tasks on the software project should be adhered to. For example in Chapter 1 I stressed the fact that software documentation should have a high degree of traceability. This same principle holds for HCI documentation: a reader of the HCI documentation of a project should be able to trace from the task specification to the HCI design, from the HCI design to the individual specification of screens, windows and menus, and from these to the modules which implement the interface. As well as this, there should also be traceability through HCI from the requirements specification to the task specification and hence into the remainder of the HCI documents.

10.7 QUALITY MANUAL REQUIREMENTS

The following documents which are concerned with the human–computer interface should be found in a quality manual. Normally, they are bound as one document which is often called the *Human–Computer Interface Standards and Procedures*:

1. User/environment questionnaire checklist
2. HCI design rationale standard
3. HCI design rationale procedure
4. Task specification standard
5. Task specification procedure
6. Task specification review standard

7. Task specification review procedure
8. HCI design review standard
9. HCI design review procedure
10. Screen and window design guidelines
11. Screen and window specification standard
12. Interface evaluation procedure
13. Interface evaluation guidelines
14. HCI evaluation report standard.

10.8 SUMMARY

Consideration of the human–computer interface is often omitted from quality systems. This is a major mistake. The interface is the part of a system which initially gives the user his or her first impression of its quality. A good quality system should offer staff a number of facilities connected with the development of the human–computer interface: these include facilities for specifying and evaluating an interface, together with guidelines which describe the overall design of the interface and the design and implementation of components such as screens.

10.9 FURTHER READING

Preece, Benyon *et al.* (1993) is a book written by a number of my colleagues at the Open University. It is an excellent introduction to the human–computer interface and provides a splendid overview of the process of developing customer-friendly interfaces. Schneiderman (1987) is a slightly academic book which, however, contains plenty of material that can be used for writing standards and procedures which govern the process of developing the human–computer interface.

PROBLEMS

10.1 For the first four bullet points on page 149 describe why these questions are important to the system developer.

10.2 What would you expect in a standard for a *textual* notation for task specification?

10.3 What sort of problems do you think HCI evaluation would pin-point?

SOFTWARE METRICS

AIMS

- To describe what a software metric is.
- To outline some of the uses of software metrics.
- To describe the relationship between software metrics and quality assurance.
- To briefly describe some of the main product metrics.
- To outline a methodology for the development and use of metrics.

11.1 INTRODUCTION

The aim of this chapter is to provide an introduction to the subject, describe some of the more useful metrics and show how even the least ambitious software developer can derive metrics which are useful.

11.2 AN EXAMPLE

In order to describe what metrics are, and how they can be useful, it is worth looking at an isolated software task: that of module programming.

System design is the process of defining a modular architecture of a system and specifying the processing that occurs in each module of a system design. Programmers take module specifications, program them and then test them using test data which checks the functionality of the module and exercises the program code. There are a number of factors which make the programming task difficult.

First, there is the module specification. The larger or longer this description, the more effort will be required to produce the module. The second difficulty is the degree to which the control flow of the module is unstructured. For example, the more criss-crossing of control flow the more difficult it will be to understand the logic of the module and test it.

A third problem is the way in which a module is connected to other modules. For example, if a module calls a number of other modules, then the process of debugging this module will be very difficult: keeping details of data affected by called modules can clutter up the programmer's memory to the extent that errors in tracing control flow in the module being debugged occur.

These, then, are three ways in which structural features of a module can affect the programming, testing and debugging process. These can be possibly quantified and expressed as numbers. For example, the length of the narrative describing a module's functionality could be a good indicator of the difficulty in implementing the module or the number of control flow criss-crossings might be a good indicator of the degree of difficulty of testing a module.

Self Assessment Question 11.1 Do you think that the derivation of the number of criss-crossings in a module is a difficult process?

Solution Done by hand it is tedious and error-prone. However, a software tool which extracts the control structure of the code of a module would calculate this metric easily.

The aim of metrics research is to derive key features which can be quantified and which can then be used for quality assurance processes. In software engineering there are a myriad of possible numeric quantities that can be extracted which may have a relationship with some activity which a quality system addresses. Some examples are shown below:

- The number of modules in a system design being an indicator of the amount of resources needed for implementation.
- The number of parameters in a module being an indicator of the amount of resource required to implement the module.
- The number of bubbles in a data flow diagram being an indicator of the size of a system to be implemented.
- The number of variables in a module being an indicator of the degree of difficulty that a programmer will find in debugging the module.

The main activity that metrics researches carry out is deriving such metrics and validating them: showing that they correlate with some key project activity such as system testing or programming.

Self Assessment Question 11.2 Why would the number of parameters in a module be an indicator of the amount of work required to implement the module?

Solution The number of parameters in a module is usually a good indication of the amount of functionality bound up in the module. For example, a module which has a single integer parameter often just updates that parameter, while a module which has a number of array parameters usually carries out quite a degree of looping amongst the arrays.

11.3 DEFINITIONS

Before looking at some of the main families of metrics it is worth looking at some definitions.

First, a *product metric* is a measure which can be extracted from a document or file which forms part of a quality system. Typical documents include the program code or system design. A *process metric* is some number which can be extracted from a process on a software project. One example of such a metric is the time taken to design a system. A *predictor metric* is a metric, normally a product metric, which has the potential to predict another metric known as a *result metric*. So, for example, the length of a module used to predict the amount of resource required to implement the module is a predictor metric while the amount of resource is the result metric.

11.4 THE USES OF A METRIC

There are a number of uses of a metric including the predictive use outlined in the previous chapter.

- *As a numerical quality threshold.* This is probably the most popular use of a metric currently. If a metric has been found to have a good relationship with some result metric, then a quality standard might insist that staff carrying out a particular task do not produce artefacts whose metric values exceed some threshold. For example, assume that a company has discovered that the number of control flow criss-crossing in a module determines the number of errors in that module, then they might insist that programmers do not create modules which exceed a particular value of criss-crossings.
- *As a predictive mechanism.* This is the aim of all metrics research: to be able to take a value of a particular predictor metric and then predict some result metric. This is not much used within a project for technical activities but there are now some metrics-based techniques which are used for project costing.
- *To keep track of the degradation of a software system.* During the software maintenance process the structure of a system usually degrades. Random patches applied by members of the maintenance department often result in a system structure which

looks tackier and tackier. Gradually the system becomes more and more difficult to maintain. System design metrics can be used to keep track on the degradation of a system and alert a project manager to the fact that he or she needs to allocate staff to the process of cleaning up the system.

11.5 A TOUR OF SOFTWARE METRICS

The aim of this section is to describe some of the main categories of product metric which are available.

11.5.1 Code metrics

These metrics are those which can be directly extracted from program code. A typical code metric might be the number of declarations in a program.

Code metrics have been the most popular metrics with both researchers and industrialists. There are two reasons for this: first, they are easily extractable since program code is always held in files; and, second, they are quite easy to extract. The development of the program code of a tool for extracting code-based metrics is a regular exercise given to second-year computer science students.

Much of the work on code metrics that has been carried out has been inspired by the late American computer scientist Maurice Halstead (Halstead, 1977). He postulated that useful properties of programs can be found by extracting the operands and operators from the programs. An operand is typically an identifier, while an operand is either some arithmetic operator such as * or a sequencing operator such as repeat.

Halstead's work was all-pervasive. The vast majority of metrics papers written in the seventies directly cited his work. However, in the eighties it has fallen into disrepute. There are two reasons for this. First, a number of researchers have pointed out that very little statistical correlation can be found between the counts that Halstead specified and important tasks such as debugging. The second reason is that you cannot do anything really useful with a metric extracted from program code. By the implementation stage of a project much of the project's developmental resources will have been consumed and there will be very little scope for using the metrics information, for example in modifying a system design.

11.5.2 Detailed design metrics

These are metrics which can be extracted from a detailed design: they are often called *graph metrics* or *control flow metrics*. They arose from work carried out by the American computer scientist Thomas McCabe, who developed probably the most famous detailed design metric known as the *cyclomatic complexity metric*. A tool for extracting detailed design metrics examines the control flow of a module or program and extracts the sequence of instructions that make up conditional statements and loops. It then calculates some metrics based on the degree of unstructuredness of the module or program.

The main use of a detailed design metric is as a quality threshold. Often programmers are instructed not to exceed a cyclomatic complexity number for the modules which they program.

11.5.3 System design metrics

The major problems with both code and detailed design metrics is that they are extracted too late in a project where little can be done if poor values are discovered. Because of this the eighties saw an increasing trend towards the development of system design metrics: numbers which can be extracted from a document that describe the modular architecture of a system.

The driving idea behind the vast majority of system design metrics is that the quality of a good design can be quantified by examining the degree of coupling and cohesion that can be found in the design. Coupling and cohesion measure the degree to which a module in a system is connected to other modules. A module which is lightly coupled can be read, developed and understood in isolation and, hence, can be debugged more easily and integrated more easily.

Normally, system design metrics try and extract features which are related to coupling and cohesion. Tools for extracting these measures count entities such as the amount of access there is to global variables and the degree of calling of other modules there are in specific modules. The most popular system design metrics are due to Kafura and Henry (Henry, 1981) and Shepperd (Shepperd and Ince, 1990).

11.6 THE DERIVATION OF METRICS

One of the problems with the use of metrics is that industrial users tend to take an off-the-shelf attitude towards their use on a project: in effect they pick one well-known metric and hope that it works. The aim of this section is to counteract this tendency, and outline a more goal-oriented method for devising metrics for both a company and the software projects it undertakes. The method is due to Victor Basili and his co-workers at the University of Maryland (Basili and Rombach, 1988). The method is known as the Goal Question Metric method (GQM).

The main starting point in GQM is a goal. Any metric extracted in a project must reflect some purpose, and the first thing that someone who wishes to use metrics has to do is to ask some questions about what the reason for gathering metrics is.

Once the goals have been decided, the next stage is to ask a number of questions which clarify the goals (the Q part of GQM). Most goals tend to be expressed in nebulous terms and the questions enable staff to focus in on some metrics. For example, a company may wish to employ a metric to satisfy the goal that their projects deliver fewer residual errors through more thorough testing. A number of questions suggest themselves from this:

- What sort of thoroughness is implied in the question?
- Does the question imply thorough functional testing?
- Does the question imply thorough structural testing?
- Do the errors that are left in a system through poor testing arise from poor performance on a particular phase?
- How can we identify errors which remain in a system which have arisen from poor testing?

Once these questions have been answered, the next stage is to identify the metrics which are important. Let us assume that the company who have asked the above questions have identified the fact that the vast majority of errors that emerge during operation are due to inadequate module testing: that programmers tend to inadequately test certain paths and conditions. One metric which might be identified as helping to reduce structural testing errors is the condition coverage achieved by a programmer: that if every condition that was exercised in a module was executed for its true and false values, then there would be a considerable reduction in the number of testing-related errors from operation.

The next stage is to identify a hypothesis or set of hypotheses which can be tested in the developer's projects. Let us assume that a possible hypothesis is this:

> That by insisting on 100 per cent condition coverage we will reduce the number of residual errors due to inadequate module testing by 98 per cent.

This is rather a strong hypothesis, both in terms of the hard numbers used and also in terms of what might be possible on a software project, since deriving test data for 100 per cent condition coverage is mightily difficult. The hypothesis can be relaxed to a lower percentage.

Once the hypothesis has been derived the next stage is to plan the measurement process on some sample projects which attempt to validate the hypothesis. For example, this might involve, for the testing example, activities such as writing a small software tool which tracked condition coverage, modifying test documentation to include details of condition coverage, introducing an extra procedure for those staff charged with fielding errors from customers and providing resources to track down the source of the errors.

Once the measurement process has been planned, the next stage would be to collect the data. With the example used here this would mean collecting coverage percentages and defect data identified as being due to module errors. Once this data is collected the next stage is to use statistics to validate it. The statistics would be used to check out the hypothesis. Sometimes the hypothesis has a high degree of truth in it, since after all it is conjectured by experienced staff, but it may need some amendment. For example, it might be discovered that the size of the interface of the module has an effect on the number of residual errors due to inadequate testing.

Eventually, after trial and error, the developer will either validate the hypothesis or a variant. The final stage, then, is to apply the metric to all future projects. For example, if the hypothesis above was modified to:

> That by insisting on 85 per cent condition coverage we will reduce the number of residual errors due to inadequate module testing by 95 per cent.

Then programmers on future projects would be directed, via a module programming and test standard, to provide evidence that their functional tests have covered 85 per cent of the true and false outcomes of the conditions in a module.

The stages in this process of metrics identification and eventual application in the GQM method are:

- The definition and clarification of goals.
- The posing of questions in order to make the goals clearer.

- The derivation of metrics.
- The identification of hypotheses which involve these metrics.
- The planning of the measurement process.
- The collection of data from the measurement process.
- The validation of the data.
- The analysis of the data.
- The application of the derived metrics on future projects.

It is worth stressing that this is rarely a strictly linear process. For example, the posing of questions often modifies the goal and the analysis of the data often results in the modification of the hypotheses. Nevertheless, it forms a useful way of developing metrics which can lead to considerable process improvement.

11.7 FURTHER READING

Fenton (1991) is a good introduction to metrics technology. Be warned, however, that it occasionally becomes quite mathematical. Kitchenham (1992) is an excellent tutorial on metrics. An excellent feature of this book is a large annotated bibliography. Two excellent books on the implementation of metrics on industrial projects are Grady and Caswell (1987) and Goodman (1993). The former describes the implementation of a metrics programme at Hewlett-Packard; the latter is the distillation of one of Europe's most experienced metrics practitioners. A good project-specific case study can be found in Durst, Stark and Pelnik (1992).

PROBLEMS

11.1 What aspects of a module expressed in a third-generation language do you think could be quantified and used as a metric for characterizing difficulty of debugging?

11.2 Write down part of a procedure which describes the fact that a programmer is not allowed to develop a module which has a cyclomatic complexity higher than 10.

11.3 How might you use a detailed design metric to influence the integration activities on a software project?

11.4 Can you think of some metrics which can be used to determine the degree of readability of a requirements document, say a statement of requirements produced by a customer?

12

PROCESS MODELLING AND PROCESS ASSESSMENT

AIMS

- To describe the rationale behind process modelling.
- To describe some notations used in process modelling.
- To outline the nature of process assessment.
- To describe some process assessment schemes.
- To describe how process assessment is able to guide process improvement.

12.1 INTRODUCTION

When you ask to look at a company software quality manual, more often than not you will be given a large, but rather unorganised document to look at. Some pages will be written in natural language, some might be documented as flow charts and others may only be sketched in the most abstract way. To read and extract information from such a document can be a very difficult process; for example, it might be very time-consuming to discover the source of a document which forms part of an important process such as system testing. One of the aims of the research topic known as *process modelling* is to provide notations which can be used to describe the processes that make up a software project in such a way that information about these processes required by managers, technical staff and quality assurance personnel can be obtained quickly and efficiently. It is worth re-emphasizing that process modelling is still a research topic. However, I would consider it sufficiently advanced that the results from research should start impinging on projects in the near future; hence, its brief inclusion in this book.

Probably your first reaction to reading this chapter is: why should we go to a great deal of trouble in researching this area? Software projects are all rather similar; they merely consist of a series of tasks which are executed sequentially, with the output from one task being input into the next. All that is needed is simple descriptions. This is far from the truth; the sequential model of software development which I presented in Chapter 2 is almost a myth. This will become clear from the following two examples.

The first example is the large project which has a long duration. Such projects will be affected by requirements changes throughout their life. These changes will often necessitate simultaneous changes to the requirements specifications, system design, program code, and test suites. The changes give rise to a large amount of parallelism; for example, redesign due to a requirements change may be carried out at the same time as programming. To keep track of all these changes—within a number of parallel processes—requires a fairly complicated configuration management system, particularly if the developer produces software packages. Because of the high degree of parallelism, and the information needs of a large number of staff, there is a requirement for some sort of process modelling notation to let staff know what is required to happen when changes need to be processed.

The second example is the prototyping project which has a number of subsystems that are being prototyped in parallel. Each analyst or programmer assigned to the prototyping process will be modifying his or her subsystem in response to change requests by the customer. Normally, in such a project, there will be some central data architecture which each analyst or programmer needs access to via the prototype they have constructed. Now during the process of prototype development analysts will want to make changes to this data architecture in response to customer change requests. Unfortunately, a change arising from the prototyping of one subsystem may slow down another system or even invalidate some of its functions. Clearly, there is a need for some coordination and a way of specifying how it is executed. This coordination is carried out in parallel, and ways of specifying it using natural language may give rise to major problems in interpretation.

Self Assessment Question 12.1 From your reading of the previous section could you sum up in a sentence why process modelling is useful?

Solution Process modelling is useful because it is a way of documenting and controlling the immense complexity that occurs in modern software projects.

12.2 PROCESSES AND PROCESS MODELS

Before looking at process modelling it is worth defining what I mean by a *process*. This is a task in a software project which progresses the project towards one or more of its goals. For example, a design review is a process, as it progresses the project towards its goal of achieving the correctness quality factor and, if the design review included a checklist which evaluated maintainability, then it progresses the project towards achieving its maintainability quality factor.

A process will consist of a number of *process steps*. These are actions which cannot be decomposed into any further subatomic actions; for example, a process step of booking a room may make up the process of carrying out a design review. While a pedant may point out that the task of booking a room could be split up into other steps, such as using a telephone and talking to the clerk in charge of room bookings, within the context of a project where using a telephone and speaking to a booking clerk are well understood a process step would be at a higher level.

Self Assessment Question 12.2 Would the activity of carrying out a requirements elicitation meeting with the customer be an example of a process step?

Solution No, it really consists of a number of steps such as filling in a form after the meeting, updating the requirements specification and, perhaps, booking a room.

A process model is a description of the interlinking processes that occur in a software project with irrelevant detail, such as the use of a telephone in booking a room, omitted. There are a number of uses for process models (Kellner, Curtis and Over, 1992):

- *To support human understanding and communication.* This is the use alluded to above. For example, if a company has a well-defined notation for expressing the processes in its projects, and it is used in all these projects, then there will be few problems in interpreting process descriptions when staff come to carry out a process.
- *To support process improvement.* Chapter 16 of this book stresses that a company should always aim to monitor the effectiveness of its quality system. It should also aim to improve its development processes. Process modelling aims to help both these tasks. For this, a company should have a well-established set of standard processes which can be measured; for example, the process of module programming would have a number of measures associated with it, including time to complete the module, length of the module, and a metric such as the density of Boolean conditions in the program code. By having standard process templates, a developer is able to easily compare the effect on, say, productivity, of a change in technology—for example, the effect of a configuration management tool from project to project—since each project would effectively employ the same standard process template.
- *To support project management and quality assurance.* In Chapter 1 I described the fact that in developing a quality plan and project organization, a manager will consult a quality manual and select those aspects of the manual suitable for the project. In carrying out this selection the project manager would consider quality factors, the current business policy of the company, the risk inherent in the project, and the nature of the customer. This tailoring can be immensely difficult if the processes which are available to the manager—both developmental and quality assurance processes—are expressed in a non-standard way in the quality manual and its associated documentation. The eventual aim of process modelling is to enable a project manager to consult a database of process descriptions, tailor all or some of the processes to the particular project that is started, and, eventually, join up the process descriptions in the same way as a jigsaw. The 'jigsaw' would form an overall description of the process architecture of the system in terms of entities such as process details, data flows, documents, and decision points. This description can then be given to a project manager who

ensures that his or her project enacts the process architecture by carrying out the processes in a designated way.

- *To provide automated guidance for staff performing a process.* Again, the eventual target which researchers in process modelling aim for is the ability to automate processes in such a way that a member of staff who is carrying out a process, such as system testing, can call up, via software tools, information such as procedures, standards and guidelines which enables him or her to carry out his or her jobs effectively.

- *To aid automated execution support.* The eventual aim of process modelling research is to be able to develop notations for expressing the process architecture of software projects, so that staff who carry out developmental activities are provided with software tools which not only help them to carry out their developmental tasks, but also generate data which can be used by project management or by the quality assurance department. For example, defect data used in the process of evaluating the effectiveness of a quality system, and defined in the process model, can be used to improve technical processes such as design. The dream of many process modelling researchers is of a central database which holds the process architecture of a project. When staff carry out a particular process, such as module testing, they would be prompted by a tool which would consult the database and guide the user through the steps required to carry out the process, calling in any tools that were required automatically, based on information within the process model database.

12.3 NOTATIONS FOR PROCESS MODELLING

Much of the research currently being carried out on process modelling concerns notations used to construct process models. Indeed, perhaps one of the main criticisms that one can make about the research is the panoply of notations that have been proposed, including those based on programming languages; mathematics; object-oriented technology; grammars; graphical notations similar to those used for requirements analysis; notations used to express concurrency; artificial intelligence notations; and project planning notations. Indeed, this book contains an example of a fragment of notation on page 186.

A fragment of a graphical notation based on data flow is shown in Fig. 12.1. It shows the initial stages of the process of programming and testing a module. The circles represent standards which are to be used for a process, while the three-edged objects represent products of the process which could be reused by that process or another process. It is important to point out that this is only a fragment of the module programming and testing process. The arrows which lead to mid-air point at the remainder of the process.

Self Assessment Question 12.3 Can you give two reasons why the notation shown in Fig 12.1 is a good one for process modelling?

Solution It can be understood by all staff on a project, both technical and managerial. It is also a notation to which CASE technology can be applied.

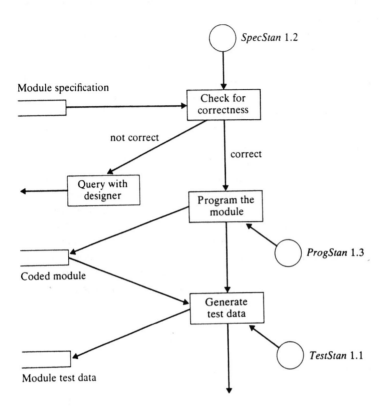

Figure 12.1 An example of a graphical process modelling notation.

There are three aspects to a notation used for process modelling. First, it should describe the processing which occurs; for example, when a test procedure is applied it should detail the tasks that make up that process. Second, it should describe who carried out a particular process. This may be expressed as a single person, group of persons or, more likely, in terms of job function. Third, it should give details of the data and information that is required and generated when a process is carried out. For example, a process description for programming a module should describe the process steps involved in the programmer receiving a module specification, producing code and testing the code; standards for programming and module testing; and the production of a coded module, a test suite and a quality record which confirms that adequate testing has been carried out.

A good process modelling notation should not only include these features, but should also provide facilities where each of the features can be isolated from the others. For example, a manager who wants to know the flow of a document through a project—who initiates the document, who reads it, who signs it off and where it is eventually stored—does not want the tool that he or she uses to browse through a process model database to display information such as step-by-step procedures which would clutter up the process of finding out about data flow.

One of the main arguments currently being fought out by researchers is how formal the language for process modelling should be. On the one hand, there are proponents who, motivated by the need to develop project support environments and software tools, say that the notation used to model processes should be as exact as a programming language—indeed, should look like a programming language. On the other hand, there are researchers who point out that human beings require other qualities apart from formality in a notation which describes the tasks that they are expected to carry out on a software project. They state that, for example, human beings are quite good at carrying out instructions which are ambiguous, but require expressiveness and comprehensibility from a notation (Kellner, Curtis and Over, 1992).

It is difficult to predict the way that process modelling notations will move. If this was the eighties I would say that they would progress towards becoming more formal. However, one of the lessons that we learnt in the eighties was that different users of a technology required different facilities from that technology. For process modelling, the range of users of process notations is so large—ranging from business managers to programmers—that I suspect the process modelling notation which is totally formal will be a rarity. I suspect a more likely scenario is of a core process modelling notation which might be formal but which will have a number of instantiations depending on the user who is employing the notation. For example, project managers may have an instantiation of the notation which is graphical, programmers may see an instantiation which looks like a programming language, and customers may see a sort of constrained natural language version of the model.

12.4 INDIVIDUAL PROCESS IMPROVEMENT

As an example of how process modelling can be useful for the company which at least has ISO 9000 certification comes from technical reviews. A technical review is a meeting of staff who examine a particular document, usually a requirements specification, system design or program code, and then attempt to discover defects. Normally technical reviews are used as a validation technique; in a company which is at least at a high level 3 within the process maturity framework, the results of these reviews can be used to improve a number of development processes as well as technical reviews themselves.

A company which does not have a well-defined process may have technical reviews available in their quality system; however, since they are not well-defined the amount of variation between reviews will give rise to so many parameters that a statistical analysis which attempted to answer questions such as: 'Is our design notation at fault?' or 'Are particular parts of a design prone to errors?' would be difficult to answer without a prohibitively large amount of generated data. However, if technical reviews are strictly governed by process descriptions which describe factors such as who attends, maximum duration, the accompanying documentation that is to be used and the documentation that is to be issued after a review, then there is a much greater chance that conventional statistical analyses can be carried out—although it must be said that it is only companies that have generated a large amount of data, and regularly update a statistical database, that are able to take full advantage of the process improvement opportunities offered by process modelling.

A typical process improvement sequence for a very advanced company is:

- The company has a strict design notation standard which all software engineers have to adhere to.
- Technical reviews are governed by a process template which can be instantiated for different reviews.
- A review is held according to the process template.
- Errors are detected in the design.
- These errors are rectified by the designer and the chair of the review issues a defect report which details *what* errors occurred and *where* they occurred.
- The error data is entered into a database of past errors and correlations are made between the location of the errors and some metric which measures design complexity. It is discovered that the errors are highly correlated with the design metric.
- At the next revision of the quality system the design procedure is modified to insist that designs should not normally be developed which have a metric value higher than some threshold. If a designer wishes to exceed this threshold he or she must gain the permission of the technical member of staff he or she reports to.

12.5 AN EXAMPLE OF PROCESS MODELLING IN ACTION

The special issue of the journal *Information and Software Technology* (Vol. 35 No. 6/7 July 93) describes a case study from IBM of process modelling in action. What is interesting about this case study is the fact that fairly low-tech ideas were used to carry out process improvement based on the process model that was discovered and documented by the IBM staff. For example, for the most part, pencil and paper drawings were used.

The Federal Systems Company in IBM develops software for government and state bodies in the USA. A team based in the company have used process modelling to try to integrate the processes that they use for software development. This activity arose because of problems the company encountered with confusion about roles and responsibilities, poor communication about the products of software development, the omission and duplication of work, the limited spread of new technology and sluggish response to customer and business needs.

The team led by a senior manager at IBM, Mike Dyer, used relatively low-level technology to document the various processes. The main notations they used were system flow diagrams and tables. Even with such low-level technology the modelling produced major gains. One of the main areas they identified for improvement was reuse. The modelling that was carried out identified a large scope for reuse over and above that already practised at IBM. The team identified major opportunities for the reuse of parts of requirements documents and also major chunks of testing documentation; they even managed to identify reuse potential in areas such as product training and field support.

The second benefit, over and above those being sought, was that the ability to collect measurements on a software project had been greatly increased. IBM are very advanced in their use of defect data generated from technical reviews to improve software tasks such as programming. However, a number of activities generated data on defects which were ignored. The process modelling that occurred led the team to discover that defect data on activities such as system engineering and integration testing could be treated in the same way as existing defect data and provide a fuller view of the efficiency of individual projects.

12.6 PROCESS ASSESSMENT

Software companies vary in their competence. They range from those companies which are short-lived and who have virtually no forms of quality assurance to successful companies who have a quality system and have quality systems which are mature and are being regularly examined and improved. The last decade has seen a number of attempts to try and develop schemes which attempt to give an idea of where a company is in both developmental and quality terms.

There are a number of reasons for having such schemes. First, customers are naturally interested in the capability of a software developer and an independently developed assessment of a software company's competence would be the main determinant of whether to use a company for some software task. Second, many companies well understand that their software processes are not perfect and wish to know where they are in terms of some technical baseline and where improvement is needed. There have been a number of software assessment schemes. Virtually all are implemented by means of site visits, checklists and questionnaires by some independent body. The first of the significant schemes was developed by Watts Humphrey at the Software Engineering Institute in Carnegie-Mellon University.

Humphrey was an ex-senior staffer from IBM. He was tasked by the American Department of Defense (DOD) to produce some form of questionnaire which could be used to appraise their subcontractors. The DOD had had some very poor experiences with subcontractors during the seventies and early eighties; this had led to large numbers of cancellations and of software being delivered which has not satisfied many of its critical requirements.

The DOD wanted some scheme whereby they could appraise software contractors and eliminate poor developers before development started.

The resulting questionnaire developed by Humphrey enabled the DOD to categorize software developers from level 1 to level 5:

- Companies at level 1 are in anarchy. There may be a quality system or, more likely, a quality manual; however, whether a project takes on standards, procedures and individual quality controls depends on the whim of project managers.
- Companies at level 2 have more control over their projects. This is established by means of proper project planning, task monitoring, the proper management of subcontractors and decent configuration management. At this stage process modelling starts to become a useful tool.
- At level 3 a company has an organisation-wide process which can be tailored to individual projects. The process model becomes an asset which can be refined through experience.
- The big change comes at level 4 when processes are instrumented and measurements are made. Typical measurements would involve product metrics and defect statistics. At this level industrial statistical quality control can be employed in order to ascertain the effect of changes to the process model. For example, a developer may use facilities provided in a level 4 quality system to examine whether technical reviews of code are more productive than module testing.
- Level 5 companies use the data generated by metrics in order to continually drive improvement programmes.

> **Self Assessment Question 12.4** At what level would a company be who had a quality system which applied a quality plan to each project, but where there was no auditing of projects to ensure that they adhered to the quality plan?
>
> **Solution** The company would be at level 1.

It is at levels 4 and 5 where process modelling comes into its own, and is most useful because of its link with process improvement.

This initiative was followed by a number of others. There are in existence about ten process assessment programmes. The best known British one was developed by the Institute of Software Engineering (now MARI Northern Ireland). While such programmes are very useful, many companies can carry out relatively quick health checks by asking a selection of questions.

Some typical questions are shown below; a full selection, cross-referenced to the chapters of this book, is reproduced as an Appendix:

- Does your system documentation have built-in traceability?
- What efforts do you take to validate a design?
- Do you always use the same quality manual, or do you orient your quality plan to each project by extracting or removing elements from the quality manual?
- How do you evaluate the effectiveness of your quality system?
- What records exist which demonstrate that a programmer has carried out a test?
- Does your quality manual cover the risk analysis that a project manager often has to carry out at the beginning of a project?

12.7 SUMMARY

Process modelling is a term used to define the process of describing the individual tasks that make up a software project in some standardized way. Process models have a number of uses: to support human understanding and communication; to support process improvement; to support project management and quality assurance; to provide guidance to staff carrying out a software process; and to aid automated execution support. Process assessment is concerned with making some judgement—usually carried out independently—of a company's capability to develop software.

12.8 FURTHER READING

Process modelling is a topic that has interested researchers since the early seventies. However, the work which caused a huge flurry of interest in the subject is Humphrey (1989). This is an excellent book about managing the software development process. At the heart of the book is the 1 to 5 categorization that Humphrey developed for the DOD. Good descriptions of Humphrey's ideas in practice can be found in Gilchrist (1992) and

Hinsley and Bennet (1993). Humphrey has also described a case study which applied his ideas in Snyder, Humphrey and Willis (1991). Almost certainly the best tutorial introduction to process modelling is Kellner, Curtis and Over (1992). Details of a large number of process modelling notations can be found in this article.

PROBLEMS

12.1 Develop an outline questionnaire that can be used to judge whether the configuration management system used by a company is adequate.

12.2 Develop an outline questionnaire that can be used to judge whether the module testing standards used by a company are adequate.

12.3 How would you organize an assessment visit to a software company?

13

STANDARDS AND PROCEDURES

AIMS

- To describe the nature of standards and procedures.
- To give examples of standards and procedures.
- To show how standards and procedures can be formally developed.

13.1 INTRODUCTION

The aim of this chapter is practical: it is to show how standards and procedures are developed.

> **Self Assessment Question 13.1** Can you remember what the distinction between a standard and a procedure is? It was detailed in Chapter 1.
>
> **Solution** A standard specifies what a project document looks like, while a procedure is a description of how a particular task is to be carried out.

Something like 80 per cent to 90 per cent of the effort of implementing a quality system is spent on writing documents which specify how certain tasks are to be carried out (procedures), and how information on documents is to be presented (standards). One of the options taken by software developers when constructing a quality system is to hire a consultant in quality assurance to work on the task of writing standards and procedures; normally, what this consultant would do is to take a pre-written quality manual, and adapt it to the company for whom he or she temporarily works. There are a number of drawbacks in this approach. The first is that even general pre-written standards and procedures tend to require a major effort to adapt them to a company's circumstances—almost as much effort as writing the standards and procedures anew. The second drawback—and probably the most important—is that the adaptation of existing standards and procedures tends to be something of a solitary exercise, with little interaction between the consultant and staff in the company: since the standards and procedures exist there is little incentive for the consultant to involve staff in their construction.

This is a major mistake: it is an important principle that when a quality system is developed, the staff who have to operate under that system must feel that they have had a major say in its construction.

13.2 THE STARTING POINT

The starting point in writing a standard or a procedure for a task is to question the staff involved in carrying it out. The first step is to question the staff, either directly or via a questionnaire, about the problems they have found with a particular task. Typical questions that you should ask are:

- Do you consider part of the task to be too time-consuming?
- Where do you find yourself making errors?
- What do you enjoy doing in the task?
- What do you not enjoy doing in the task?
- In the past, has an error committed in this task led to major problems in other tasks?

It is also worth while questioning project managers in order to see how poor performance of that task has affected their work. Typical questions to ask are:

- Has the poor performance of a task badly affected any of your projects?
- Is enough documentation issued from a task to allow you to monitor its effectiveness?
- Are you able to effectively monitor the completion of a task?
- If a task is a quality control, is there adequate evidence that the control has checked the quality factor that it was meant to check?

It is vitally important that the process of questioning is also applied to staff carrying out maintenance, as it is this category of staff who will provide the majority of material which enables you to develop a standard. Staff who carry out a task from new do not seem to be too concerned with standards and procedures; however, it is the staff who have to read specifications and program code for understanding, modify the documents and program code, and chase errors, who seem keenest on standards and procedures, and seem the most ready to answer questions about problems with software development.

In order to demonstrate how standards and procedures are developed I shall look at two tasks: unit or module programming, together with its associated testing activities, and carrying out a design review.

13.3 UNIT PROGRAMMING

This task involves the programmer receiving a specification of a module, programming that module, and then testing it. This is often one of the most poorly performed tasks on a software project—mainly because of inadequate standards. In order to describe the process of developing the standards and procedures for this task it is worth looking at some of the answers that might be obtained when staff are questioned about problems with the task:

1. I enjoy programming and I also enjoy testing the modules that I produce, but what I do not enjoy is the process of retesting. Often, a module is returned to me a number of weeks later for reprogramming. There are a number of reasons for this: sometimes the designer has made an error in the system design, more often there has been a requirements change from a customer, and occasionally I have made an error in programming. I really do not enjoy trying to think up my original test data again.
2. Sometimes I am asked to make a change to an existing module. I usually encounter two problems with this. The first is that it is often quite difficult to understand what the module is aiming to do. The second follows on from the first, in that when I have major difficulties in understanding the functionality of a module I have to find the programmer who wrote the module in order to ask him or her about it. This often means I have to spend a lot of time looking through past project files.
3. Many of the modules which I have to maintain are littered with variables which act as control flags. These pass information from one part of the module to another part. Often these flags just have names such as *flag1*, *flag2* and *flag3*, with little indication of what they do. Moreover, they seem to contain so much information that when I change one part of a module which contains references to these flags, I have to change other parts which reference the same flags.
4. I have major problems understanding the program code of a module. Some of our programmers nest their control structures to a horrendous depth. I once had to modify a program which had 16 loops and *if* statements. By the time I got inside the tenth control structure I was having great difficulty understanding what was happening in the module.
5. In the past we have had some major problems with programmers who have inadequately tested the modules that we have given them to program. In one case, a programmer felt so arrogant that all he did was to clean-compile a module and pass it on to the system testers. We have found that rectifying errors during system testing, which should have been detected during programming, is immensely expensive.
6. When I test a module I have to construct software which turns the module into an executable program; feeds test data to the program; calls the module; and displays the results of the module execution. This extra coding is relatively easy to write, but it is a repetitive task which I think could be automated.
7. One of the problems I have to face, particularly on the real-time systems that I maintain, is that of coding tricks where a programmer has implemented some strange piece of coding, either to increase response time or to save memory. Although this trick is usually very clever, it is terribly difficult for me to understand it. It wouldn't be so bad if the programmer was readily available; however, he or she has often left the company.

8. I wish I understood what the program variables mean.
9. I am often asked to apply some changes to a module. It can take me ages to find the file which contains the module and the name of the directory in which the file is held.
10. I have to spend a large amount of time finding out what progress has been made in programming a system. We instigated weekly meetings during which the programmers would report progress. However, I still feel it could be done better: meetings are valuable and I don't like cluttering them up with routine reporting.
11. I often receive the specification of a module which is poorly written. I have major problems in finding someone who can explain to me what the specification means. The design team are always so busy.
12. I don't know whether it is me, but I have real problems in debugging a module. In the end I have to insert a lot of debugging code and monitor the values of variables during execution. Can a quality system help me in this?

Self Assessment Question 13.2 What facility would a quality system offer to alleviate the problems detailed in the first point above?

Solution It would insist that all test data was stored and a proper convention was used to name the files containing this data.

Self Assessment Question 13.3 What facility would a quality system offer to alleviate the problems detailed in the fourth point above?

Solution It would specify as part of a programming standard that programmers were not allowed to nest control structures to more than a certain figure.

Self Assessment Question 13.4 What facility would a quality system offer to alleviate the problems detailed in the eighth point above?

Solution It would provide directions to the programmer for variable naming in the programming standard.

The first remark is quite a common one which emanates from staff who are involved in a wide variety of activities: it reflects the difficulty they have in retrieving a document, source code or data which they believed was in a final state. Many quality systems do not provide direction to staff about the storage of these various entities.

In this case, a programmer has not been instructed to store test data and test outcomes in a file. Also, the names of these files have not been specified. The solution to this problem is to include in the procedure an instruction to staff to create files to hold the test data, test output and, if a test harness is used, a file to hold the test harness. In addition, the programmer should be instructed to place the files in the directory which has been assigned to the project in which the modules have been developed. Moreover, the programmer should be told to name the files in such a way that the module name can be traced from the file name and vice versa, for example by using the first n characters of the module, where n is sufficiently large that duplication of file names will not occur. Also, the test data, test outcome and test harness files should each be distinguished in some way, for example by using the extension *tda* for test data, *to* for test outcomes, and *hr* for the test harness. If these instructions were followed, then hours would be saved when a change has to be applied to an existing module. Given that this is a common activity on a software project it can lead to a large amount of resources being saved from this measure alone.

The second remark is also a fairly common *cri-de-coeur*, which is not just associated with program code, but with designs and the functional specification part of the requirements specification. The solution to the problem is not easy: at a trivial level it requires the function of the module to be embedded in the module as a comment. The major problem here is that it is all too easy for staff responsible for specifying the functionality of a module—usually designers—to write a poor specification. The only solution to the problem is to hold a design review, and for the checklist for the design review to include a check that the functions of modules whose design is presented at the review are understandable, unambiguous and can be interpreted in software terms.

The sign-off of the parts of the system design considered in the review would be the quality control. It is also important that if functional descriptions of a module are passed to a programmer, say when a design review has not taken into account part of the functional description, then there should be a clearly defined way of communicating any problems in the functional description. As you will see in the following description, this means that the programmer should consult the member of staff to whom he or she reports. The other point made concerns who to ask if the functionality of a module is not clear. This is relatively trivial; however, it is surprising how much time that a programmer can spend chasing up staff who he or she believes was the author of the module whose functionality is difficult to discern. The solution to this problem is straightforward: it is to have a standard for module documentation which insists that the designer of the module is included as a comment inside the module.

The third remark concerns variables which have poorly chosen names. The quality system should insist that the names are well chosen and give examples. However, this remark conceals something much more serious than misnamed identifiers. Very often when a module contains flags, that module is carrying out a number of functions, and the flags are used to communicate and pass information between these functions. A well designed system will contain only modules which carry out one function and communicate with other modules by means of small interfaces. Such systems contain modules which are easy to read and understand in isolation, test in isolation, and integrate. The existence of modules with flags often indicates multi-functionality. These modules are horrendous to maintain, since a change to a function in the module often means a change to one of the flags, which further necessitates a change to other parts of the module.

This is an example of where a grumble about a problem during programming has ramifications for the quality assurance of another activity: in this case, the activity of design. While it is obviously a good thing to insist that programmers use meaningful identifiers, it is also important that, as part of the design standards, staff should always be instructed to develop designs which only contain modules that implement one function. The quality control which would ensure this would be the signing off of a design by the chair of a design review which, as part of its checklist, contains a directive banning multi-functional modules.

The fourth point, concerning the gross nesting of control structures, is connected with the previous point about flags. It is obviously very difficult to understand a module which contains a large degree of nesting. However, the programmer responsible for developing the module could have been given a module specification which is too big, and which attempts to implement a number of functions. The programming standard should obviously include directions about the maximum level of nesting; however, it should also contain directions about what to do if the programmer finds that he or she is unable to write a module which is smaller in terms of nesting. This would involve reporting the fact to a senior member of staff.

Problem five—inadequate testing—is also a common one found in the software industry. You will remember that in the first chapter I stated that the further into a software project an error remains undetected, the larger the amount of resources that are required to rectify the error. It is vitally important that modules are tested thoroughly and that evidence is presented that this has been done. There are a number of solutions to this problem: the first is to include, in the procedure governing module testing, an instruction to document each test case, and provide a reason why each case was chosen. This, at least, provides evidence that the programmer has thought up the test data. It also has the spin-off that it actually forces the programmer to think about the reasons why the test data was chosen—once someone starts thinking about a task, inevitably that task will be more efficiently carried out.

Confirmation that the tests have been carried out can be shown in a number of ways. The simplest is for the programmer to provide a printout or a screen dump which shows the results of each test. A more expensive method would be to use a *dynamic analyser*. This is a tool which instruments a module and produces a report on which parts of a module a test has executed. The more sophisticated dynamic analysers also provide summary information for a number of tests; for example, they often produce histograms which show the frequency with which statements or branches are executed and also identify any which remain unexecuted. The quality system could insist that the report from this tool is bound in with the remainder of the module documentation.

Point six concerns software used to support testing. It is typical of something which often comes up during the process of asking staff to comment on the way in which they currently produce software. It is not directly relevant to quality assurance; however, a procedure could be of help to programmers who find the development of such a harness software time-consuming. As part of the procedure governing module programming, staff could be told to use a pre-written piece of code which carries out many of the functions of a test harness. Obviously, some extra coding would be required in order to cater for the input and output of values to and from a module but, nevertheless, there is still quite a degree of common coding which occurs and, hence, considerable savings can be achieved.

Point seven concerns devious coding tricks, and was obviously made by a maintenance programmer. The effect of coding tricks can be totally eliminated by having a decent programming standard which, for example, banned low-level coding. Probably a more realistic standard would be to insist that if a programmer used a piece of tricky code, then it should be flagged and documented by means of a comment.

Points eight and nine have already been covered. Point eight could be handled by means of a programming standard which gave examples of what meaningful variables were. Point nine can be covered by means of standard naming conventions for files.

Point ten was obviously made by a project manager who has problems tracking project progress. The answer to this problem is relatively simple: ensure that an item of documentation is filled in when the programming of a module is complete. This documentation could be processed by a clerical assistant, entered on a spreadsheet, together with the estimated times of completion of modules, and displayed in an easily assimilable form for the project manager.

Point eleven—the problems encountered with poorly written specifications—can be handled by having an explicit procedure whereby the programmer informs the member of staff to whom he or she reports of a problem with a module. That member of staff will usually have sufficient seniority to make the design team sit up and take notice when the problem is discovered.

The final point about debugging can be covered by having an explicit defensive programming standard. *Defensive programming* is the term given to the insertion of debugging code into a module before the module is tested. A defensive programming standard will insist that the programmer insert this debugging code in places such as on entry to a module, after a module has been called, and after a particularly complex calculation.

Once the points made by staff in questionnaires have been processed, a standard and procedure for a task can be developed. However, before actually doing this, there are a number of questions that need to be asked in order to ensure that nothing is missed. These questions are common to each of the activities on the software project, and in many ways, they reflect quite a large number of the concerns addressed by the questions discussed above. They are reproduced below:

1. What are the inputs to the task that is to be carried out? For example, the main input to the task of system design is the requirements specification.
2. What are the outputs produced by the task that is to be carried out?
3. What reports should be generated from the task which will help project management to monitor and control the task and the project?
4. Is the task associated with a quality control? If so, how should evidence that the quality control has been successfully carried out be documented? Who should sign off the quality control?
5. What archival material should be produced for staff who are to carry out maintenance?
6. Is there any checkpoint in the task which requires permission to proceed before the task is completed?
7. What should be done when the input to a task falls below expected quality?

The answers to these questions for module coding are fairly straightforward. The input is the module specification taken from the system design. Another optional input might be a project-specific standard for testing the module. For example, the normal standard might insist that testing occurred with 100 per cent of all statements executed, and with 85 per cent of the branches executed, but the software that is being developed is so critical that the standard requires modifying so that 90 per cent of all branches are executed. The output is the coded module, which is then passed to the staff who are responsible for integration.

The main report that is generated to help project management is some form of document which indicates that programming of the module has been completed and signed off. Another form of documentation which should be produced when problems occur in programming and testing is some form of exception report. This explains why work on the module has ceased and what is happening about restarting the process. Normally, every developmental task is associated with a quality control, and module programming is no exception.

The main quality control will be the insistence that the tests which have been applied have been documented and that evidence that the tests have been carried out correctly has been produced. This is normally found in the unit folder, and will be signed off by the senior member of staff responsible for the programmer who produced the module.

The question concerning archival material is usually easy to answer. In the case of module programming, the source code of the module should be stored together with its object code, test data and test outcomes. It is also a good idea to store the harness which was used to test the module.

Question six, relating to module programming, is easy to answer: that there is no intermediate checkpoint which requires permission to proceed. The answer to the seventh question will be virtually the same, irrespective of the task: that if the input to the task is defective, for example the module specification is ambiguous, then whoever carries out the task has to report the problems that have been found to the senior member of staff to whom he or she reports.

Given this simple algorithm of asking staff about the problems they encounter, and asking a few general questions, the process of producing a standard and procedure can be carried out. It is worth stressing here that whenever you write a standard or a procedure it is important to try and minimize the amount of documentation that staff have to fill in. For example, try and use tools such as word processors, which provide glossary facilities. The standard and procedure for module programming is shown below. It is important to point out that the procedure is generic in that it covers any language X:

Procedure P17. V3 (Module coding and testing)

Task
This procedure covers the coding and testing of modules written in the X programming language.

Tools used
Borland compiler for language X. The dynamic analyser tool ANALYSE.

Input
The input to this task will be a module specification. This will contain a list of parameters and global variables, together with the function of the module expressed in natural language. Further details of this document can be found in Standard S13.V2 (Module specifications). A minor input to the process may be a project-specific directive which overrides the current test completion criteria.

Task description

The programmer will take the module specification and produce program code in the X language which satisfies the specification. If the specification is deficient then the programmer will notify whoever he or she reports to about the problem. A simple form will be used for this. Details of this form can be found in Standard S55.V4 (Module incident form). Until the problems that have been noted in the form have been cleared up the programmer will suspend work on the module.

If the module specification is in a form which is adequate for programming, then the program code is produced. This code must adhere to the programming standard used by the company for programming language X. This can be found in Standard S43.V2 (Programming language X coding standard). If in coding the module the programmer discovers that it is impossible to keep to the standard, this fact must be reported to the manager the programmer reports to. That manager may suggest a way in which the module could be coded which respects the coding standard, or may decide that the module is so functionally large that it has to be queried with the designer. In the latter case a error incident form has to be filled in by the programmer; details of this form can be found in Standard S55.V4 (Error incident form).

Once the module is coded and clean-compiled it should be shown to a colleague, and the function of the module explained in terms of its source code. If a substantial number of errors are discovered by your colleague, then another meeting should be scheduled after the errors have been rectified and the module clean-compiled again. Once no more errors have been discovered by this static analysis, the colleague should sign off the module as being correct. The unit folder will contain space for the signature to be inserted, see Standard S44.V1 (Unit folder).

The next task is for the programmer to test the module. A test harness will be built which turns the module into an executable program. It is then instrumented using the ANALYSE tool. The programmer will then generate test data which will test the functions of the module. The various testing strategies that can be used can all be found in the company's manual of good developmental practice. All the test outputs should be channelled to a file. This file should be retained as it will eventually be stored in the project library.

The main aim of testing is to ensure that a module works correctly in terms of the functional description provided by the designer. However, the programmer should also provide proof that the tests which have been carried out have executed all the module statements. The ANALYSE tool will produce a histogram which will show the statements that have been executed and the frequency of execution of each statement. If any statement has not been executed, then more test data should be generated which achieves 100 per cent coverage. Once this coverage has been achieved, the programmer should complete the test data section of the unit folder. Here, he or she should describe why each test case was chosen in terms of the test strategies described in the company manual of practice. The histogram which is produced by the ANALYSE tool should then be placed in the unit folder; finally, a printout of the source code of the module should be placed in the unit folder.

Once these tasks have been completed the member of staff who the programmer reports to signs off and confirms that the unit folder is correct. What this implies is that the member of staff confirms that all the standards have been adhered to, and that adequate testing of the module has taken place.

Outputs

There are a number of outputs from this task: the source and object code of the module; the test data; the test outcomes; and the test harness. These should be stored in separate files. Each file should consist of the name of the module together with an extension. In the unlikely event of the module name being more than 12 letters then it should be abbreviated to 12 letters. The extensions used are *tda* for test data, *tou* for test outcomes, *sor* for source code, *obj* for object code, and *tha* for the test harness. Thus, the test data for the module update will be stored in the file *update.tda*.

The associated standards for the unit folder and for the programming language X are shown below:

The unit folder will contain a number of sections. The template for this document can be found in *Templ:unitf.doc*. This template should be copied to the programmer's directory and the sections edited to include the information generated by module programming and testing.

Section 1. Module specification

This is the module specification that is provided by the designer. Normally this will be provided as a file so that it can be copied directly into the unit folder.

Section 2 Source code

This section of the unit folder will contain the source code of the module that has been programmed. The display should be obtained by running the source code through the prettyprinter tool FORMAT, and directing the output to a file which can then be edited into the unit folder.

Section 3 Test data

This section should contain the test cases that were used to test the system. You should have stored these test cases on a file, so all that is required is for you to edit the file and annotate each test case with TEST CASE N enclosed within square brackets.

After each test case you should describe why you chose it, for example that the test case represents a boundary condition, or it was devised to bring the test coverage up to 100 per cent statement coverage. Your description should again be enclosed within square brackets. An example of a test case is shown below:

[TEST CASE 1] 33, 45, 22, 12 [This test case checks whether the first name on the database is recognized as being valid]

Once each case has been annotated, the resulting file should be edited into the unit folder. The summary file of test coverage obtained by running the ANALYSE tool should also be edited into this section of the unit folder. Once this file has been completed, it should be stored in the project library. It should be printed off and signed by the manager to whom the programmer who developed the module reports and the programmer who statically checked it. The file should be given the name of the module followed by the extension *ufo*. If the name of the module contains more than 12 characters it should be truncated to 12 characters.

The associated programming standard for language X might be as shown below:

The start of the module should be annotated with bureaucratic information. This consists of the name and extension number of the programmer who developed the module, the name and extension number of the programmer who applied the last major change to the module, a list of the modules the module calls, a list of the global variables which the module references, and a list of the modules which call the module.

A module should also contain a comment which describes what it does. This can be copied directly from the module specification produced by the designer of the system. This narrative should follow the bureaucratic information described previously. Normally, for the X programming language, the following restrictions will hold for a module:

1. No *goto* statements are to be used.

2. No more than four boolean operators such as *and* and *or* should be used in a condition.

3. On no account should more than two *not* operators be used in a condition. If possible, restrict boolean conditions to one *not* operator.

4. Control structures such as *if* and *repeat* should not be nested to a depth greater than 8.

5. Identifiers should be meaningful at all times. No identifiers such as ID009 should be written unless, of course, ID009 has a specific meaning in terms of the application.

6. Modules should be no bigger than 100 lines of code after they have been processed by the FORMAT tool.

7. Variable initializations should be written at the head of a module, the only exceptions being variables used to count loops.

8. If non-array variables in the program have a definite relationship with each other at a point in the module, for example the sum of variables a and b is greater than variable c, then defensive programming code should be inserted which checks for this and displays an error message if the condition is not true.

9. Arithmetic expressions should contain no more than 10 operators such as * or +. If they do, split them into subexpressions and assign them to variables which have meaningful identifiers.

10. Use only single letter variables for loop counters; do not use them in any other context.

If the programmer feels that these restrictions cannot be adhered to, he or she should communicate the fact to the member of staff to whom he or she reports.

13.4 DESIGN REVIEWS

To conclude this chapter it is worth looking at another activity and writing a procedure for it. This time I will use a slightly more rigorous notation for the procedure—one modelled on a detailed design notation which has facilities for control flow specification.

> **Self Assessment Question 13.5** This is more of the nature of an exercise than a self assessment question. However, it is worth doing at this point in the text. Cover up the remainder of this page and write down the problems which you think might afflict a design review.
>
> **Solution** The majority of the problems are detailed below.

Some of the problems with design reviews are described below:

1. Sometimes we are given a design to review which is nowhere near to being ready for review. We just waste our time looking at an incomplete document.
2. The reviews which I attend are often appallingly chaired. We seem to spend hours just going over 'pet' points that are brought up by the more loquacious members of the review team.
3. Managers often seem to invite staff to a review at a moment's notice. I've been to one review where all the staff, except myself, have only had an hour's notice that the review was to take place. Consequently, they had not carried out enough preparation.
4. I have turned up at the venue for a review which is occupied by another meeting. We spent a considerable amount of time looking for an empty room which had not already been booked by another meeting.
5. Some of the reviews that I have attended have degenerated into informal design meetings where, in response to one problem, the whole design review team just spent the time redesigning the system in order to eradicate the error.
6. When a new member of staff first attends a review, he or she often has no idea what a review is meant to achieve and what we should be looking for in a review.
7. Sometimes I do not receive material to review sufficiently in advance to be able to adequately prepare for a review.
8. It would be nice for me to be able to discover progress on a project, in particular how close we are to completing a system design.

9. I am aware that reviews are rather a tricky thing to chair. Therefore, I would really like data on the number of errors that a review threw up and the number of errors that were missed. If this data is consistent—for example, reviews chaired by one member of staff were consistently letting major errors go undetected—then I can do something about it, such as sending the individual involved on a training course.

10. Sometimes my work is reviewed and problems discovered. Usually when a review takes place I am in the middle of another task, and when I return to rectifying the errors I have forgotten what some of them were. I make notes, but because of the nature of reviews they are always hurriedly done.

11. When I started work for the company, reviews were a rude awakening. Here I was, a young graduate, thrust into meetings where two or three other members of staff tore my work to pieces. I felt terribly dispirited, and almost left the company.

These are a selection of problems which I almost invariably encounter in companies which are trying to make reviews a success, though they are by no means all the problems I encounter. It is worth considering them in order.

The first problem is quite a common one; time and time again staff tell me that whoever submitted an item for review has done it in a hurry, and hence it is incomplete or too abstract. The solution to this problem is to direct whoever chairs a review to read the item before deciding whether a review can take place; if the item is not good enough, then it is returned to the originator for rework.

The second is the most common one that I find. A quality system's scope for improving the chairmanship qualities of staff is limited. There are a number of points about chairmanship that can be written into the company manual of good practices, such as instructions to keep to an agenda, but the scope is limited. Where a quality system can help is in detecting whether a review—or, more realistically, a series of reviews—has not gone well because of poor chairmanship. A proper error-reporting procedure, together with the minuting of the problems discovered during a review, will enable a project manager to home in on a poorly executed review.

The third problem is one of poor planning. This can be solved by writing into the project planning standards an instruction that all reviews should be explicitly planned for and, furthermore, that staff should be allocated at least two hours in order to prepare themselves for a review.

The fourth problem is trivial, but it can give rise to a large amount of wasted time. The solution is to write an instruction into the procedure for holding the review: that the chair should book a meeting room well in advance of the review taking place.

Again, a quality system cannot prevent the poor chairmanship which the fifth problem indicates. Obviously, a review is a much better medium for detecting errors than solving problems, and a good chair should clamp down on any attempt to carry out redesign. Unfortunately, a quality system can only provide advice on good chairmanship via a manual of good practice. Where a quality system is of help is in detecting the consequences of poor chairmanship. This is discussed with respect to problem nine.

The sixth problem is one which not only affects reviews, but also almost every activity that a software company carries out. Although many companies have induction courses, many are of insufficient duration to show new staff exactly what is required of them for a particular task. There is, in fact, a good argument against induction courses which only try to deal with minor detail. A quality system can generally help, as it is in effect a collection of detailed descriptions of the tasks which staff members have to carry out and good practice governing these tasks. In the case of a design review, the design review checklist and the design review procedure would be the medium which a member of staff would use to understand the nature of the review process.

The seventh problem is again a minor planning deficiency; it can be remedied by including a directive in the review procedure to circulate review material at least two days in advance of a review meeting.

The eighth problem is obviously voiced by a project manager. It calls for some form of documentation to be issued after a review which gives some indication of its outcome.

The ninth problem is obviously articulated by a project manager who is concerned with the quality of the processes which he manages. It is a call for documentation which is issued after a review to give some idea of the quantity and seriousness of the errors which were detected by the review. It is also a call for something much bigger: a proper defect reporting system which provides data on errors discovered throughout the software project. Documentation which provides data on the number and incidence of errors discovered by design reviews would be just one component of this system.

The tenth problem is again a common one. It can easily be solved by including a directive in the design review procedure for a member of the review team to make detailed notes on the errors that were discovered. This documentation can be read and checked by the chair of the review, and signed off if he or she is satisfied that enough detail is included for the staff who are to rectify the errors.

The final problem can be addressed by including material in design review guidelines about the proper way to conduct a review; it also requires some material to be inserted in the induction material given to new technical staff. The first requirement is a procedure for running a design review. It is written in a specific notation which resembles a detailed design notation or programming language, with the subtasks which make up the task of running a design review specified in terms of control structures. The capitalized references within brackets are to standards, CHECKLIST DES2 is the standard for the checklist used for design reviews, while REV REPORT FORM is the standard for the report form which is issued when the review is completed:

```
DESIGN REVIEW PROCEDURE
REPEAT
    Designer informs chair of review that design is ready for review
    REPEAT
        Chair reads design and checks for readiness
        IF the design is not ready THEN
            It is rejected
        ENDIF
    UNTIL design is ready for review
    Chair books meeting room
    Chair announces time for review
    Chair selects review participants
    Chair generates review material
    Participants review material and make notes. [CHECKLIST DES2]
    Participants meet
    Chairman reads the review material in textual order
```

```
FOR each problem DO
        The secretary notes down the reason [REV REPORT FORM]
        for the problem
ENDFOR
CASE problems OF
    No problems:      Review successful
                      Chair signs off the design
    Small problems:   Review mainly successful
                      Designer modifies design
                      Chair signs off design
    Major problems:   Designer modifies design
    ENDCASE
UNTIL chair signs off design
Review report form signed off [REV REPORT FORM]
Design added to project library
```

This looks very much like some program coding. However, it does convey the essence of the design review process. Obviously some things are missing; for example, it does not contain a description of best practice for reviewing. Nevertheless, it is an excellent medium for describing the step-by-step process whereby designs are produced.

A design review will also need a standard for the documentation which is issued. Here, what is required is a document which tells the reader what was reviewed, who did the reviewing, and what was the result. A standard is shown below:

Design review documentation

The only piece of documentation issued from a design review is the design review minutes. This will consist of a number of sections.

The header

This will contain bureaucratic information: the staff who attended, who chaired the meeting, who took minutes, the item that was reviewed, and the person or persons who produced the item. The header will also consist of a unique identifier which distinguishes this review document from any other document. Normally, a design review identifier is made up of the project name followed by a letter *d*, followed by an integer one greater than the number of the last review.

The list of problems

This consists of a sequential list of problems which are each uniquely identified by means of the design review identifier followed by an integer. The integer starts at one for the first problem, and is incremented by one for each subsequent problem. Each problem should be given a seriousness rating, starting at 1 (trivial) to 4 (serious).

Review outcome

This section of the review minutes contains a description of the outcome of the review. This is filled in by the review chair. There are essentially three outcomes to a design review. The first is that no problems were discovered; this means that the review process is complete for the item being processed. The second is that a relatively small number of not very serious problems were discovered; in this case the item being reviewed is reworked, then shown to the review chair and the review signed off. The third outcome—and the most serious—is that major problems were discovered; if this occurs the item has to be modified and completely re-reviewed.

Sign-off

This part of the form just contains space for the chair to sign off the reviewed item if the review was successful, i.e. if the first two outcomes above occurred.

The guidelines for a review are shown below:

Review guidelines

We have found that reviews are a highly effective way of validating a project document or source code. In general, the earlier a review occurs the more effective it is. The following guidelines are not prescriptive, but our experience has been that if they are followed, then the vast majority of errors in an item are picked up well before expensive system testing starts. We would normally expect a project manager to follow them for the vast majority of the time.

1. A review should normally involve no more than five members of staff and no fewer than three, including the chair of the review.

2. Care should be taken in selecting staff for a review. The member of staff who produced the item being reviewed should always attend, as should a member of staff from another project in order to provide an independent viewpoint. A staff member who carries out the same task as the developer of the item being reviewed should be invited, as well as other members, depending on the type of review. For example, the customer should be invited to attend requirements specification reviews, staff responsible for system testing should also be invited to a requirements specification review, and an analyst who was concerned with the development of the requirements specification should be invited to a design review.

Consideration should be given to inviting new members of staff who have not experienced reviews before. It is often a good idea to invite them as observers so that when, and if, their material is reviewed, the process of reviewing will hold no surprises for them. It is important that senior members of staff do not attend reviews. Staff whose material is being dissected often feel that if a senior member of staff is present, their performance is being evaluated. This often means that they become very defensive and their attitude hinders the validation process. The company has well-defined procedures for evaluating staff and a review is really not one of them.

3. The chair of a review shall, at all times, ensure that the review concentrates on validation. Discussion on possible solutions to a problem, similar problems which were encountered on other projects, gossip, and over-concentration on one error, should be firmly discouraged.

4. We have found that if reviews are working well, the participants become very tired and their work becomes less effective after about two hours. The amount of work scheduled for a review should therefore not result in meetings which last more than two hours.

5. Having one's work reviewed can be a very painful experience, and the chair of the meeting must ensure that the pain is reduced to a minimum. For example, if the chair feels that one member of staff's validation contains some personal criticism of the originator of the document being reviewed, then steps must be taken after the review to remind the member of staff that a review is meant to be an appraisal of a document or source code, not a criticism of the person who produced it.

6. It is important that the minutes produced after a review meeting are legible and understandable. The chair should check them before they are issued.

13.5 SUMMARY

The development of standards and procedures can consume up to 90 per cent of the resources devoted to the implementation of a new quality system. The main point stressed in this chapter is that the development of such standards and procedures should be driven by the needs and problems of technical and managerial staff on projects, and that the first step in writing new standards and procedures is to ask such staff what they feel is required.

13.6 FURTHER READING

There has been very little written on the development of standards and procedures. However, two good documentation books which have helped me a great deal are Bell and Evans (1989) and Williams and Beason (1990). Strunk and White (1979) is a good pocket-sized introduction to writing clearly, and both Gowers (1988) and Jenkins (1992) are excellent reference books.

PROBLEMS

13.1 Write down a standard for a document which would be used to propose changes to a system. Such a document would be processed by a configuration management system.

13.2 Write down a procedure for costing a project using the conventional work breakdown structures discussed on page 55.

13.3 If you were going to develop a procedure and standard for system testing what sort of replies do you think you might get after asking staff charged with this activity about the problems they encounter?

13.4 Write down a procedure which might be used by staff charged with the improvement of a quality system.

14

ISO 9001

AIMS

- To introduce an important external standard: ISO 9001.
- To interpret the twenty sections of ISO 9001 in software quality terms.

14.1 INTRODUCTION

This chapter has a number of aims, the main one being to describe the increasingly important international standard ISO 9001. The standard, which has been adopted for use by more than 130 countries, is becoming increasingly important as the main means whereby customers can judge the competence of a software developer. One of the problems with the ISO 9001 series standard is that it is not industry-specific: it is expressed in general terms, and can be interpreted by the developers of diverse products such as ball-bearings, hair dryers, automobiles, sports equipment, and televisions, as well as software. A number of documents have been produced which relate the standard to the software industry, but do not go into a huge amount of detail. It is the aim of this chapter to describe what ISO 9001 means in terms of the quality elements and development techniques described in the book. For the software industry the relevant standards are:

- *ISO 9001 Quality Systems—Model for Quality Assurance in Design, Development, Production, Installation and Servicing.* This is a standard which describes the quality system used to support the development of a product which involves design.
- *ISO 9000-3 Guidelines for the Application of ISO 9001 to the Development, Supply and Maintenance of Software.* This is a specific document which interprets ISO 9001 for the software developer.

- *ISO 9004-2 Quality Management and Quality System Elements—Part 2.* This document provides guidelines for the servicing of software facilities such as user support.

The requirements are grouped under 20 headings:

Management responsibility	Inspection, measuring and test equipment
Quality system	Inspection and test status
Contract review	Control of non-conforming product
Design control	Corrective action
Document control	Handling, storage, packaging and delivery
Purchasing	Quality records
Purchaser supplied product	Internal quality audits
Product identification and traceability	Training
Process control	Servicing
Inspection and testing	Statistical techniques

Before discussing each heading it is worth looking at a small excerpt from ISO 9001. This gives the reader an idea of the level at which ISO 9001 addresses the QA and development process. The extract chosen comes from section 4.11:

4.11 Inspection, measuring and test equipment

The supplier shall control, calibrate and maintain inspection, measuring and test equipment, whether owned by the supplier, on loan, or provided by the purchaser, to demonstrate the conformance of product to the specified requirements. Equipment shall be used in a manner which ensures that measurement uncertainty is known and is consistent with the required measurement capability.

The first thing to notice is its generality: it could apply to the developer of any product. The second thing to notice is the difficulty in interpreting the paragraph—it is obviously aimed at standard engineering processes where equipment such as thermocouples, calibration gauges and potentiometers are the norm. An interpretation of the paragraph is that the supplier shall ensure that any software tools used for testing are of at least the same quality as the software that is to be developed, and that any test equipment which produces measurement values, for example, performance monitors, has an accuracy which is acceptable when compared with the accuracy specified for performance in the requirements specification.

This, then, is the type of level of text contained in the ISO 9001 standard. The aim of the following 20 subsections is to examine each of the sections in the standard and produce an interpretation in terms of the contents of the previous chapters of this book. Whenever numbers appear in brackets they refer to the specific paragraph in the ISO 9001 standard. The final section of this chapter summarizes the components of a quality system which is able to satisfy ISO 9001.

14.2 THE ELEMENTS OF ISO 9001

14.2.1 Management responsibility

This part of the standard (4.1.1) describes the fact that the management of the software developer should publish its commitment to software quality via company policy. The statement of this policy would appear in broad form in prominent company publications, and in more detailed form in the introduction to the company quality manual. The broad form of a company's commitment to policy might appear in statements such as: 'The company believes that good quality assurance is something that occurs throughout our projects, involves both our staff and the customer, and cannot be built in as an afterthought.' The more detailed form might involve a statement such as: 'We believe that an error discovered during development, no matter how trivial, should be rectified and the cause of the error determined and documented.' Both the broad and detailed statements should be displayed prominently in documents which are widely available to staff.

Staff should be made aware of the quality policy of the company by means of training and induction courses. Not only should a company produce a quality manual, but it is also a good idea to produce a short guide to the quality manual which would reiterate the detailed quality aims and objectives of the company, and provide a rationale for company quality procedures in terms of a history of projects which have had quality problems.

This section also details the fact that staff who are to carry out either a quality or a developmental function should have their responsibility, authority and interrelationship defined (4.1.2.1). This would include answering questions such as:

- How a quality assurance department is organized.
- If a company is not big enough to have a separate quality assurance department, what is the managerial relationship between staff responsible for quality assurance activities, the project manager, and the senior member of staff responsible for quality matters.
- What power a member of quality staff has when a problem is discovered, such as an audit discovering that a quality control has not been properly executed.
- Whether the team structure for a project is adequately defined, and its relationship with the quality function and other external agencies specified.
- Whether an adequate development model is employed by each project.

Such details should be found in two sources: the job descriptions of staff categories employed by a software developer, and the staffing section of the project plan which would detail project-specific responsibilities which may not be contained in broad job descriptions.

In this part of the standard (4.1.2.1) there is an implication that as far as possible quality staff should be independent of developmental projects. A further part of this section (4.1.2.2) specifies that the software developer should identify in-house verification requirements and provide adequate resources for these. This means that the developer should have identified all the main tasks used for checking both customer-related quality attributes and developer-related attributes, and have qualified and experienced staff who can carry out these tasks; normally, this information would be found in the company's overall resource plan. Also, if certain quality controls are carried out using software tools, these tools should be widely available, documented, and staff trained in their use.

Staff should also be trained in the quality control activities used by the company. If a company sometimes requires external staff to carry out some quality controls, for example complicated real-time testing, then there should be a procedure which describes how such staff should be contracted. There is also an implication that training provision should be regularly reviewed by management.

This section also states that there should be a designated member of management who is responsible for ensuring that the requirements of ISO 9001 have been implemented (4.1.2.3). Normally, this should be a member of staff who is at a very senior level in the developer's company—either at board level or just below it. Such a manager would receive reports from staff carrying out the quality function about serious violations of the standard. These would usually be reported as a result of project audits. In addition, the manager should have the power to order a thorough investigation of a project which starts emitting warning signals about budget exhaustion or late delivery.

The final part of this section describes the fact that the quality system should be regularly reviewed. The frequency of review will depend on a number of factors. If the quality system is new, then it should be reviewed more frequently than if it was mature and was seen to be coping well. A review could also be scheduled as part of the preparation for the implementation of new technology such as CASE tools. There are a number of potential inputs into such a review: a report from the senior manager responsible for ensuring that the quality system meets ISO 9001 requirements; project debriefing reports which highlight concerns about the operation of the quality system; a staff questionnaire; summaries of audit reports; quality records such as the level of defects discovered during operation, and the cause of the errors; and data on project performance in terms of profit and delivery time.

Self Assessment Question 14.1 Would the fact that a company specified that the skills and background of developmental staff is specified in the project plan be related to this part of the ISO 9001 standard?

Solution Yes, it covers the fact that staff who are to perform a specified task should have the skills to carry out that task.

14.2.2 Quality system

This section of the standard (4.2) specifies that the software developer should establish and maintain a documented quality system which satisfied ISO 9001 and that it should be effectively implemented. The first requirement is really a reference to the fact that there should be a widely available set of standards and procedures. These standards and procedures should constitute a dynamic document, and should be updated in response to any management reviews and any developments in technology such as a new programming language being adopted by the developer.

The part of the section that deals with the effective implementation of the quality system (i.e. its standards and procedures) has two implications for the software developer.

The first is that audits of software projects should be held to ensure that the agreed quality controls in a project's quality plan have been implemented, and that the standards and procedures governing developmental activities and the quality controls have been correctly carried out. These audits should be carried out with a frequency that is determined by a number of factors, including the criticality of the activity that is being audited (for example, requirements analysis is a much more important activity than programming, and one would expect more auditing of tasks associated with requirements analysis), and the experience of the members of staff (a quality manager may ask staff responsible for the quality assurance function to audit the work of a new member of staff).

The second implication of this section of the standard is that adequate quality records should be kept which enable staff concerned with quality to identify either that staff on a project are not complying with standards or procedures, or the existence of deficiencies in the quality system. There are two types of quality records.

The first detail the number and seriousness of errors discovered during each phase and the phase in which the error was committed. By producing a plot of percentage of errors committed, and percentage of errors discovered on a phase-by-phase basis, a software developer will be able to detect which parts of the quality system may not have been implemented correctly by a project.

The second consists of documentation which provides proof that a quality control has been successful and has checked that a particular quality attribute has been implemented in a system. A typical example is a test report.

An important part of the quality system is that the company should document at least one process model which can be tailored to particular projects. This topic was described in Chapter 12. It is worth pointing out here that one model may not be adequate; for example, a software developer may develop third-generation systems using a development philosophy which is process-driven, and may also develop commercial data processing systems using a philosophy which is data-driven. In this case, one process model may be inadequate and two would be called for.

Implicit in this section is that each project should produce a quality plan which details how controls described in the quality manual are to be used to check that quality attributes specified at the beginning of the project are present in the final software.

Self Assessment Question 14.2 Would the process of project auditing, i.e. the execution of detailed checks on software projects to ensure that they are adhering to their quality plan, be relevant to this part of ISO 9001?

Solution Yes, this activity is an important part of the quality system— without it there would not even be a point in developing a quality plan for a project.

14.2.3 Contract review

This part of the ISO 9001 standard describes what the software developer should do to ensure that the contract to produce a software system is a valid document (4.3). This sounds innocuous to any reader who thinks that a contract is just a straightforward legal document. The response of anyone reading this part of the standard might be to ensure that there is a procedure which details how the legal department should be involved in this process. While this is an important activity, it is by no means the only one. For example, a contract will specify a delivery date and a price and, usually, a document which forms part of the contractual bundle associated with a contract is some form of requirements specification. Thus, the developer has to ensure that customer requirements are adequately defined, properly specified, and that the software can be delivered on time and to budget.

These are major implications which have quite a lot of ramifications for the quality system. First, let us examine those connected with the requirements specification. There are a number of models of contracting in the software industry. One is to issue a tender for a system which is split into two phases: first, the software developer produces a detailed requirements specification (which he would then be paid for); he would then be contracted to produce a system which is based on this specification. A second model is where a contract is awarded on the basis of the customer statement of requirements, and a third is where a contract is based on an outline requirements specification which may, or may not, have been paid for by the customer. In the first and third cases, the quality system should provide direction on how the requirements specifications are validated with respect to the original customer statement of requirements. This will mean outlining the various techniques which can be employed, for example technical reviews, walkthroughs, and prototyping. The main activity to ensure this will be a requirements specification technical review, and the software developer should certainly have standards in place to determine the conduct of these reviews (described in Chapter 4 of this book).

When the second model of contracting has been adopted, the quality system should provide direction on how to ensure that the software developer incorporates a description of his or her perception of the system to be developed in the contract. This document should be of at least the quality of an outline requirements specification, and should be reviewed in the same way as a full requirements specification.

This section of the standard also emphasizes the fact that any requirements differing from those in a tender produced by the customer are resolved. A software interpretation of this is that there should be adequate documentation of contact with the customer, to show that differences between the contractual requirements document and the original statement of requirements document have been notified to the customer and have been agreed by a customer's representative.

This part of the standard can also be addressed by documentation that links the requirements specification document to the original statement of requirements produced by the customer. Details of this form of documentation can be found in Chapter 4.

The final part of this section concerns the fact that the supplier should ensure that he or she has the capability to meet contractual requirements. The most important is, of course, delivery to the requirements detailed in the requirements specification, but this also deals with the ability to deliver on time and to budget. Reviews and feasibility studies are normally used to implement this part of the standard. The quality system should provide standards and procedures for carrying out a feasibility study: a mini-project which determines whether all the requirements including cost can be met.

A requirements review is used to determine whether individual requirements can be met. For example, the customer may insist in the statement of requirements that a particular requirement well beyond the state-of-the-art of software development has to be implemented. A requirements review should, as part of its remit, address this aspect. A project plan review is used to determine whether the set of tasks, resources and schedules specified in the plan will meet the target date for delivery, and enable the profit called for by the company's business plan to be met. The review should ask questions such as:

- Do we have the expertise to carry out this task?
- Is the project so risky that even if we built in risk avoidance techniques there is still a high probability that we will lose money on this project?
- Are the resource requirements for these tasks reasonable?
- Can we have confidence that the customer will carry out specific tasks within the time period that we have specified in the project plan?

Within this section there is an implicit requirement that the eventual requirements specification produced is complete, and describes all customer requirements, and that eventually the final design and program code of the system can be checked to ensure that it meets those requirements.

14.2.4 Design control

This part of the ISO standard (4.4) is divided into six subsections. The first (4.4.1) describes the fact that a supplier shall have standards and procedures which control and verify the design of the software system in order to ensure that customer requirements are met.

There are a number of implications behind this. First, that adequate notations for expressing the design are provided by the quality system, i.e. a notation which produces designs which can be checked against user requirements and which represents a global, physical view of the system. Second, that adequate standards for validation and verification activities are detailed in the quality system; for example, the quality system should provide a standard and procedure which governs the conduct of system design and detailed design technical reviews. The quality system should also provide facilities whereby traceability documentation, such as the verification matrix described in Chapter 5, is constructed. Another feature which should be offered by the quality system is directives which specify how the developer is to check the functional quality attributes and non-functional attributes, such as response time, against a design. The normal medium for this is the technical review.

Another important feature of this subsection of the standard (4.4.2) is the specification that the organizational and technical interfaces between different groups shall be identified and their interface documented. This is a reference to the provision in the quality manual of details of how the relationship between the software development team and other agencies, such as hardware developers, should be managed. It should also detail the relationship between the design teams who are designing subsystems and how the relationship between the analysts and the designers on the project is handled. The quality system should document the means of communication, the standards for the documents used for communication, and aspects such as the querying of the functional properties of the system by the designers. If there is any need for liaison between the designers and the customer, this should also be the subject of standards and procedures.

The third subsection (4.4.3) specifies that design input requirements relating to the system to be developed shall be identified and documented, and that poorly specified requirements shall be resolved with the staff who drew them up. This is a reference to the fact that the requirements specification, which is the main input into the design process, should accurately reflect the customer requirements which were initially detailed in the statement of requirements. Details of what exactly this means can be found in Chapter 4 of this book. The implication for the quality system is that there should be a standard for expressing a system design, and if detailed design forms part of a company's development practices, a standard for detailed design; there should also be a procedure which describes the processes of both detailed and system design.

Another important issue touched upon by this part of the standard is that of poorly expressed requirements. The part of a quality system describing design should include a procedure for describing what a designer should do when a poorly expressed requirement is found.

The next subsection (4.4.4) is concerned with the documentation of the design that has been produced by the software developer, and specifies that the output from the design process—the system design or detailed design—must meet the design input: those requirements detailed in the requirements specification.

Subsection 4.4.5 deals with the output from the design process, and concentrates on outlining the fact that the developer should plan, initiate, document and resource the process of verifying that a design meets its input. A software interpretation of this is that standards and procedures should be available for activities such as design reviews, prototyping, simulation, and response time calculation, and that proper planning should precede these activities.

The final subsection (4.4.6) is a reference to the configuration management practices adopted by the developer: that all changes should be documented, reviewed, applied and checked, and that any related documents which also need to be changed are processed correctly.

Other implications in this part of the standard are: that the outputs from developmental phases are documented and reviewed, and that when an item is identified as not conforming to requirements it is tagged as such, and not used in subsequent development until it does conform.

14.2.5 Document control

This section of the standard (4.5) is split into two subsections. The first (4.5.1) describes the fact that documents produced during a software project should be reviewed and approved for adequacy before they are used for developmental activities. The implication of this for a software quality system is that each task which produces a document, for example the system design task, should be accompanied by a sign-off which acts as a quality control. Sometimes this sign-off will be carried out by a member of staff who has inspected the document; sometimes it will be signed off by the chair of a meeting such as a technical review.

The second subsection (4.5.2) discusses the application of change control to project documents. It specifies that changes to project documents such as the requirements specification should be reviewed, approved or rejected, and the body which approves changes should have access to all the information on which it is necessary for them to base their judgement. This includes the reason for the change; the effect of the change on the system; and the resources required to implement the change.

This part of the standard also implies that a configuration management system capable of keeping data on versions of documents and the change history should be used by the developer.

14.2.6 Purchasing

This section details what issues a quality system needs to address when software projects have to purchase or use external products—either software or hardware. These external products could either be subcontracted or could be provided by an external agency, such as the customer or a government department. It describes what a software developer should do to ensure that these external products have the same level of quality as the software which will incorporate them.

The first subsection (4.6.1) is a general statement that all purchased products which form part of a system should conform to specified requirements. This is a general directive. However, underneath this statement there are a number of major ramifications for the software developer who is to handle a purchased product. The first is that the requirements specification to be produced for someone like a subcontractor should be of the same standard as the requirements specification used in the project, and should receive the same degree of validation. Also, the procedure whereby this software is system and acceptance tested should be of the same level of thoroughness as that employed within the project that uses the purchased software. The implication of both these requirements is that the software developer should have carried out some form of assessment of the capability of a subcontractor to act according to the requirements specification and testing standards that will be used.

Subsection 4.6.2 deals with the assessment of subcontractors. It places an obligation on the developer to ensure that subcontractors who are competent to meet the quality goals of the overall system are selected. There are a number of ways of carrying out this selection: keeping records of subcontractor performance during a software project which can be consulted by a project manager who is thinking of employing a subcontractor, carrying out an external quality audit by visiting the subcontractor, or by asking previous clients of the subcontractor about their experiences. Ideally, all three measures should be employed.

Subsection 4.6.3 deals with the identification of product to be purchased. This is normally taken to be a directive to the software developer to specify any subcontracted software correctly and to ensure that adequate change control applies to this software as much as to the software and documentation produced in the project.

The final part of this section (4.6.4) deals with the verification of purchased product. In software terms it is interpreted as a directive to the software developer to provide an adequate set of quality controls, usually implemented as acceptance tests, to ensure that any software which has been purchased meets the requirements specified by the software developer.

The issue of external software used on a project is a slightly complicated one, as software projects which do not use subcontracted, purchased or customer supplied software still, in a sense, use external software; for example, testing tools and compilers are external software. The software developer has to make a decision as to whether extensive tests need to be carried out on such software. Normally, the answer to this would be no; however, there are certain occasions when even software which is regarded by the industry as reliable might need some acceptance tests to be carried out on it. For example, a compiler used to produce code for an ultra safety-critical application, such as nuclear plant control, would need to be formally accepted by the software developer, either by carrying out tests which check the generated code or by appraising tests carried out by independent agencies.

Self Assessment Question 14.3 Would a check on a compiler to ensure that it generated correct code—carried out as part of a safety-critical project—be relevant to this part of the standard?

Solution Yes, even though the compiler might have been purchased far in the past, it may only have been used on non-critical projects.

14.2.7 Purchaser supplied product

This short section (4.7) simply re-emphasizes the important principle that software supplied by the purchaser should be checked for correctness as much as externally subcontracted software, and that configuration control should apply to these items as much as to software developed within a project. An important implication of this is that the purchaser should supply not only the software, but also the requirements specification of the software.

14.2.8 Product identification and traceability

This is a direction that elements of the system to be developed—not only software, but documents such as the requirements specification—should be adequately identified and documented and that traceability should be maintained between related documents.

In order to illustrate this, consider an example taken from testing. At the beginning of the software project, the developer will have identified a number of quality factors. These factors will each be uniquely identified and will be cross-referenced to statements in the requirements specification. These will be documented in the quality plan and will be checked by a quality control. The quality control will be given a unique identification and will be cross-referenced to the quality factors. Those quality controls which represent user-related functional quality factors will give rise to a test design. This test design will again be identified and cross-referenced to the quality control, and may give rise to a test procedure. This test procedure again would be documented and cross-referenced to the test design. Associated with the test procedure there may be a number of test files which will be given a name that enables them to be cross-referenced to the test procedure. In this way, each element of the system is uniquely identified and traceability is built into the system—from the requirements specification down to the test data used to check a customer-related functional quality factor.

Another requirement of this section is that some form of version information should be attached to components of a developed system.

14.2.9 Process control

This part of the standard (4.9) describes the requirements upon development processes such as system design. The major part of this section concerns the execution and planning of these processes.

A major interpretation is that the developer should adequately plan the development process. This means that the project should be split into its various tasks, the right people should be assigned to the tasks, task details such as duration and effort should be documented, and the resource estimate for the project should also be calculated.

The standard places stress on the fact that adequate documentation which describes the work being carried out is given to the staff who are to execute a task; for example, that adequate direction is given to staff who are to test a system based on their knowledge of the system; that the quality system provides adequate standards for a task; that a proper design methodology is specified; that in design not only functional attributes, but also any residual design directives that the customer has insisted on, are communicated to the designer. It also places great emphasis on standards for activities such as design and programming, and the documentation in the quality system of good practice for developmental activities.

Another feature of this part of the standard is that adequate monitoring and control of both the processes and products of a software project should occur. The main tools for implementing this aspect of the standard are the audit and the process of signing off items by senior members of the project.

The final part of this section (4.9.1) describes special processes. These are tasks for which the result cannot be predicted during a software project and where deficiencies can only be identified during actual use. The standard specifies that these processes should be identified, and that even if they are regarded as special the same level of care should be taken over them as over processes which can be checked.

An example of this type of process is where a system is developed which has a specified response time for a particular hardware configuration, but where an element of that configuration, say a new memory device, is not available well into the operational life of the system. The process of calculating the response time of the system with such a device should be regarded as a special process, and although it would be carried out according to the developer's best practices, it would need to be identified during the project planning. It should be marked as special, with the customer being informed that although a guarantee of response time can be given for the first version of the system without the new memory device, no guarantee can be given of a better response time for the full hardware configuration.

14.2.10 Inspection and testing

This important part of the standard (4.10) is split into four subsections. Subsection 4.10.1 describes the fact that a system or part of a subsystem should not normally be released to a customer unless it has been checked as conforming to requirements. This will normally be carried out as system or acceptance testing.

The final part of this subsection specifies the action to be taken if a system, or part of a system, is released for urgent reasons. Typically, this might occur when the business circumstances of a customer change during the development of a system, and the customer may ask for early delivery of a system containing some subsystems which have not been acceptance tested. The developer should document those parts of the delivered system which have not been adequately tested; this documentation would be used in a number of ways: as reporting data to high-level management, as information to staff carrying out field support, or to staff who are responsible for the subsequent upgrade to the software which would be fully tested.

The second subsection (4.10.2) deals with process testing and inspection. It requires the developer to carry out testing during development—normally interpreted as integration testing, unit testing, and system testing—and specifies that the developer should use mechanisms to ensure that such tests have been carried out adequately, and that the test results conform to what is expected. In software terms, the developer should have documentation standards which describe the tests that are carried out during unit, integration and system testing, and include sections that describe the actual test output. Such documentation would be checked by a member of staff signing it off and also by staff responsible for auditing.

This subsection also specifies that a software system should not normally be released, either to the acceptance testers or the customer, until all the tests and reviews which should occur during development have been carried out. The final part of this section specifies that the software developer should be able to identify parts of the system which are non-conforming, i.e. in terms of inspection and test, modules and partial versions which have either not been tested or have failed their tests.

Subsection 4.10.3 concerns what it calls final inspection and testing, but which in software terms should be interpreted as acceptance testing. It specifies that the final acceptance tests should be carried out in accordance with the quality controls described in the quality plan for a project, and that software should not be released until all the quality controls have been carried out and confirmed.

The final subsection (4.10.4) states that the software developer should maintain records which provide evidence that a system, or parts of a system, has correctly passed all its tests—that, for example, the project manager can call for module documentation and see that the modules have been tested and that no problems have been raised by the tester.

14.2.11 Inspection, measuring and test equipment

This section specifies that when any software tools such as dynamic analysers are used, the developer should be confident that these tools work properly, and that records are available—both internally and externally—to demonstrate that the developer has actually checked their functioning. This is vitally important not only for testing tools which are produced by the developer but also for bought-in tools. However, the degree of testing applied to such tools will depend, in the main, on two factors: the maturity of the tools and the criticality of the application. For a new software testing tool which has just been released and which is to be used on a safety-critical application, it is important that the developer tests such tools thoroughly. Even for mature tools employed on non-critical applications, it is still worth keeping test sets for checking out the tools; such tools do undergo revisions and can be issued in versions which include new errors. For tools which are developed within a project, it is vitally important that the same quality regime used to govern the developed software is used to oversee the development of the tools.

14.2.12 Inspection and test status

This section of the standard is related to that described in Section 14.2.13 of this chapter. It stipulates that software products such as modules should be properly identified in order that staff can easily discern their test status; for example, whether a module has passed tests which confirm that it satisfies certain requirements. This identification, which is usually implemented at the subsystem level, should ensure that when a system is assembled prior to release to the customer, no part of the system that is untested or poorly tested is included.

> **Self Assessment Question 14.4** Would a direction to the programmer to include details of when a module was tested be relevant to this part of ISO 9001?
>
> **Solution** Yes, indirectly: it would at least give an indication that the module had been tested.

14.2.13 Control of nonconforming product

This section of the standard (4.13) describes what is necessary in order to cope with a software product which does not satisfy specified requirements. Examples of this include:

- A module which has failed some of its unit tests.
- A subsystem which has failed some of its system tests.
- A design which has been reviewed and in which a number of design errors have been discovered by the review team.

There should be adequate checks to ensure that subsequent development tasks do not use items which have not satisfied requirements. For example, as part of the process of installation, a check should be made that every module has been signed off by a senior member of the development team certifying that the module has been adequately tested. Another example is where the chair of a design review carries out a preliminary check that the part of the requirements specification which describes the design to be reviewed has also been certified by a senior member of staff as having no residual errors.

One area where it is easy to produce non-conforming product is during maintenance or during the process of modifying a configuration item that has been baselined. Here, a designer or programmer may carry out the task which was specified, for example rectifying a design fault, but may, at the same time, insert some extra code which affects functions of the system which should not have been affected. A quality system which detects a non-conforming product should address this issue. This means that checks should be carried out to ensure that a change only addresses the area which it was intended to address. There are a number of ways of doing this: one is to run a series of tests which check out the functions which should be unaffected; another is to have all changes reviewed, perhaps not by a large review team but by one or two other members of staff.

14.2.14 Corrective action

This section (4.14) describes the process of carrying out tasks when a defect is discovered, a defect being something which prevents a software system, or part of it, from meeting requirements. This part of the standard has a number of themes.

The first theme is that when a product is discovered as not meeting requirements—usually during system or acceptance testing—the developer should investigate the reason for this and carry out any corrective action. Thus, if a test fails because of a fault introduced during requirements analysis, then the developer should amend the requirements specification, the system design, and the affected program code; furthermore, there should be an audit trail which leads into and out of the configuration management system that documents this.

A second theme is that the developer should be continually monitoring the causes of defects via documentation such as test reports and customer complaints in order to discover whether non-conforming software is being produced because of a deficiency in the quality system. The implication here is that a main driving force in the continual improvement of the quality system is that of monitoring non-conforming software.

A third theme is that the quality system should specify the actions to be taken when a defect is discovered. For example, when an acceptance test fails, there should be a clearly defined reporting procedure which results in a member of staff, usually a designer or senior programmer, carrying out a mini post-mortem. The quality system should also specify what should happen after the result of the post-mortem has discovered the cause of any defects, i.e. that work instructions should be issued to eliminate the error.

14.2.15 Handling, storage, packaging and delivery

This part of the standard (4.15) describes the process whereby the developer assembles the final software product ready for delivery to the customer. This reads very much like a set of directives to companies who produce non-software products, as it mentions deterioration and secure areas. However, it does have relevance to software development: the product which is to be sent should be software which has been adequately tested, and the methods for detecting non-conforming software detailed in the previous sections should have been applied and have easily been seen to be applied.

The company for whom this section is the most relevant is the package developer. This company will perhaps have developed a small number of products but might have sold thousands of copies of each product, with every copy being different because it satisfies the local circumstances of the customer. This part of the standard places an onus on the developer to ensure that the right version of a package is delivered and, moreover, that when updates to parts of the system have been produced, the subsequent deliveries of the system are the correct ones.

There is also an implication that software and project documents should be safely stored and precautions taken against events such as fire, flooding and virus attack.

14.2.16 Quality records

Section 4.16 places an obligation on the software developer to establish, store and maintain quality records. Such records are the visible confirmation that a software system meets the quality attributes specified in the quality plan. An important point made in this section is that this includes not only quality records generated by the prime developer of a system but also those which arise from subcontractors.

Typically, these quality records will either be test reports (as described in Chapter 7), the minutes of technical reviews, or documents which have been signed off by senior members of the development team. This part of the standard effectively states that for every quality attribute defined during the early stages of the project there should be documentary evidence that the quality attribute has been met by the developed software.

> **Self Assessment Question 14.5** Would the production of documentation that showed that a module was clean-compiled be relevant to this part of the standard?
>
> **Solution** No, this is not a quality record: it states that the module does not have any syntax errors; however, it could have many functional errors.

14.2.17 Internal quality audits

Section 4.17 specifies that the developer should initiate a series of quality audits which check that the quality system is being applied correctly; that is, that standards and procedures are being adhered to, and that the controls associated with the quality attributes defined in the early part of the project have been applied. A subsidiary point made in this section is that quality audits should be scheduled on the basis of the status and importance of the activity; for example, I would expect a company to audit more frequently during requirements analysis than during programming, although the latter activity should not be ignored.

The standard describes the fact that the result of the audit should be documented and brought to the attention of relevant staff who are concerned with quality policy. Deficiencies that are found should then be followed up by staff responsible for quality assurance. This follow-up may range from the harsh—a reprimand—to the less harsh—an investigation as to why a particular facility of the quality system is being ignored by a number of project managers.

14.2.18 Training

This section (4.18) places a responsibility on the software developer to establish a system whereby the training needs, both of the company and of individuals, are identified and sufficient training is put in place to meet these needs. The standard specifies that all staff whose work affects quality should have training provided for them. I take this to be a directive to provide training for all staff. The standard also specifies that training records should be maintained. Such records would normally be consulted by managers when they are carrying out the process of staffing a project. The training plans of the company should also be periodically reviewed.

14.2.19 Servicing

This section (4.19) specifies that when a software system is to be serviced, there should be standards and procedures in place which govern servicing, and the supplier should have developed checks which ensure that the desired level of servicing has been achieved; for example, a service contract may specify that all queries from the customer will be answered within 48 hours. The software developer should hence have developed some standards which require staff responsible for servicing to fill in the time of user request and the time when the request was answered.

14.2.20 Statistical techniques

This section is really intended for the developer of mass-produced goods such as ball-bearings and hair dryers, where statistics are frequently used to check on product acceptability and the efficiency of the processes used to create a product. In software terms, its interpretation is more problematic. There is a body of research which is attempting to predict metrics such as the mean time between failure from test results. However, this work is still in its early days, and the standard does stress that, *where appropriate*, statistical techniques should be employed. I would say that, except for the software developers with the most mature quality systems, this paragraph currently has little meaning over and above the collection of error data from activities such as reviews, but that in the next five years it will become increasingly important. Chapter 16 discusses these issues in more depth.

Self Assessment Question 14.6 Would the use of data which detailed the number of tasks carried out, the number completed on time and the number over time be relevant to this part of the ISO 9001 standard?

Solution Yes, this would be valuable data for staff who might want to improve the estimating process.

14.3 MAIN SUMMARY POINTS

This final section summarizes the points made in the previous 20 subsections. It outlines the components of a quality system which should satisfy ISO 9001.

Management responsibility

- General quality aims and objectives in prominent company documents such as the annual report.
- More detailed quality aims and objectives in the quality manual.
- A short guide to the quality manual.
- Training courses for staff which introduce them to the quality system.

- Accurate and up-to-date job descriptions being maintained by the company which detail broad staff responsibilities.
- A staffing section in the project plan which describes project-specific responsibilities for all the staff involved in the project—both development and quality assurance staff.
- A section in the company's overall resource plan, detailing staff levels for staff carrying out activities such as testing.
- Adequate documentation of any software tools for implementing quality controls.
- Adequate training for staff using software tools used for implementing quality controls.
- Adequate training in quality control activities, such as system testing or technical reviewing.
- A procedure for hiring staff required for carrying out project-specific or one-off quality controls.
- A senior manager responsible for overseeing the operation of the company quality system and its adherence to ISO 9001.
- A regular review of the effectiveness of the quality system, based on documents such as project debriefing reports and summary project audit reports.
- A regular review of training provision.
- As far as possible, quality assurance being performed independently of the software projects.

Quality system

- The existence of documented standards, procedures and guidelines which have to be adapted and adopted by all the software developer's projects.
- A standard and procedure which describes how auditing is used to check that project standards and procedures are being adhered to by individual projects.
- The collection and retention of quality records, which would normally describe defects on a phase-by-phase basis.
- The production of quality records which detail that a particular quality control has been carried out.
- At least one process model which can be tailored to specific projects should be provided as part of the quality manual.
- The production of a quality plan for every project which describes the quality attributes for the software system that each project produces.

Contract review

- A technical review of the customer statement of requirements as preparation for requirements analysis.
- A technical review of the requirements specification for adequacy against the customer statement of requirements.
- Documentation of the interaction between the customer and the developer.
- Traceability documentation, which relates requirements specified in the statement of requirements to those contained in the requirements specification.
- Standards and procedures for carrying out a feasibility study.
- The use of a requirements review to determine infeasible requirements.

- The use of a project plan review to determine whether a project plan provides an adequate framework for the production of a software system with the desired quality attributes.
- The production of a requirements specification which contains all customer requirements.
- Traceability should be built into project documents so that customer requirements can be traced to program code via the system design and detailed design.

Design control

- An adequate notation for design is employed by the developer.
- Adequate validation and verification activities which can be applied to a design are described in the quality manual.
- Traceability between the requirements specification and the design should be built into project documentation.
- The interface between the design team and other agencies should be documented in the project plan.
- Procedures should be available to govern the process of querying the requirements which are fed into the design process.
- There must be explicit documentation produced which reflects the fact that the input to the design process—the requirements specification—has been satisfied by the design.
- The design must come under configuration control, i.e. all changes to the design must be rigorously reviewed, applied, checked and documented.
- The outputs from a development phase such as system design should be documented and reviewed.
- If any developmental item such as a subsystem design is found not to conform to requirements, it should be tagged and not used until it does conform to requirements.

Document control

- All the main documents generated during a software project should come under formal change control.
- There should be standards and procedures for notifying change and considering whether a change should take place.
- Standards and procedures should be contained in the quality system to enable staff concerned with evaluating change to decide whether a change should be approved or disapproved.
- The configuration management facilities offered by the quality system should be capable of keeping version data and change history data.

Purchasing

- The same level of requirements specification used on a project should be employed to communicate with software subcontractors.
- A proper acceptance procedure should be adopted for all software which is purchased.

- There should be explicit evidence that subcontractors are capable of producing software of the same quality as the developed software.
- The same level of change control should be adopted for purchased software that is employed for the developed software.
- An adequate acceptance testing regime should be applied to any external software.

Purchaser supplied product

- Software supplied by the system purchaser should be checked as rigorously as the software that is being developed.
- Software supplied by the system purchaser should be placed under configuration control.
- Any purchaser supplied software should also be accompanied by its requirements specification, and possibly its design.

Product identification and traceability

- Each element of the system, be it documentation or code, should be uniquely identified.
- As much traceability as possible should be built in between elements of a system.
- Version information should be held for elements of a software system.

Process control

- Tasks which affect quality should be identified and properly planned.
- Such tasks should be specified and associated with planning information such as duration and sequence in time.
- Adequate documentation which describes the developmental tasks to be carried out should be provided for the staff responsible.
- Adequate facilities for monitoring the execution of a task *vis-à-vis* the project plan should be provided.
- Adequate facilities for monitoring the adequate completion of a task should be provided.
- Adequate facilities which enable quality staff to check that a quality control has been carried out correctly should be provided; for example, there should be standards for auditing in place in the quality manual.
- Standards should be provided for all tasks which affect quality.
- A project should specify an adequate development methodology.
- Good practice for tasks which affect design should be publicized in the quality manual.
- Special processes should be identified during planning, and marked as such in any contractual documents.

Inspection and testing

- The quality system should provide checks that no system or part of a system is released to the customer unless it has been checked as conforming to requirements.

- The quality system should ensure that the developer documents those parts of a system which have not been adequately tested.
- Adequate testing such as unit testing should be carried out in advance of acceptance testing.
- Adequate documentation should be provided for testers which not only details the test(s) to be carried out, but what the outcome of the tests should be.
- Software should not be released to acceptance testers until all testing activities which precede it have been correctly carried out.
- Final acceptance tests should be derived from the quality attributes described in the quality plan.
- Adequate documentation should be generated which confirms that a system or part of a system has passed all the tests which have been applied to it.

Inspection, measuring and test equipment

- Where necessary, test and inspection tools are tested and test records are made generally available.
- For tools developed internally, the same quality regime that is used for the project on which the tools are to be used is employed during their development.

Inspection and test status

- Parts of the system that are separately tested should be documented with their test status.

Control of nonconforming product

- Adequate checks should be implemented, prior to a task such as system design, that all inputs into the task have been certified as being correct.
- That a maintenance change, or change to a baselined item, has not affected any other parts of the item which should not be affected by the change.

Corrective action

- When a defect is discovered, at whatever stage in a software project, the cause of the defect should be investigated and documented.
- Corrective action, when carried out, should not only affect the part of the system in which a defect was found, but should lead to the modification of all connected documents, such as designs.
- The developer should monitor the cause of defects in order to improve developmental practices and the quality system.
- There should be well defined standards and procedures which govern what should happen when a defect is discovered.
- There should be adequate standards and procedures which govern the reworking that occurs when a defect is discovered.

Handling, storage, packaging and delivery

- When the final software is assembled for delivery, standards and procedures should be in place which ensure that it does not contain nonconforming product.
- The correct versions of the components of the system should be assembled into the system that is to be delivered.

Quality records

- Quality records should be maintained by all projects. These records describe whether a particular quality control has checked that a specific quality attribute has been built into a software system.

Internal quality audits

- The quality system should contain standards and procedures which determine the conduct, frequency and relevant documentation of quality audits.
- The quality system should also detail how the results of an audit are to be used.

Training

- The company should have a training plan which covers not only the training needs of individuals but also those of the company.
- The training plan should be periodically reviewed.
- Training records should be readily available to staff carrying out project planning.

Servicing

- Where servicing of a software product is carried out, the developer should have standards and procedures which ensure that any services specified in a contract are being delivered to the customer.

Statistical techniques

- Appropriate statistical techniques should be used for prediction. These techniques should, however, be mature, and not the result of untried research.

14.4 FURTHER READING

There has been very little written on ISO 9001. However, a few case studies and short articles containing advice have been published. Chan (1993) describes the implementation of an ISO 9001 certified system, and Hemington (1993) provides excellent advice on implementation.

PROBLEMS

14.1 Write down what you think is an adequate statement of policy on quality assurance which addresses the management responsibility part of ISO 9001.

14.2 Detail some of the questions that you might ask a subcontractor to judge their competence in order to satisfy the part of ISO 9001 which deals with purchasing.

14.3 Give examples of the type of documentation required in the part of ISO 9001 which deals with quality records.

14.4 Write down a procedure which might satisfy the needs of the part of ISO 9001 which deals with internal quality audits.

15

CASE STUDY

AIMS

- To show how one company went about improving their quality system.
- To describe some of the quality problems encountered by one particular company.
- To detail some important points about quality improvement which are universal.

15.1 BACKGROUND

MonitorMaster PLC was a company which produced systems for industries where real-time monitoring was involved. Its customers included chemical companies, avionics companies and, more recently, water utility companies. It was set up by two men who worked in the chemical industry and had seen the large amount of profits which had been generated by real-time system subcontractors who had delivered what they regarded as substandard systems. They left their employment with a large chemicals company and started up *MonitorMaster PLC*. The first two or three years were very difficult: many of the systems suppliers were established, and had very good relationships with potential customers. However, the company managed to get two key contracts for metering systems which went well: the systems were delivered on time, to budget and, more importantly, the two customers thought the systems were, in quality terms, far in excess of what had been supplied previously. After this success, other potential customers soon got to hear of the quality of the work of the company and started placing orders. Soon, *MonitorMaster* was an extremely successful company. During the seventies it expanded its staff to 15, and the boom period in the eighties saw further expansion to around 35 staff.

Unfortunately, the eighties saw another phenomenon which gave rise to many problems: the microprocessor. During the seventies, the systems produced by *MonitorMaster* were predominantly hardware-oriented; occasionally a system was developed which was made up of as much as 20 per cent of software, but this type of system was something of a rarity.

Because of the hardware-oriented nature of the *MonitorMaster* systems, the staff employed by the company were a mix of hardware engineers and process engineers. If software was required then, to quote the words of the technical director: 'somebody just wrote a program'. The advent of the micro changed all that: during the early eighties the systems supplied by *MonitorMaster* contained as much as 50 per cent software; towards the end of the decade as much as 80 per cent. Because of this increase, *MonitorMaster* hired five software staff to replace hardware engineers who had left to form a company geographically close to *MonitorMaster*.

It was in the late eighties that trouble started to occur. Three projects experienced difficulty. The first of these used a new hardware device for which there was inadequate documentation, and the project had to employ a simulator as the device was not available until acceptance testing. The system tests for the project went well, including response time tests. However, when the device was delivered and used in acceptance testing, the software developer realized there was a major problem: the actual hardware device differed in characteristics from the simulator. In particular, it led to the response time dropping considerably. This meant that *MonitorMaster* had to redesign and reprogram the system to increase the response time. This took eight months, and cost the company a lot of overtime payments. The system was eventually delivered six months late, and *MonitorMaster* made only a tiny profit.

The second project involved a customer who continually changed his mind; *Monitor-Master* staff would meet with the customer at progress meetings, only to be faced with some further change in requirements. This process continued well into the coding phase of the project. The system which was delivered was received enthusiastically by the customer; however, it differed quite radically from the system described in the customer's original statement of requirements. The profit made was much less than was expected.

The final project was a major disaster. It was a large project contracted to a German chemical company, and the statement of requirements given to *MonitorMaster* was extensive and detailed. It was an English translation of the original German document, and in the translation process much of the subtle meaning behind a number of sentences had been lost. Also, one key member of the customer's staff with whom *MonitorMaster* had to liaise spoke poor English. The system contained seven subsystems; unfortunately, because of problems with the statement of requirements, three of these subsystems did not meet requirements. This was only discovered during late system testing in Germany. The project was heavily delayed while these problems were rectified and, because of the cost of reworking and of travel and accommodation for a software team in Germany, the company made the first project loss in its history—and it was a big loss.

During the third project the company was also coming under pressure in its strongest market: the United Kingdom. In particular, the company set up by the five hardware engineers who had left *MonitorMaster* had gained a number of medium-sized projects at the expense of *MonitorMaster*.

MonitorMaster was still financially healthy, but the three projects which were not successes had perturbed the senior managers of the company. I was called in to do an autopsy on these projects. After about an hour it was clear what the problem was: that *MonitorMaster* had no effective software quality system.

All the projects that failed exhibited signs in their early stages that trouble could be expected: signs that a good risk analysis could have picked up—at least two of the electronic engineers who worked for the company were aware of some hardware problems that the supplier of the device for the first project had experienced in the past, and had formed the opinion that this was not a reliable supplier. It was clear at the initial meeting with the customer who was involved with the second project that his requirements were very fluid indeed, and it was also clear during the early stages of planning for the third project that there were some worrying aspects of the statement of requirements provided by the German customer.

The problem was that no adequate risk analysis was carried out which could have resulted in proper project planning and quality controls and, furthermore, the quality controls were not available as the software quality assurance system was rudimentary: the quality manual extracts for software occupied ten pages, while the hardware part of the same manual was over 150 pages in length.

I submitted an initial report which described what the problems were, and how they could be avoided. The report did not concentrate on a large amount of technical details, but did provide detail on three of the 50-odd problems that I encountered to give a flavour of the depth of the quality assurance difficulties. What the report did focus on was how poor software quality assurance was affecting the business of the company—in the long term, its future growth, and in the short term, its ability to resist an economic downturn in British industry. I did not make the mistake which I often see in post-mortem reports of hiding a very strong message about the business effects of poor quality behind a massive amount of technical detail.

In the first project, a risk analysis procedure would have asked searching questions about the hardware and provided advice about what to do if there was a suspicion that the hardware was going to be delivered late. The results of the risk analysis would have led to *MonitorMaster* bidding more for the project to take into account possible manpower overruns at the end of the project. It would also have led to them concentrating on including a large amount of maintainability quality attributes in the system. For example, the programming language C was used for implementation, and a good information-hiding standard could, I estimated, have reduced the rework costs by a minimum of 30 per cent.

In the second project, a good risk analysis would have detected the chance of volatile requirements being present. Again, this would have resulted in the developer building contingency into the project cost, and also organizing the project to address the maintainability quality attribute. Moreover, a proper change handling system incorporating a costing procedure which gave each change a monetary cost that had to be confirmed and paid for by the customer, would have made the project a very profitable one. It would have dissuaded the customer from asking for some of the more outlandish changes that were requested.

Again, in the third project, a good risk analysis would have shown that the project had a high probability of getting into trouble. As well as the measures which could have been adopted for the first two projects, the developer might have been prompted to use a limited form of prototyping, such as employing a screen generator to produce an early version of the human–computer interface, to check requirements well before development started.

The problem with the company was that the quality assurance manual, which simply consisted of a few, not very well thought out standards, provided no guidance for planning, risk analysis and requirements specification. Because of this, the three projects failed in that a profit well in excess of £1 200 000 could have been made, when in fact for the three projects a loss of £200 000 was made. This alone made the managing director determined to implement some form of quality system.

15.2 FIRST STEPS

The senior management of the company decided that they wanted a software quality system. My post-mortem report had listed about 50 deficiencies in developmental and quality assurance practices, and the result of these in terms of lost resources. The initial decision by the company was to contract the development of the quality system in two stages. The first was a design study in which the broad outline of the components of the quality system were sketched out, together with an indication of how the quality system would affect the working practices of the company; the second was an implementation stage, in which the details of the quality system were specified in terms of a quality manual and were introduced into the company software projects.

The decision to carry out the introduction of a quality system in two stages was made because the senior management of the company wanted to know what they were committing themselves to, in both financial and organizational terms, before a huge amount of resources were spent. As a by-product of the process of carrying out the post-mortem on the three projects, I advised the company that their staff technical mix in terms of hardware and software experience was wrong: that hardware staff dominated in terms of numbers at a time when the software component of their projects was increasing at a rapid rate. As a consequence of this observation, the company made a decision that when hardware staff left they were to be replaced by software staff until the mix was approximately 25:75 per cent hardware to software. Also, when interviews for new staff were held, the company made a big effort to interrogate potential staff members about their experience and views on quality systems. During 1988, when the first part of the quality system design and implementation took place, four hardware engineers left, two of them joining the company that had been set up by ex-hardware engineers who worked for *MonitorMaster*. They were replaced by four software engineers, three of whom worked for large software developers who had well defined, mature quality systems.

The first half of the quality system implementation—the design phase—was commissioned by the company, and I started work in 1988. I expected it to take about three to four weeks. The first step I took was to form a steering group, which would nominally be responsible for the design of the quality system. This group consisted of four members of staff.

The first member was a project manager who effectively represented the board of directors' viewpoint. I felt it was important that very senior members of staff were not seen to take part in the design of the quality system. The main reason for this is that when a company has problems with aspects of development such as errors, budget overshoots, and unsatisfied requirements, the blame does not lie mainly with the technical staff: there are often major problems with the attitude of senior staff to quality. For example, senior staff who are neurotic about profit will order a project to skimp on system testing if a customer makes enough noise about delivery: in the short term this might seem to make economic sense; however, in the long term it loses money.

Both technical staff and senior staff should be actively involved in the development of the quality system, but I am a great believer in dealing with each group separately as they can then be completely honest about each other's failings. I included the project manager to represent the directors' point of view. The person chosen was fairly close to the financial circumstances of the company and could, if required, point out the financial implications of a decision to the steering group. The second reason for picking the project manager was that he represented a major group of users of the future quality system. The third reason, specific to the company, was that he had a hardware background and had managed one of the projects that had failed. He was the link to the hardware engineers who, at the start of 1988, when hardware staff were being replaced by software staff, were beginning to sense, wrongly, that they were being threatened by a software quality system. The project manager was there because he talked their language and could reassure them.

The second member of the steering group was one of the 1988 hirings. He was an analyst who had worked in London for a very large software company with a well developed, if rather bureaucratic, quality system, and had moved back to the area where *MonitorMaster* was based. He was on the steering group because he could at least provide confirmation to the sceptics that quality systems were not a hindrance to creativity, but something to help staff.

The third member of the group was a hacker. He was a highly skilled electronic engineer who produced some of the fastest C code that I had ever seen, but whose code was grossly unreadable: he tended to reject any facility in C—and there are not many of them—which promoted readability. He had, however, worked on the third project which had gone very wrong. His presence on the steering group was important: *MonitorMaster* produced the sort of fast-response system which required very efficient coding, and I thought that it was important to include someone who would be able to provide advice on designing a quality system which would cope with the type of coding that sometimes, of necessity, had to be carried out.

The fourth member was a woman who carried out the customer support function. *MonitorMaster* transacted their business in two areas: they produced bespoke systems from scratch, and had also produced a number of packages which were created from the same design but which could, by means of altering a number of tables, be oriented towards the needs of a particular customer. These packages generated a large proportion of the income for *MonitorMaster*, and the customer support function was oriented towards fielding problems and modifying the system whenever an error occurred.

The two most popular packages were quite old and were both programmed in BASIC, a language which was once an excellent teaching language, but which was not the ideal medium to maintain, particularly since there were no designs for the two packages. The packages were becoming increasingly popular, but there were ominous signs that the rather rudimentary configuration management system being employed was gradually breaking down. I wanted someone on the steering group who maintained other people's code who could point out the consequences of poor quality assurance and who was also involved in maintaining multiple versions of systems.

15.3 THE DESIGN STUDY

It took me five weeks to complete the study. This comprised a number of sections.

15.3.1 Introduction

This introduced the remainder of the study; gave an outline of what a quality system consisted of (similar to that contained in this book); and described three case studies. These case studies outlined deficiencies in the rudimentary QA system currently used by *MonitorMaster*. The three studies involved poor specification notations being employed by company staff, the inadequate configuration management system that was currently being used, and the poor quality of the unit testing phase. They outlined the problems which had occurred in the past; for example, for the configuration management case study, the degree of miscommunication that led to different designers having different versions of the functional specification was described. In each of the case studies the financial impact was outlined (I deliberately chose three areas where the financial impact was heavy). Each of the three case studies concluded with an outline description of the future possible QA changes which would have led to significant savings. The message given by this section was that a quality system was an investment and, in a comparatively short time, could pay large dividends to the company.

15.3.2 Major deficiencies

During my analysis of the company's approach to quality I discovered about 50 deficiencies, which were listed in this section. Each was described in no great length; on average I devoted about 50 words to each deficiency. They were uniquely numbered so that I could refer back to them later in the plan. An example of one of the deficiencies is shown below:

> **d1** When staff carry out unit testing the test data for the unit test is not usually retained. It is a simple matter to do this and place the file containing the test data in the project library. Failure to retain test data leads to extra expense if a module has to be changed.

As can be seen above, each failure was accompanied by a sentence which described why the failure was serious.

15.3.3 A process model

The major problem with the company was that it did not have a defined process model. Many of the staff worked to what they perceived was the process model, and because communication was quite good in the company many had in effect agreed, via informal working practices, what the process model for the company was. This section described what I perceived was the process model in terms of activities and the flow of documentation in the company. This documentation was not only existing documentation, such as unit test standards, but also documentation such as standards, procedures and specifications which were currently non-existent. These items were differentiated from existing items by means of dotted lines.

An important point that is worth repeating many times is that it is an act of folly to develop a quality system which is not based on even a simple process model. Without an idea of the way in which a company works, or wants to work in the future, there is little chance of developing the correct components of a quality system. In effect, what I am saying is that developing a quality system in this way is analogous to producing a software system with a poor or non-existent system specification.

15.3.4 Required components of the quality system

This section described what was required of a possible quality system for the company. It outlined the standards and procedures that were required, the staffing that was needed and the relationship of staff who carried out quality assurance activities on software projects to the senior management of the company. One of the problems with *Monitor-Master* was that it was a comparatively small company, and I felt that economically it could only justify one extra member of staff responsible for quality. There were certainly no resources available for a quality director, and so I suggested that a board member should have a part-time responsibility for overseeing the quality function.

Each standard and procedure was listed and related back to the process model detailed in the previous section of the plan. They were also cross-referenced back to the list of 50 deficiencies detailed in the second section of my plan, so that the reader could see what deficiencies a standard or a procedure would address. It was in this section that I placed great emphasis on the fact that the member of staff who carried out the day-to-day quality function should have quite a degree of power over individual projects; for example he or she should be able to insist that a project adopt the mandatory parts of the quality system, such as the system specification standard that was to be developed as part of the future quality system. However, I also stressed that, although individual project managers had a right of appeal to the director who was partly responsible for quality assurance, it would be unusual for many appeals to be upheld.

15.3.5 Implementation plan

This section gave a broad outline of how the quality system could be implemented. It was, in fact, three separate plans which catered for a number of possible scenarios of investment in a quality system. The first plan was one which assumed that the company was able to commit a substantial amount of resources in one chunk. It started with activities such as placing a quality system infrastructure in place by hiring a quality specialist, writing the job descriptions of some staff to give them quality responsibilities, and also organizing lines of responsibility. This was followed by plans for the implementation of standards, procedures and guidelines for developmental activities in the order in which they occur in the life-cycle that I sketched out for the company. The development of the configuration management system was also planned to take place in parallel with the implementation of the QA functions associated with development, and I assumed that its implementation would be complete before the sections of the QA manual dealing with design had been finished.

The second possible plan assumed that resources were available but that they were stretched over a longer time period. In effect, I split the first plan into two halves, with each half corresponding to a half of the first plan. However, I did include in the first half plan some cheap but effective measures which I was confident would produce some very visible savings that would persuade the company to commit fully to the second part of the plan—for example, I included a programming standard which contained instructions on defensive programming.

The final plan was one which assumed that resources were very tight. This was the worst of the plans, and was the one I hoped would not be adopted. It represented the dilemma faced by a quality consultant time and time again in the software industry—when faced with a shortage of resources provided by a customer, what do you do: tell the customer directly that the resources available for quality assurance were inadequate, or make an attempt to solve some of the customer's problems? I made the decision to do the latter, but provided plenty of written warnings about the problems of this third plan. The plan included tasks which would lead to the improvement of the requirements specification process, together with the early generation of test data. This was accompanied by a number of small, cheap measures which would provide some large gains; for example, I advocated a programming and unit testing standard to be implemented.

Happily, *MonitorMaster* adopted the second plan, and work started on the implementation of a quality system about nine months after receipt of the plan. The long gap was occasioned by the fact that the company had received a major contract which diverted its attention from considerations of a quality system. This contract, which again pointed up major quality problems within *MonitorMaster*, both paid for the first half of the implementation of the quality system and focused the minds of the management on implementing the second half as soon as possible.

15.3.6 Tasks

This section included a list of tasks which had to be carried out either by consultants or by staff of the company. Typical tasks were:

- Write standard X
- Write procedure Y
- Write a statement of responsibility for Director Z
- Review procedures P, Q and R
- Procure documentation software
- Develop templates for documentation W.

At this stage I did not include detailed timings for these tasks or when they were to be carried out. However, the three alternative plans outlined in the previous section gave a broad indication of the progression of the implementation.

15.4 IMPLEMENTATION

The company agreed to the implementation in two parts. The first stage of this implementation involved producing a more detailed plan. I took the tasks which were specified in the previous section of the plan, assigned staff to these tasks, and planned which tasks had to be carried out in series and which could be carried out in parallel. I felt that the quality system which was going to be devised would only succeed if there was full involvement of the *MonitorMaster* staff. To that end, I arranged that any tasks which I envisaged being carried out by a consultant would have a member of staff from the company shadowing him or her. The role of the shadow would either be to help in the task allocated to the consultant, for example help to write a standard for unit testing, or have a role in reviewing the work of the consultant. *MonitorMaster* was distinguished by the fact that many of its staff had very little experience of software quality systems. Consequently, I envisaged that most of the initial work of the development of the quality system would be carried out by consultants. However, some of the recent signings to the company had excellent experience of modern quality systems, and so I allocated them to the production of some of the elements of the quality system.

All the work produced—introductory documents, standards, procedures, guidelines, statements of responsibility, etc.—was reviewed and commented on by staff in the company. Two of the best reviewers of this material were programmers who had been with the company for some time and who, when I met them initially, were totally against the concept of a quality system. Both voiced objections that such a system would totally stifle their creativity. In conversation with a senior member of staff, I discovered that the company was looking to assign staff to maintaining an existing system which had been developed with little concern for quality—a system which was grossly unstructured and almost impossible to read. I suggested that the two members of staff might, as part of their responsibilities, be asked to help out in the maintenance. This is what happened, and I found that within a short time they became pretty hawkish over quality. Days spent poring over printouts which, to say the least, were unhelpful, developing new test data, and trying to understand the functional characteristics of a monolithic software system, turned them into hard-line quality propagandists. Indeed, their experience of maintaining a disastrous system made them less efficient than they could have been initially, as they tended to write standards and procedures which were exceptionally detailed, and which gave the users of those standards and procedures no leeway at all. However, they quickly became valued members of the team allocated to the process of developing a quality system.

The process of writing standards and procedures was a three-stage one. First, the staff involved in an activity were interviewed and asked what they thought the problems were in that activity; a questionnaire was used for some of the tasks. A consultant then went away and wrote a standard or procedure. This was later reviewed by the staff involved in the task. If the comments from the staff were minor, then the document was revised and frozen. If there were major worries, the document was revised and then re-reviewed. It is worth stressing yet again the importance of always involving development and managerial staff totally throughout the construction of a quality system. It is those companies where the staff feel they played a part in the development which have had the most successful quality systems in terms of adherence and commitment.

15.5 THE CURRENT POSITION

The position in *MonitorMaster* at the time of writing (January 1993) is that the first half of the plan has been fully implemented, and the company is working to a quality system which covers planning; system specification; early generation of system and acceptance tests; and configuration management. It is obvious, even after a year, that major savings are being made—savings which have prevented *MonitorMaster*, in a time of deep recession, from laying people off and retrenching their business commitments. However, the recession has had an effect in that it was originally envisaged that implementation of the second half of the quality plan would start six months ago. The company made the decision to delay it by nine months. However, at the time of writing their commitment to a start in three months time has already been shown by the fact that they are beginning to plan longer projects to allow some of the key staff involved in the implementation of the second half of the quality system not to have a full commitment to these projects.

15.6 SUMMARY

There are a number of important points that arose from the *MonitorMaster* project which are universal:

- As with many software projects, the problems encountered by *MonitorMaster* mainly occurred during the early stages of a project: during requirements analysis, system specification, and project planning.
- Always concentrate on business issues in any evaluation of a software quality system. By all means give technical examples of where, for example, money is being lost, but the important message that should come from a report on poor quality is how it can radically affect the business health of an enterprise.
- From the first, it is important to involve staff in the development of a quality system. As far as possible they should feel that it is their system—only then will they respect it and work under its constraints.
- You cannot even think of implementing a quality system unless a company has at least one process model—it is equivalent to developing a software system without a requirements specification.
- There are some cheap but effective quality changes such as a defensive programming standard which will bring savings almost immediately and which, if implemented, can persuade a company to go for a full implementation of a quality system.
- The implementation of a software quality system is a project, and should be treated like any other project: it should be planned, monitored and controlled.
- Assignment to the maintenance function, particularly if the maintained software is of poor quality, can radically change development staff's perception of the utility of a software system.
- If a quality system is to be implemented in a number of phases, it is vital that the elements of the system which deal with front-end activities such as requirements analysis are put into place in the first phase. These elements tend to have the best potential for achieving large savings.

16

IMPROVING A QUALITY SYSTEM

AIMS

- To outline the need for quality improvement.
- To describe one way in which quality improvement programmes can be implemented.

16.1 INTRODUCTION

A number of companies have expended a large amount of resources on installing expensive quality systems which have remained in place for many years, without any modification to them taking place. This is a mistake—a mistake which becomes increasingly costly as time proceeds. There are a number of reasons—over and above the very pragmatic one that the ISO 9001 series insists on it—why a company should be monitoring, reviewing and evolving their quality system: examining patterns of non-adherence to the system; examining where software errors have occurred; looking at the effect of new technology on the quality system; and discovering whether changes in business strategy will have an effect. These are:

- There will always be a tendency for staff to skimp in terms of their adherence to the quality system. This is not because they are unprofessional, but rather because there is a pressure on staff to deliver on time and to budget. Staff in a hurry to deliver a system may ignore parts of a quality plan. If a company is certified to ISO 9001, then a record of non-adherence is enough for the certification to be invalidated.
- The first version of a quality standard is never perfect. There will be parts of the system which still allow an unacceptable level of errors or require staff to carry out too much work. It is important, during the early stages of the use of a quality system, that particular care is taken in monitoring what are perceived to be these weak spots. Even quality systems which have been in place for a number of years contain processes which can be considerably improved.

- Chapter 9 discussed some of the ways in which new technology—both tools and development methods—can give rise to new requirements on a quality system. It is important that these new requirements are detected in advance of the implementation of new technology.
- Changes in business policy and strategy can give rise to the need for major changes in a quality system. For example, a company whose main business is producing bespoke software may decide that, with users increasingly looking to package-based solutions, the time has come to develop software packages which can be tailored by the company to a specific customer's requirements. This could have two major impacts on the developer. First, there will be a need to tighten up the configuration management parts of the quality manual; these parts may be adequate for bespoke system development but, almost invariably, are inadequate for a situation where there are a number of versions of a system in existence. Second, design standards and procedures will need to be tightened up in order to cope with techniques such as table-driven development which are used for producing packages.

16.2 THE QUALITY IMPROVEMENT TEAM

One strategy which can be adopted to cope with the improvement and evolution of the quality system is to appoint a quality improvement team. Its brief is to continually examine the functioning of the quality system, business policy and technological developments, and to specify tasks which need to be carried out in order to develop the quality system.

Such a team would come from diverse areas in a company. First, it should contain a senior member of the company—preferably at board level. The reason for this is that it is important for senior management to show their commitment to improvement of the quality system, and, after all, they are a user of the system.

A project manager should also be part of the team. Project management use parts of a quality system different from those used by senior management and technical staff. A member of technical staff, say a designer or an analyst, should also be part of the team, together with a programmer who currently works on the maintenance of a system. If the company is large, then it may have an R & D department; if so, then a member of that department should also be part of the team. An important input into the deliberations of the team is an indication of technologies which will affect the company and which are just over the horizon. If the R & D department are doing their job properly, then they should be continually monitoring and disseminating the spread and effect of new technology. The final member of the team should come from the quality assurance department.

The team will base its deliberations on a number of inputs:

- Project debriefing reports. A quality system should have a standard and procedure which directs a project manager to fill in a questionnaire after a project has been completed. Such questionnaires are a useful repository of experiences, and an important component in such documents are questions about the effectiveness of the quality system.
- Reports on technology which will affect the company in one-, two- and five-year time spans. As mentioned previously, these reports should emerge from the R & D

department. If the company is too small to support such a department, then they should be commissioned by external consultants.

- Reports from validation activities, such as reviews, which detail the extent and level of errors that are being discovered at each phase of a project. These reports will not be read in a raw form, but will be presented to the team in summary form. Normally, staff responsible for the quality function will carry out limited post-mortems on these reports and provide some indication of the reasons why certain categories of error have occurred.

- Summaries of audit reports from quality staff which indicate where deviations from the quality system are occurring.

- Unsolicited letters from staff on projects who, for example, may be having trouble using a standard.

- Business policy statements from the board of directors.

- Questionnaires filled in by staff asking them about their perceptions of the effectiveness of the quality system.

- If the company has implemented quality circles, then reports from these circles should be used.

- The contents of suggestion boxes.

- Reports from consultants who have been called in to periodically review the quality system.

- Reports from staff who provide a servicing function. Such staff will have a good idea of some of the problems with a software system, for example the poor quality of an interface, which may be ascribed to deficiencies in the quality system.

- Reports from quality staff who have traced back selections of errors which have been detected during validation to their source. It is important to point out that this is quite a time-consuming activity, and only a small number of errors can be treated in this way. Nevertheless, if it is possible to produce this report then it can be very valuable indeed.

It is worth pointing out that very rarely do I find a company using all the above documents; the points described above merely constitute an exhaustive list which can be tailored to each company's particular circumstances.

In many ways, the quality improvement team functions in the same way as a Change Control Board, the only difference being that it is responsible for changing the quality system rather than a software system and that version control is a much easier task.

A quality improvement team will usually meet relatively infrequently; a realistic interval between meetings is three months. Its task is to examine the type of reports detailed above and decide whether any changes to the quality system are required. Once it has made this decision, it then needs to categorize the importance of the changes. This is one of the reasons why the spread of people on a quality improvement team should be as wide as possible: a team consisting solely of developers will often prioritize those changes which affect technical activities, and may be tempted to give a low priority to changes which relate to the business strategy of the company.

I normally advocate that changes are given a five-point rating, together with an ideal date by when the change should be implemented. Normally, a rating of five means that the change has to take place immediately, with all other ratings used to indicate that the changes should be batched up so that they can be implemented in the next revision of the quality system. Having a five-point rating when there are two outcomes might seem strange: the reason for having it is to give the quality department, which is responsible for implementing change to the quality system, some idea of priorities; for example, when resources are scarce and a major revision has to take place. A further task, over and above identification and prioritization of a change, is to specify exactly what the change is and why it is being asked for. An example of such a specification is shown below:

> There is a relatively urgent need to develop a C^{++} programming standard. We have perceived that many of our potential customers are asking for systems written in this language. Also, one of our projects has already used C^{++}, and it is obvious from the reports from system testing that a large number of errors which have been detected have arisen from an undisciplined use of a number of C^{++} facilities. We have also had a report from staff who maintain this system that coding styles range from the eccentric to the pragmatic and sensible. We have also had a number of complaints and suggestions from programmers on the project that they felt they were producing poor quality software because of the lack of a standard. We suggest that the starting point for staff engaged in the development of this new standard is the report from the maintenance department and the letters from the programmers.
>
> **Priority** 4. **Date required** 9 months from now.

It is vitally important that lists of these changes are posted up in highly visible parts of a company. Much of the input to the process of quality improvement comes from staff on the ground, and a company should provide visible evidence that their suggestions are being taken seriously.

16.3 SUMMARY

One of the indications that a company has an excellent quality system is, paradoxically, that they do not think it excellent, but are continually attempting to improve the system. Another indication is that in improving a quality system the company involves staff at every level, not just those who have to implement the quality system.

16.4 FURTHER READING

Two excellent books which concern process improvement are Humphrey (1989) and Harrington (1991). The former describes the process of converting a rudimentary quality system into a sophisticated system which represents a zenith. The latter is a book about business process improvement; however, it can easily be adapted by staff who are interested in software process improvement.

APPENDIX A: SOME QA QUESTIONS

A.1 INTRODUCTION

This appendix contains a list of twenty-five questions which will usually enable someone to detect major weaknesses in a quality system. Consider it, if you like, as a short version of the questionnaires discussed in Chapter 12. I often use it when quickly assessing companies for a customer who wishes to place a software contract. Each question is cross-correlated to the chapter that it is relevant to and the page number of the most relevant part of the book. The page number is written in bold and enclosed by square brackets.

A.2 THE 25 QUESTIONS

A.2.1 Functional traceability

One of the first questions I ask concerns traceability, a concept detailed in Chapter 5. I ask a developer to show me some of the listings of the program code of a completed project. I place my finger on a module and then ask him or her to tell me which functions in the project's requirements specification that module helps to implement.

If they can point to the functions in a comparatively short time, say less than ten minutes, then it is an important sign that the company has a good quality system. If the retrieval time is measured in hours, then I normally suspect a poor quality system. Chapter 1 [18] described why traceability is important: staff in a software project are continually tracking between requirements specifications, designs and code, and a quality system with standards which insist that a high degree of traceability is maintained will encourage a reduction in errors and an increase in efficiency. Traceability is also dealt with in more detail in Chapter 5 [91].

A.2.2 Project monitoring

A good question to ask a project manager concerns his or her ability to monitor the progress of a project. I usually ask whether he or she can easily monitor the progress of a project in terms of tasks completed, tasks which are slipping, and the amount of resources expended at a certain point in a project as compared with the amount of resources which were planned to be expended.

If a project manager can point to procedures which enable him or her to get this information easily, then the part of the quality system dealing with planning and project monitoring is excellent. It means that the planning is carried out at a task level, and there are good facilities for staff to report on task completion. This topic is dealt with in Chapter 3 [**58**].

A.2.3 Validation of designs

It is always worth asking a developer what efforts he or she takes to validate a design; for example, what quality controls exist which provide evidence that a design meets its corresponding requirements specification—both functional and non-functional. An answer which simply states that a senior member of staff signs off the design is not adequate. If the developer states that methods such as technical reviews and prototyping are used and that standards and procedures exist for these activities, then that is a good answer. Reviews, within the context of the validation of requirements, are described in Chapter 4 [**75**].

A.2.4 Quality planning

A very revealing question to ask a developer concerns the construction of the quality plan. If the developer simply states that each project uses the company quality manual, then this is a poor answer. The correct answer, described in Chapter 1 [**22**], is that the company has a quality manual, but that the elements of the manual relevant to a project are extracted after quality factors have been identified and a risk analysis has been carried out. This process is described in Chapter 3.

A.2.5 Review of the quality system

An important question to ask a developer who claims to have a quality system concerns its evolution. The question is: how does the company evaluate the effectiveness of the quality system and, also, how does it evaluate the potential changes that new software development technology and business policy might have on the quality system? A quality system is an evolving entity, and it is important that mechanisms are in place to evaluate what the degree of evolution should be. A company should receive information such as project debriefing reports, error statistics, and project audits which should be periodically reviewed and then used as input into the process of evaluating the effectiveness of the quality system—both in the present and in the future. This process is described in Chapter 16 [**222**].

A.2.6 Unit test records

A question concerning unit testing is: what records exist which prove that a programmer has actually carried out a test? Many quality systems do not provide enough standards for this part of the software project. If it is not obvious that a programmer has carried out testing, but that all that might have happened is that a clean-compiled module has been passed to staff who carry out integration, then there is a weakness in the quality system: it allows programmers to pass untested modules to staff who carry out system and acceptance testing at a later stage in the project.

Discovering errors in a module when it is embedded in a whole system is many times more difficult than discovering errors in a module when it is tested by itself. A good quality manual would include directives which ask the programmer to provide evidence that a module has been tested; for example, by detailing the data that was used, and including the output of the tests with the other module documentation that is generated. Quality assurance and unit testing is dealt with in Chapter 7 [**109**].

A.2.7 Planning for system and acceptance testing

A very revealing question to ask about system and acceptance testing is: when does your quality manual insist that you start planning and thinking about system and acceptance tests? If the answer is that this occurs during the later stages of the project, say, during programming, then this is a poor answer. The correct answer is that as soon as the requirements specification has been validated as being correct the system and acceptance tests should be developed in outline.

There are a number of reasons for this: the project manager wants to know about the level of resources required for system and acceptance testing, and can only calculate this if he or she has a good idea of what the testing involves; there may be a need for special-purpose hardware for testing which needs to be fabricated in advance; and there could also be a requirement for special-purpose testing tools which need to be specified and developed in advance.

However, the main reason for developing the tests early, in outline form, is that they give the project manager confidence in the requirements specification. If a good tester is able to generate a series of outline tests from a requirements specification, without too many problems, then the requirements specification—a key document in the software project—is in good shape. The derivation of these outline system and acceptance tests— known as *verification requirements*—is dealt with in Chapter 4 [**79**].

A.2.8 Risk analysis

A question concerned with project planning is: what standards and procedures does your quality manual contain which deal with the identification of risks? All projects are risky, some more than others. A good quality system should provide standards and procedures which direct the processes of organizing and planning a project based on an appraisal of the possible risks in the project. The effect of events which are risky can be mitigated through careful planning. A quality manual should provide procedures for analysing the risks in a particular project and guidelines which provide advice on how to minimize the effect of risk. This is dealt with in Chapter 3 [**45**].

A.2.9 Configuration management practices

It is worth investigating how the process of change is managed. A favourite question of mine is: show me what happens when an error is discovered during operation and it necessitates changes to the requirements specification, system design and program code. This is a question about configuration management: the process of documenting, appraising and implementing changes to a system. In answer to this question, the developer should point to standards and procedures which describe how errors are notified to the software developer; how any proposed changes arising from the error are communicated to staff in charge of configuration management; how a decision to carry out the change is made; how the change is applied and validated; and, eventually, how staff who should know about the change have details communicated to them. This process is described in Chapter 8 [**122**].

A.2.10 Training

One of the aims of project planning is to ensure that staff who are qualified to carry out a task are experienced in that task or, as a minimum, have been trained in that task. If a company does not keep adequate records of training—whether carried out externally or internally—a project manager is unable to access important information needed for planning. The question to ask in this case is: do you keep training records and could I have a look at them? It is worth looking at these records to see what training the company regards as useful: if staff are just sent on hacking courses on languages such as C, then this is not a very good sign. However, if staff are sent on a variety of courses on topics such as requirements specification, system design, project management, quality assurance and testing, then that is a much better sign. Planning is dealt with in Chapter 3 [**42**].

A.2.11 Integration testing

Integration testing is a term used to describe the process of validating a system as it is being built up incrementally, with coded modules being added a few at a time. Developing a system in this way enables errors to be discovered more efficiently than if the system was not integrated and just collected together prior to system testing. The reasons for this are described in Chapter 1 [**19**], while Chapter 7 [**113**] describes standards and procedures for testing. A good question to ask is: have you got standards and procedures to describe the process of integration testing which, for example, provide advice on integration strategies and describe the documentation to be generated from integration testing?

A.2.12 Procedures for costing

A good question to ask is: are there standardized procedures which every project has to use in establishing a cost estimate? It is important that projects use the same costing technique, as the results from previous costings can be used for future projects. This may not seem to have much to do with quality; however, projects which make erroneous costs usually start running out of budget during testing and often have to skimp on testing. This topic is dealt with in Chapter 3 [**55**].

A.2.13 Checking costs

It is important that there are standards and procedures which enable a project manager to check the estimated cost of a project. Searching questions should be asked about the existence of such standards and procedures. For example, are there modern metrics-based costing methods whereby a project manager can compare the cost of part of a finished system which is similar to part of a proposed system by looking at historical costing data, or even the actual amount of resources spent on the finished system?

A.2.14 Early checking of a system

An excellent question to ask a company is: when is the earliest point in a project that a system and its documentation are checked against customer requirements? The answer to this should be that the requirements specification is checked just before it is frozen, and the developer is happy with it; the validator may use a technique such as a requirements review or prototyping. Errors detected early are much cheaper to rectify than if they were detected at a later stage in a project. Requirements reviews are described in Chapter 4 [75]; prototyping is described in Chapter 9 [133].

A.2.15 The storage of test data

A question that is intended to discover how seriously a company takes maintenance is: do your standards insist that, as far as possible, test data for module, integration, system and acceptance testing is stored? This ensures that if retesting occurs, then little extra effort is expended in redeveloping old test data. Quality assurance and testing is described in Chapter 7 [106].

A.2.16 The effect of new technology

As described in Chapter 9 [133], new technology can give rise to major new demands on a quality system. It is worth questioning a developer as to whether he or she monitors the growth of new technology, and ascertains whether this technology threatens to affect the quality system. This is dealt with in Chapter 16 [222], which details steps for the improvement of the quality system in response to a number of factors—one of which is new technology.

A.2.17 Standards and procedures for the human–computer interface

Systems are often built which, although they satisfy functional requirements, ignore the capabilities, environment and skills of the user. You should closely question a developer about standards and procedures which govern the process of discovering user characteristics, and about guidelines for designing the human–computer interface. Chapter 10 [147] details the quality assurance aspects of developing the human–computer interface.

A.2.18 Traceability into testing

A question which pinpoints problems in testing is: can you easily trace from a function, expressed in your requirements specification, to the individual tests which check out that function? If the company can retrieve these tests from past project documentation in under 15 minutes, then there is a good chance that the part of the quality system concerned with testing is in good shape. Traceability was dealt with in Chapter 1 [**18**], and testing is dealt with in Chapter 7 [**106**].

A.2.19 Rationale for decision making

It is important that when a major decision is made in a software project the responsible person provides a rationale, or set of reasons, for making the decision in the way that it was made. You should closely question a developer to check whether standards for project organization, system design and module testing include a directive which specifies that the staff carrying out these activities provide this rationale. For example, a designer should be asked to explain why a particular design was adopted for a system. By asking staff to explain themselves, a quality system encourages them to think more deeply about a task.

A.2.20 Standards and procedures for auditing

A question which often enables you to discover how seriously a company takes quality is: do you have explicit standards, procedures and guidelines which govern the process of checking that projects follow standards and procedures? They should cover the process of auditing, when to audit, how frequently to audit, what reports are generated from the auditing process, and what actions are taken when a project fails an audit. I have come across quality manuals which contain good standards for activities such as system design and requirements analysis, yet omit any mention of auditing.

A.2.21 The structure of the functional specification

It is worth exploring the standards that a developer uses for the requirements specification. A good question to ask is whether the functional part of the requirements specification is structured in such a way that all functions which are connected with each other are physically adjacent—whether, for example, the functional requirements concerned with stock ordering in a purchasing system can be found together. A requirements specification organized in this way is much easier to access by both software development staff and the customer and, hence, gives rise to fewer errors. This topic is dealt with in Chapter 4 [**83**].

A.2.22 Defect data

Validation of a software system gives rise to defect data which describes the errors that have occurred and their seriousness. A good question to ask is: what happens to this data? Is it, for example, used to improve the technical processes employed by the software developer and also the quality system? This topic is outlined in Chapter 16 [**222**].

A.2.23 Design guidelines

Design can have a major effect on the amount of resources expended during maintenance and the number of residual errors that occur during this process. A good quality system should have design guidelines which detail what practices are regarded as good or poor design; for example, it might state that a design which contains multi-functional modules is poor. You should ask about the existence of these guidelines and read them thoroughly.

A.2.24 Test failure

Ask the testers in the company what happens when an acceptance test fails. The wrong answer is: we rectify the error, repeat the test and carry on. The correct answer is: we rectify the error, repeat the test and then re-execute those tests which exercise modules that have had to be changed in order to rectify the error. There is a high probability that a change necessitated by the discovery of an error will have caused further errors which can only be discovered by rerunning previous tests. The procedure for acceptance testing should insist that this always happens. System testing and acceptance testing are dealt with in Chapter 7 [**106**].

A.2.25 Project debriefings

Project debriefings are a useful source of information used for improving the quality system. You should closely question a company about the existence of standards and procedures governing the conduct of a debriefing meeting and the associated documentation that is produced. This topic is dealt with in Chapter 16 [**223**].

BIBLIOGRAPHY

A J Albrecht and J R Gaffney. Software function, source lines of code, and development effort prediction: a Software Science validation. *IEEE Transactions on Software Engineering*, 9(6):639–648, 1983.

C Ashworth and L Goodland. *An Introduction to SSADM*. McGraw-Hill, 1990.

W A Babich. *Software Configuration Management*. Addison-Wesley, 1986.

V R Basili and H D Rombach. The TAME project: towards improvement-oriented software environments. *IEEE Transactions on Software Engineering*, 14(6):758–773, 1988.

P Bell and C Evans. *Mastering Documentation*. John Wiley, 1989.

M Ben-Menachem. *Software Configuration Management Guidebook*. McGraw-Hill, 1994.

J L Bentley. *Writing Efficient Programs*. Prentice-Hall, 1988.

D Benyon, J Preece *et al. A Guide to Usability*. Addison-Wesley, 1993.

E H Bersoff. Elements of software configuration management. *IEEE Transactions on Software Engineering*, 10(1):79–87, 1984.

B Boehm. *Software Engineering Economics*. Prentice-Hall, 1981.

B W Boehm. Verifying and validating software requirements and design specifications. *IEEE Software*, 1:75–88, 1984.

B W Boehm. *Software Risk Management*. IEEE Press, 1989.

G Booch. Object-oriented development. *IEEE Transactions on Software Engineering*, 12(2):211–221, 1986.

F P Brookes. *The Mythical Man-Month*. Addison-Wesley, 1975.

P W Chan. Installing an ISO 9001 accredited software quality management system. In G Staples, M Ross, C A Brebbia and J Stapleton, editors, *Software Quality Management, Proceedings of 1st International Conference on Software Quality Management*, pages 13–26, 93.

R N Charette. *Software Engineering Risk Analysis and Management*. McGraw-Hill, 1989.

R H Cobb and H D Mills. Engineering software under statistical quality control. *IEEE Software*, 7(6):44–54, 1990.

J L Connell and L Brice-Shaffer. *Structured Rapid Prototyping*. Yourdon Press, 1989.

P B Crosby. *Quality is Free*. McGraw-Hill, 1979.

A M Davis. *Software Requirements, Analysis and Specification*. Prentice-Hall, 1990.

R Dunn and R Ullman. *Quality Assurance for Computer Software*. McGraw-Hill, 1982.

R C Durst, G E Stark and T M Pelnik. Evaluation of software testing metrics for NASA's mission control centre. *Software Quality Journal*, 1(2):115–132, 1992.

C Easteal and G Davies. *Software Engineering: Analysis and Design*. McGraw-Hill, 1989.

M E Fagan. Advances in software inspections. *IEEE Transactions on Software Engineering*, 12(7):744–751, 1986.

N E Fenton. *Software Metrics: A Rigorous Approach*. Chapman and Hall, 1991.

J M Gilchrist. Project evaluation using the sei method. *Software Quality Journal*, 1(1):37–44, 1992.

A C Gillies. *Software Quality— Theory and Management*. Chapman and Hall, 1992.

P Goodman. *Practical Implementation of Software Metrics*. McGraw-Hill, 1993.

E Gowers. *Fowler's Modern English Usage*. Oxford University Press, 1988.

R B Grady and D I Caswell. *Software Metrics: Establishing a Company-wide Program*. Prentice-Hall, 1987.

M H Halstead. *Elements of Software Science*. Elsevier - North Holland, 1977.

P G Hamer and G D Frewin. M. H. Halstead's Software Science — a critical evaluation. In *Proceedings 6th International Conference on Software Engineering*, pages 197–206, 1982.

H J Harrington. *Business process improvement*. McGraw-Hill, 1991.

W T Harwood, B Cohen and M I Jackson. *The Specification of Complex Systems*. Addison-Wesley, 1986.

W Heitzel. *The Complete Guide to Software Testing*. QED Information Sciences, 1985.

J Hemington. ISO 9001: Moving from requirement to reality. In G Staples, M Ross, C A Brebbia and J Stapleton, editors, *Software Quality Management, Proceedings of 1st International Conference on Software Quality Management*, pages 3–12, 1993.

S Henry. Software metrics based on information flow. *IEEE Transactions on Software Engineering*, 7(5):510–518, 1981.

D S Hinsley and K H Bennet. A process modelling approach to managing software process improvement. In G Staples, M Ross, C A Brebbia and J Stapleton, editors, *Software Quality Management, Proceedings of 1st International Conference on Software Quality Management*, pages 189–204, 1993.

W S Humphrey. *Managing the Software Process*. Addison-Wesley, 1989.

D C Ince. *Software Development: Fashioning the Baroque*. Oxford University Press, 1988.

D C Ince. *Object-oriented Software Engineering with C++*. McGraw-Hill, 1991.

S Jenkins. *The Times Guide to English Style and Usage*. Times Books, 1992.

C Kaner. *Testing Computer Software*. TAB Books, 1989.

M I Kellner, B Curtis and J Over. Process modelling. *Communications of the ACM*, 35(9):75–90, 1992.

B A Kitchenham. Software metrics. In P Rook, editor, *Software Reliability Handbook*. Elsevier, 1992.

R O Lewis. *Independent Verification and Validation*. John Wiley, 1992.

J Martin and C McClure. *Structured Techniques: The Basis for CASE*. Prentice-Hall, 1987.

T J McCabe. A complexity measure. *IEEE Transactions on Software Engineering*, 2(4):308–320, 1976.

J A McCall, P K Richards, and G F Walters. Factors in software quality. Technical report, Rome Air Development Center, 1978.

J A McDermid. *Software Engineer's Reference Book*. Butterworth-Heinemann, 1990.

S N Monanty. Software cost estimation: present and future. *Software Practice and Experience*, 11(2):103–121, 1981.

G J Myers. *The Art of Software Testing*. John Wiley, 1979.

M A Ould. Quality control and assurance. In J A McDermid, editor, *Software Engineer's Reference Book*. Butterworth-Heinemann, 1990.

M Page-Jones. *The Practical Guide to Structured Systems Design*. Prentice-Hall, 1988.

D L Parnas and P C Clements. A rational design process: how and why to fake it. *IEEE Transactions on Software Engineering*, 12, 1986.

R S Pressman. *Software Engineering. A Practitioner's Approach—European Edition*. McGraw-Hill, 1994.

F J Redmill. *Dependability of Critical Computer Systems 1*. Elsevier Applied Science, 1988.

P Rook. Project planning and control. In J A McDermid, editor, *Software Engineer's Reference Book*. Butterworth-Heinemann, 1990.

M J Shepperd and D C Ince. The multi-dimensional modelling and measurement of software designs. In *Proceedings ACM Annual Conference*, 1990.

B Shneiderman. *Designing the User Interface*. Addison-Wesley, 1987.

T Snyder, W S Humphrey and R Willis. Software process improvement at hughes aircraft. *IEEE Software*, 8(4):11–23, 1991.

D A Stokes. Requirements analysis. In J A McDermid, editor, *Software Engineer's Reference Book*. Butterworth-Heinemann, 1990.

W Strunk and E B White. *The Elements of Style*. MacMillan, 1979.

P Sully. *Modelling the World with Objects*. Prentice-Hall, 1993.

C R Symons. *Software Sizing and Estimating. Mk II FPA*. John Wiley, 1991.

P A Williams and P S Beason. *Writing Effective Software Documentation*. Scott, Freeman and Co., 1990.

E Yourdon and L Constantine. *Structured Design*. Prentice-Hall, 1979.

INDEX

Related titles are available in McGraw-Hill's International Software Quality Assurance Series